Listening to Workers

THE WORKING CLASS IN AMERICAN HISTORY

For a list of books in the series, please see our website at www.press.uillinois.edu.

Listening to Workers

Oral Histories of Metro Detroit Autoworkers in the 1950s

DANIEL J. CLARK

UNIVERSITY OF ILLINOIS PRESS
Urbana, Chicago, and Springfield

1 2 3 4 5 C P 5 4 3 2 1
∞ This book is printed on acid- free paper.

Library of Congress Cataloging-in-Publication Data
Names: Clark, Daniel J., author.
Title: Listening to workers : oral histories of metro Detroit autoworkers in the 1950s / Daniel J. Clark.
Description: Urbana, Chicago and Springfield : University of Illinois Press, [2024] | Series: The working class in American history | Includes bibliographical references and index.
Identifiers: LCCN 2024008387 (print) | LCCN 2024008388 (ebook) | ISBN 9780252045998 (cloth) | ISBN 9780252088094 (paperback) | ISBN 9780252047176 (ebook)
Subjects: LCSH: Automobile industry workers—Michigan—Detroit—History—20th century. | Labor—Michigan—Detroit—History—20th century. | Detroit (Mich.)—Economic conditions—20th century.
Classification: LCC HD8039.A82 M533 2024 (print) | LCC HD8039.A82 (ebook) | DDC 331.7/62922209227743±dc23/eng/20240324
LC record available at https://lccn.loc.gov/2024008387
LC ebook record available at https://lccn.loc.gov/2024008388

To my mother, Carolyn "Jill" Clark,
who didn't get to live very long
but who is with me every day

Contents

Acknowledgments

This book could not have been written without the generosity of so many former autoworkers in sharing stories about their lives. I am grateful beyond words to each of them, although not all of those I interviewed appear in this book.

Several people played major roles in helping me locate people to interview. Running partner Ed Lyghtel directed me to Bob Bowen, and Oakland University student and UAW member Steve Clinton introduced me to Bonnie Melton. In the early 2000s, Bob and Bonnie were UAW retiree chapter presidents who saw value in this project from the outset. They invited me to retiree luncheons and made space available in their union halls for interviews. When it wasn't clear at all that this project was viable, they nurtured it to life. Special thanks to former students Greg Miller, Paul Dusney, and Marie O'Brien for connecting me, respectively, with L.J. Scott, Dorothy Sackle, and Ernie Liles.

Marie O'Brien has been a huge part of this project from the beginning, both for her skills as a historian and as a superb transcriptionist who handled the first drafts for a majority of the interview recordings. Her interest in the details of the lives of the people whose words she transcribed helped convince me that life history narratives were the best way to convey them.

I'm grateful to various public audiences who listened to early versions of my attempts to make sense of the interview material. Feedback from people who had lived through the 1950s helped me gain my bearings. In addition, a presentation, long ago, as part of the "Our Daily Lives/Our Daily Bread" lecture series, organized by John Beck, allowed me to test preliminary findings from the interviews. So did a presentation as part of a panel, also long ago, at the North American Labor History Conference. Elizabeth Faue played an important role in organizing that panel.

A number of Oakland University students engaged with transcripts, rough drafts of narratives, or both. Lesley Chapel, Andrea Stabile, Kari Cadwell, and Chris Blaker provided excellent feedback about the approach I was taking to writing the narratives. Lesley has continued to offer sharp insight and criticism about the emerging manuscript. Several generations of students in my colleague Erin Dwyer's Public History course responded thoughtfully to transcripts. This indicated to me that the stories could have wide appeal.

The University of Illinois Press's Alison Syring has been immensely helpful and supportive throughout the process. I always value her recommendations and her creative solutions to thorny problems. The anonymous readers for the press gave the manuscript a careful reading and I'm especially grateful for their recommendations on improving the Introduction.

Not long before the Covid pandemic, Margaret Beaudry contacted me and wondered about the fate of the book I was working on. I stopped by her house and gave her a copy of *Disruption in Detroit*, my recently published book in which she appears. Margaret looked at it for a bit and responded, "Not *that* book!" All I could do at the time was offer her a rough draft of my narrative about her life, promise her that the book she wanted to see would someday see the light of day, and assure her that her story would be in it. It pains me that it took so long to complete this book and that so many of the people included in it are no longer with us. With luck, I can hand deliver a copy of this book to Margaret.

Alternate Groupings of Narratives

The rationale for the order in which the narratives appear can be found in the Introduction. There are many ways the narratives could have been ordered, however, and below are some alternate possibilities based on race, sex, those who were southern migrants, and those with immigrant parents.

African American Men: Joe Woods (chap. 5), L.J. Scott (chap. 9), James Franklin (chap. 13)

White Women: Margaret Beaudry (chap. 4), Dorothy Sackle (chap. 8), Edith Arnold (chap. 12), Katie Neumann (chap. 16)

White Men: Emerald Neal (chap. 1), Elwin Brown (chap. 2), Paul Ross (chap. 3), Les "Lucky" Coleman (chap. 6), Gene Johnson (chap. 7), Thomas Nowak (chap. 10), James McGuire (chap. 11), Ernie Liles (chap. 14), Paul Ish (chap. 15)

Southern Migrants: Emerald Neal (chap. 1), Paul Ross (chap. 3), Joe Woods (chap. 5), Gene Johnson (chap. 7), L.J. Scott (chap. 9), James McGuire (chap. 11), Ernie Liles (chap. 14)

Interviewees with Immigrant Parents: Dorothy Sackle (chap. 8), Thomas Nowak (chap. 10), Katie Neumann (chap. 16)

Listening to Workers

Introduction

This is a book of life history narratives based on oral history interviews I conducted with people who worked in auto plants in the Detroit area in the 1950s. The project stemmed from my long-term interest in contributing to the social history movement by exploring history "from the bottom up," from the perspectives of ordinary people who were not famous. Like most autoworkers in the 1950s, the ones whose lives are recounted here weren't well known outside their circles of family and friends, and few of them sought positions of union leadership or stood out for their activism. But they led profoundly interesting lives that tell us much about the experiences of workers who were at the heart of America's industrial economy in the mid-twentieth century.

Despite all that has been written about the auto industry and the United Auto Workers (UAW), not much is known about the lives of ordinary autoworkers, how auto jobs and the union looked from the bottom up. This was true long ago when I began thinking about this project. In a discussion about his 1995 book, *The CIO: 1935–1955*, Robert Zieger defended his emphasis on union leadership: "When it came time to assessing workers' views, I found little help in the existing literature. . . . The problem of most oral history and autobiographical material is that it reflects the views and interests of activists and adds little first-hand evidence about truly ordinary workers."[1] Many years later, understanding ordinary workers is still a recognized shortcoming in labor history. In a 2018 celebration of the fortieth anniversary of its Working Class in American History series, the University of Illinois Press invited prominent historians to reflect on the series. James Barrett remarked, "Neither the field nor the series has advanced far into what Robert Orsi has called the 'hidden terrain,' the personal lives of poor and working people." In addition, Julie Greene observed that "we should take care to examine all sorts of workers' activities and experiences, regardless of whether or not they are exhibiting some degree of class unity."[2] This book certainly looks at the personal lives of working people, including insights into all sorts of activities and experiences, for the most part outside of any context involving collective action.

Scholarly attention on autoworkers has indeed focused mostly on activists or leaders, particularly Walter Reuther, the longtime president (1946–70) of the UAW. It made sense for historians to explore the actions of leadership and high-level union policies because so much remained unstudied and leaders and organizations were more likely than ordinary workers to generate and preserve documents that could form the basis of scholarly research.[3] It also made sense for labor historians to focus mainly on organizing campaigns, strikes, and radical challenges to UAW leadership because those conflicts revealed much about social forces and competing visions of what America should be. It helped that strikes tended to generate plenty of sources for later researchers. As important as this scholarship was, Zieger was correct. Rarely did the existing literature provide insights into the lives of the ordinary workers involved in the events under study.

Some of the best windows into the lives of ordinary workers in the fifties come from books written by their children, for example, Jack Metzgar's *Striking Steel: Solidarity Remembered* and Cheri Register's *Packinghouse Daughter: A Memoir*.[4] For the auto industry, ordinary workers filed grievances about racism and sexism both on the job and in the union that have allowed researchers to explore these crucial workplace issues. Even with these records, however, it's difficult to gain a sense of who any of these people were beyond the circumstances of their complaints.[5] Perhaps the best example of the experiences of ordinary autoworkers is Kevin Boyle's account of a daring, hostility-provoking kiss between a Black man and a white woman during a shop-floor holiday celebration in the 1950s. The story is riveting and heartbreaking, but Boyle reached dead ends when trying to place the event in the larger contexts of the participants' lives.[6]

The scarcity of information has not prevented scholars from making claims about autoworkers' lives in the 1950s. Historians have argued that for white autoworkers the first few decades of the post-WWII era, from roughly 1945–1973, were marked by stable employment with steadily rising wages and new benefits like company-paid health insurance and pensions. Conditions were significantly tougher, however, for African American autoworkers, who experienced employment discrimination, confinement to the most difficult and dangerous jobs, and disproportionate job losses due to automation and the decentralization of the industry away from Detroit. Women autoworkers faced employment discrimination and sexual harassment on the job, often from fellow union members. Still, the literature contains little evidence directly from ordinary workers and often considers them mostly in terms of their relationship to the bargaining agendas of top-level UAW officials.[7]

In hopes of learning more about ordinary autoworkers, I began an oral history project in the early 2000s. The central question was wide ranging: How did Detroit-area autoworkers experience the 1950s? This was as far back in the past as I could go and have a realistic chance of finding people in their 70s and 80s to talk with who had been at least young adults at that time. It was also a decade recognized by historians and the general public as the heyday of the auto industry and the UAW.

Even though there were potentially thousands of retired autoworkers to interview in the metro-Detroit area, and probably thousands of others in retirement in Florida, Arizona, and other warm places, it wasn't necessarily easy to find them, and at that time there wasn't much in the way of social media or even internet search capability to help. There were, however, UAW retiree chapters affiliated with many local unions, and I attended several monthly luncheons and a regional retiree picnic. Recruitment efforts involved going from table to table, briefly explaining to potential interviewees what I hoped to learn from them. This proved reasonably but not spectacularly successful. I naively thought that everybody would want to talk with me, but it turned out that many retirees were too busy to add to their schedules. In addition, many of them had the same sense of their own history as did a good portion of the literature, that the history of autoworkers was the history of Walter Reuther. More than a few insisted that they didn't know much about the union leader and therefore had little to offer. Nevertheless, there were enough volunteers to keep me busy. Over time, referrals, some from students, bolstered the roster of interviewees and I will be forever grateful to all who agreed to participate.

I had no idea what I would discover with the interviews. Maybe I would hear stories, from white workers at least, about enjoying their relative affluence during the decade. But I was open to whatever people told me and tried to avoid assumptions that autoworkers should have thought or behaved in certain ways. I was determined to stay focused on what autoworkers thought about their circumstances and how they lived their lives. I did not want to measure anyone against standards of social justice or by allegiance or opposition to a particular set of principles, union, radical, or anything else.

In all, I conducted interviews with forty former autoworkers and two people who never worked in an auto plant but were married to autoworkers. Most of the interviewees were born in the 1920s or early 1930s, although a few were either a bit older or younger. Most reached adulthood in the 1940s or early 1950s. There was huge turnover among Detroit autoworkers, especially during World War II, in 1950, and in 1953, when tens of thousands of new hires migrated to southeast Michigan. The arrival of so many new autoworkers in the fifties prompted UAW leaders to complain that their membership had little awareness of the hard-fought union organizing campaigns of the 1930s and contractual gains since then.[8] Many of those I interviewed came to metro Detroit and entered auto work during these migration waves, including people from Illinois, North Dakota, Missouri, Arkansas, Alabama, West Virginia, North Carolina, Michigan's Upper Peninsula, and Ontario. I also interviewed several Detroit-born, second-generation immigrants whose families came from Poland and Greece. The majority of those I interviewed were white men, who were also the majority of the auto workforce in that era. Quite a few white women agreed to be interviewed, out of proportion with their share of the workforce in the fifties, which made sense because they generally outlived men of their generation and liked to socialize at retiree events. I interviewed three African American men, although by family heritage one was African Canadian, but there are no African American women represented. Very few Black women were hired to work in auto plants between WWII and the Civil Rights Act of 1964, and my interview sample reflects that history of race and gender discrimination.

No research project proceeds according to plan, and this one was no exception. While listening to the first twenty or so interview recordings, I wondered why so many of these former autoworkers, white as well as Black, recalled the post-WWII years as economically unstable and insecure. This unexpected discovery led to years of research in Detroit newspapers to see if local coverage would corroborate or contradict what interviewees recalled. As it turned out, the newspaper evidence overwhelmingly confirmed the oral history recollections and became the backbone of a book, *Disruption in Detroit: Autoworkers and the Elusive Postwar Boom*.[9] Although *Disruption in Detroit* relies heavily on that newspaper research, it never would have occurred to me to read those papers if not for the interviews. Oral history evidence does appear in *Disruption in Detroit*, usually in brief excerpts to support my larger argument about persistent instability and insecurity. That's a common way to use oral history.

And just like with many other such books, readers of *Disruption in Detroit* won't learn in any sustained way about who the interviewees were, what they wanted from their lives, what struggles they faced, and how they coped. I didn't feel that I had done justice to those I interviewed, to the richness of the lives they shared with me. They deserved to have their stories told in much greater fullness.[10]

In one sense, *Listening to Workers* is a companion volume to *Disruption in Detroit*, yet they are very different from each other. *Disruption* is a more traditional, thesis-driven, academic monograph, with each chapter advancing the overarching argument. This book is a series of life history narratives of people who were autoworkers at some point, and often several points, in their lives. The narratives don't fit easily into thematic chapters. They might if I were to slice and dice them to develop such an organizational scheme, but I decided instead to consider the interviewees' lives in a more intact form.[11] While *Disruption in Detroit* places bits and pieces from autoworkers' oral histories into the larger contexts of auto work and the auto industry, this book situates people's auto jobs in the larger contexts of their lives. Because this research project focused from the outset on the 1950s, interviews tended to wind down once we reached the 1960s, and the narratives reflect that. In hindsight, I wish I had scheduled additional interviews to explore later decades, although at the time that seemed unfeasible because of how the project developed.

Although this book isn't a traditional, academic monograph, it certainly has an argument: Ordinary autoworkers in the early postwar years were complex, multidimensional people, with a wide range of aspirations and concerns. Their lives were much richer, more interesting, and at times more confounding than we can tell from the existing literature. Specific themes will emerge implicitly and cumulatively in the narratives, and several of them will be discussed in the conclusion: family traumas, education, early jobs, religion and church, hobbies and outside interests, marriage and family, military service, secondary support systems, danger at work, relationships with the UAW, race, and working women. Although *Disruption in Detroit* challenges the belief that the 1950s were years of job stability and security for autoworkers, neither that book nor this one disputes the reality of job discrimination and harassment faced by African American men and white women in auto workplaces. Indeed, this book offers personal examples of such discrimination and harassment, while also placing those experiences in the larger contexts of people's lives.

It bears repeating that the argument in this book is not presented in the standard way of stating the thesis upfront, crafting chapters that contribute to that thesis, and advancing each chapter's argument paragraph by paragraph. In addition, no interview fits cleanly into a single thematic category. Each interview connects with numerous themes, which makes it impossible, or at least misleading, to craft tidy headings under which to group them. To do so seemed like forcing people into categories that, although relevant, might erase or downplay significant portions of who they are and were. I hope that the order of the narratives will generate a sense of curiosity and anticipation about what's coming next. However, for those who would benefit from a different method of organizing the interviews, the Alternate Groupings of Narratives page can guide readers to lists of narratives based on race, sex, those who were southern migrants, and those with immigrant parents. For those who can't wait to see what sense I make of the narratives in the aggregate, feel free to jump ahead to the Conclusion, and, I hope, return to the narratives. It's also likely that readers will think of thematic connections that are not addressed in the Conclusion. The argument of the book is probably best absorbed by getting to know each person as much as possible through the narratives and pondering how complicated our sense of autoworkers' lives would be if we were to consider them all as full-fledged human beings.

The complexities in this relatively small sample suggest how daunting the challenge would be. At various points in the fifties, there were as many as 500,000 Detroiters involved in auto work, including old-timers and recent arrivals. Their stories are the history of autoworkers in that era, but as for how most of them lived their lives, only their friends and family members will ever know, and such memories often barely survive the next generation. It might have been possible to learn more if there had been a large-scale effort to collect oral histories a few decades ago, or even if I had done more interviewing. But the time has passed for that approach. Indeed, many autoworkers from the early post-WWII era were no longer alive when I started this project. Even if I had continued to conduct as many interviews as possible, I would have talked with only a tiny fraction of people who were ordinary autoworkers. Historians never have the perfect, comprehensive sources of their dreams, and this work is no exception. Yet these narratives have great value precisely because they are suggestive of the complexity of desires and experiences among ordinary autoworkers. Moreover, I am convinced it would be a welcome discovery if a historian were to find such a cache of interview recordings and transcripts that contained the thoughts of non-famous people.[12]

The people whose stories appear here lived through dramatic decades in U.S. history. Most had memories of the 1930s, the years of the Great Depression, which affected every area of the country. The Depression hit rural areas hard, including in Missouri, Arkansas, Alabama, and the outskirts of Detroit, all places where people I interviewed were living at the time. Although none of them had experienced material plenty beforehand, the Depression made things worse. Industrial areas, such as Detroit, saw skyrocketing unemployment, hunger, and misery, with sporadic production providing occasional job opportunities. Whenever word spread that automakers were hiring in the Detroit area, people would travel long distances, or short ones, in hopes of finding work. Some of the people portrayed here began their quests to become autoworkers in the Detroit area during the 1930s, while others had relatives or friends who became established in southeast Michigan, however precariously, and encouraged family members and former neighbors to join them when circumstances looked favorable.[13]

Many thousands of Detroit-area workers supported the industrial union movement of the mid-1930s, which produced the UAW, but for the most part, these interviewees were not direct participants in any organizing campaigns. Members of the generation that came of age during the 1940s and 1950s were too young to have participated in this upsurge of unionization, and in any event, most of the people interviewed for this project lived far from any auto plants at the time and did not yet imagine themselves to be or to one day become autoworkers. Nevertheless, the unionization of workforces at major automakers and suppliers was a reality that these people encountered when they took jobs in the auto industry.[14]

World War II affected the lives of interviewees in a variety of ways. With the conversion to war production, employment in the Detroit area grew immensely, attracting tens of thousands of new workers from around the country to what became known as the Arsenal of Democracy. Those migrants included some of the people featured in this book. The war also required soldiers, and several of those profiled here served in the military during that conflict, overseas or at home. Other interviewees were married to soldiers.[15]

The automobile industry in the postwar years, it turns out, did not provide stable employment and secure incomes, and these narratives reveal how ordinary autoworkers responded to these challenging conditions. Detroit area manufacturing employment did not benefit from Korean War military production. Instead, shortages of crucial materials resulted in high unemployment for the region's autoworkers, followed by a boom in 1953 and a recession in 1954.[16] Internal migrants continued to look for jobs in Detroit, however, whether or not the auto industry offered long-term employment opportunities for them. Detroit's population peaked at over 2 million in the early 1950s before beginning a steady decline with the growth of suburbs and the decentralization of the auto industry away from the city. Officially, Detroit had a population of

1,849,568 in 1950, nearly 84 percent white, and 1,670,144 in 1960, just over 70 percent white.[17]

Quite a few of the interviewees for this project worked at Pontiac Motor, in Pontiac, Michigan, about thirty miles northwest of downtown Detroit. Pontiac was a mid-sized industrial city, increasing in population from about 70,000 in 1950 (9 percent nonwhite) to over 80,000 (17 percent nonwhite) by 1960 and closely connected with automobile production throughout southeast Michigan. A large migration of African Americans, especially during World War II, boosted Pontiac's nonwhite population and exposed fierce housing and employment segregation, similar to what took place in Detroit. Pontiac, the city, had a long industrial history, including the Oakland Motor Car Company, founded in 1907, which became part of General Motors under the Pontiac brand name in the mid-1920s. Long before then, the city had many industrial enterprises, including the O. J. Beaudette company, which built carriages in the 1890s before supplying wood bodies for Henry Ford's early Model T automobiles. The Pontiac Motor Complex, which opened in 1927, was one of the largest industrial sites in the country and remained so throughout the 1950s. GM also had truck and bus manufacturing facilities in Pontiac, which offered thousands of manufacturing jobs and made GM's Pontiac operations almost as large as the corporation's presence in Detroit itself.[18]

Several interviewees lived and worked in Ypsilanti, Michigan, a small city about thirty-five miles west of downtown Detroit and just east of Ann Arbor. Until the 1940s, Ypsilanti was mostly a college town—Michigan Normal College for teacher training, now Eastern Michigan University—with a modest industrial heritage, highlighted by the production of ladders, paper, farm implements, and underwear. Ford opened a small parts plant in the city in 1932, but only with a series of major expansions in 1948, 1950, and 1952 did it become a significant employer, with several thousand people working there at its peak. The biggest industrial transformation for Ypsilanti came in 1941 with the construction of the massive Willow Run Bomber Plant, a few miles east of the city, which drew thousands of workers to the area, many of them southern migrants, Black and white. This influx was largely responsible for the growth in the city's population from about 12,000 in 1940 to roughly 18,000 a decade later, and for increasing racial tensions. About 20 percent of Ypsilanti residents in 1950 were nonwhite, rising to 23 percent of a population of about 21,000 in 1960. After the Bomber Plant shut down at the end of World War II, businessmen Joseph Frazer and Henry Kaiser set up car manufacturing operations in the facility, and a few of the interviewees for this project worked there. Kaiser-Frazer floundered, however, and GM ended up taking over much of the factory in 1954.[19]

That type of fluctuation, whether in Detroit, Pontiac, or Ypsilanti, did much to create the options that ordinary autoworkers weighed and balanced when trying to actually be autoworkers during these years.

Methodology Notes

Oral history was instrumental in the rise in the 1960s and 1970s of the new social history, the mission to recover the perspectives of ordinary people, to explore history "from the bottom up." Books that emerged from this movement drew me to the profession in the 1980s and to an oral history seminar taught by Bill Chafe during my first year of graduate school at Duke University.[20] For that course, I conducted interviews with former textile workers who had participated in a strike in the late 1950s that resulted in the loss of their union. Those experiences reinforced for me the significance of the social-history mission and the power of oral history as a methodology. I was in the homes of people who knew what difference unionization had made in their lives and their memories of the stand they took churned up strong feelings some twenty-five years later. Those interviews were ultimately responsible for a book, *Like Night and Day: Unionization in a Southern Mill Town*, which was small consolation for what the mill workers had endured but which at least uncovered what was at stake for them.[21]

Oral history was also the driving force behind *Disruption in Detroit*, although *Listening to Workers* is closer to what I initially imagined the project would produce. Before my first interview, I developed a six-page, single-spaced list of questions to ask. Although this was a useful mental exercise, it mostly served to remind me of general topics I hoped to explore. I don't think I ever asked consecutive questions on it. At their best, oral history interviews flow more organically, with the conversational direction determined by follow-up questions about an unexpected answer or a cryptic comment.

Since I knew nothing about any of the people I interviewed, each conversation was an adventure. My first questions were about when and where the person was born, followed in most cases by discussions of childhood. This was usually a good way to develop rapport because the questions were tailored directly to the interviewees' lives and they were usually the only ones in the room who knew the answers. (Occasionally a spouse or child sat in on interviews.) Some of the people I spoke with had expected the interview experience to be like a quiz, which caused anxiety. Questions specific to their lives tended to put interviewees at ease. In addition, the icebreaking about childhood often led to important insights about the trajectories of lives, for example, the lifelong impact for a child of particularly loving or distant parents, the tragic loss of a family member, chopping cotton in Arkansas, negotiating the dangers of Jim Crow Alabama, living in a ramshackle house in the middle of a West Virginia creek, or surviving the Great Depression as kids by illegally hawking homemade beer in Missouri or selling newspapers on street corners in Michigan.

As much as I enjoyed learning from these interviews, there were always nagging concerns, mentioned above, about how many stories I needed to collect before I could say anything meaningful about "autoworkers in the 1950s." And with oral history, the problems of representativeness and incompleteness extend beyond the size of the interview sample. Those who listen to oral history recordings or read transcripts, from any project and certainly from mine, will experience frustration with questions not asked and questions not answered. During an interview, it's difficult to anticipate what other people, either the next day or decades in the future, will wish that you had covered. It's hard enough to stay in the present, listening carefully to what is said while assessing whether your own notions of what's important or revelations from the conversation should direct the course of the interview. When I listen to recordings of the interviews I've conducted, sometimes I'm impressed with how I managed these variables, while other times I can't believe how I missed obvious cues and clues about topics and insights of potential importance. An interviewer tends to get better with experience, but there are still plenty of times when fatigue, confusion, a momentary lapse in attention, or just plain cluelessness can derail a promising line of conversation. And unfortunately, it's impossible to know anything concrete about what wasn't discussed.

Moreover, the interviewer-interviewee relationship and the interviewee's personality have a bearing on what gets said. To what extent were people's recollections, or what they were willing to share, influenced by who I was, how I behaved, and the types of questions I asked? Some interviewees had an abundance of energy and carried on conversations for three hours or more, leaving me bobbing and weaving, while others seemed ready to be done in less than an hour. The pages of some transcripts are filled with words because questions elicited long, detailed responses. Other transcripts have an overabundance of blank spaces, because answers were terse, without elaboration. Some people might just be more talkative than others, and some might be more reserved than usual in the context of an interview. These factors determine to a large extent what can be included in life history narratives.

Given such limitations, it's worth considering if it's reckless to try to construct a narrative about someone from what in most cases was one interview, on a single day in a long life, decades after the main events under discussion. With what authority could I write anything at all? Yet all historians face some version of the problem of incomplete or flawed sources. In the end, historians are often left to rely on their gut sense of whether or not they believe their sources, oral or written. With oral history, if interviewees mistake basic facts or lose track of chronological bearings, or even if they intentionally mislead, they're making some sort of statement about what they think to be true, or maybe what they wish were true, and that's part of the historical record as well. On those fronts, written sources are hardly foolproof alternatives.[22]

Oral historians have come to realize that, more than anything else, their methodology reveals how people make sense of their lives at the time of the interview. That reckoning can be quite different from how the same people considered the same experiences at earlier points in their lives. The details remembered, or the ones emphasized, might vary depending on the stage of life when the interview took place. Memory is imperfect under the best of circumstances, and oral historians have long since let go of the hope that interviews with people who were there could provide an uncomplicated, direct window into the past. Nevertheless, even if the interviews for this project mainly reveal how people made sense of their lives during a specific hour or two in time, those interpretations might be the best evidence we'll ever get about the experiences of ordinary autoworkers in the early post-WWII years. And in my experience, during most interviews, including the ones for this project, there's a moment when you get to the essence of who the person is. We might not have covered everything that was important to them, and we certainly didn't cover most of what they considered to be unimportant, but more often than not we reached an understanding about many significant aspects of their life. There's an identifiable emotional pitch, sometimes a verbal recognition, when that occurs.

For all the strengths and shortcomings of the interview process, there are additional complications when trying to convert a recording and transcript to the types of narratives in this book. Just like most conversations, interviews rarely take a linear path, and sometimes bits of a story have to be cobbled together from various locations in the recording as conversations cycle back to particular themes. Chronological bearings can also be difficult to maintain. People's trains of thought don't necessarily stay confined to a specific date range. At times I had to make interpretive decisions about when I thought things happened. Sometimes the chronological fuzziness could be clarified through other markers in the conversation, or by national events, or by the research I did for *Disruption in Detroit*. Sometimes dates are seared into peoples' minds, like the day they started work in an auto plant, or the day they received their draft notice. In many cases, however, the precise date matters less than the general period, and I tried to use language appropriate to my level of confidence in its accuracy. In such cases, the goal is to be emotionally true and close enough to chronologically accurate.

Nevertheless, these narratives could contain misrepresentations, either by interviewees or by me. It's possible that interviewees tried to mislead me on occasion, but there would have been no obvious incentive to do so. The candor with which they discussed having children out of wedlock, infidelity, divorce, domestic violence, and poverty—topics that provoked shame and judgment in their lifetimes—leads me to believe that there was a tendency not to shy away from hard truths. As for me, I've made my best, good-faith effort to piece the narratives together from the interview evidence, with occasional assistance from outside research to confirm the names of towns, landmarks, events, locations, and even the occasional spot check of birth or death records. It's possible that someone could come up with different interpretations of some of the interview evidence at the core of this project, although I tried to step back from ambiguous territory whenever possible. Nevertheless, interpretive leaps, or at least short hops, were occasionally necessary to reconcile chronologies or conflicting memories. All of the recordings and transcripts for this project are available through the Walter P. Reuther Library at Wayne State University, so anyone is welcome to listen, read, assess, and quibble with how I've constructed these stories.[23]

The master of creating narratives from interview transcripts was Studs Terkel, who produced many amazing books on big topics—from the Great Depression to World War II to the American Dream—that included the perspectives of many relatively unknown people as well as famous ones.[24] The narratives in his books appear as coherent paragraphs spoken by those interviewed, with an occasional italicized question or explanation in Terkel's words. In real life, however, hardly anyone speaks in complete paragraphs, whether in casual conversation or interviews. We often don't even speak in complete sentences. Anyone who transcribes interviews will be surprised by the differences between perfectly acceptable vernacular speech and those same words typed verbatim on the page. The sentences in print often look inarticulate, like gibberish. Filler words—the ums, ers, likes, you knows, and whatnots that we tune out in ordinary conversation—can dominate a transcript if you let them. There's a question of how much faithfulness to actual speech a reader can tolerate without being distracted or annoyed. To create coherent, grammatical paragraphs, Terkel had to cut, paste, and tweak text, for grammar, syntax, and thematic consistency. When I teach oral history, students are often concerned at first by such manipulation, although many of them end up choosing that format for conveying the results of their own interviews. It's an effective and engrossing style. But it involves heavy editing. The author/editor has much to do with determining what is included and how it is portrayed, and readers should be aware of that.

I chose a similar but slightly different approach with the narratives in this volume. Although I tried as much as possible to have interviewees' words drive their stories, my voice is clearly injected into each account, providing linkages, contexts, and occasional commentary on the tone or body language with which words were expressed. It made sense to adopt this style because I was the one who ultimately decided the order in which topics appeared, what was included, and what was excluded. Each interview was a joint enterprise, for sure, but I am responsible for the final edits of the narratives in this book. Like Terkel, I cut, pasted, and tweaked transcribed text for grammar, syntax, and thematic consistency. I chose not to try to convey slang, so what sounds like "gonna" on the recording, for example, appears as "going to" in the transcript and in these narratives. Most importantly, both Terkel's approach and mine require fidelity to the meaning and intent of each interviewee's words, as best as that can be determined, subject to possible errors as discussed above. I've just chosen to be a bit more transparent about my role in creating the finished product.

Neither approach is beyond criticism or skepticism, but the alternatives aren't necessarily better. Most oral historians consider the recording to be the main document produced from an interview, but few people, including researchers, have the time and patience to listen to hours of audio, even with digital indexing. Reading a transcript is a great exercise for a class, and it's still generally the preferred way for researchers to access interviews, but it would be asking a lot to require someone to pore over transcripts carefully enough to make sense of conversations that frequently ramble and spiral forward and backward in time to their destinations. I've tried my best to do that work for you. More than anything else, I hope that readers will take from these life history narratives a sense of these autoworkers as full-fledged human beings, for whom jobs in the automobile industry were one aspect of their complicated lives.

1

Emerald Neal

(1935–)

Emerald Neal spent most of his childhood in rural West Virginia, or as he liked to say, "over the hill in the holler." The nearest town was Hinton, about twenty-two miles away, in the southeast corner of the state. Both of his parents had grown up in that area. They divorced around 1940, when Emerald was five years old. He and his sister, Willa, who was ten, went to live with their Aunt Eva "in the country." The children had a brother, between them in age, who died of pneumonia at age six. Their mother lived and worked in town, and they never saw much of their father. "My aunt raised me," Emerald explained.

Part of the weekly routine with Aunt Eva involved shopping in Hinton on Saturdays. Once, when Emerald was in high school, his cousin Maxine invited him to a birthday party in town on a Saturday afternoon. A bit shy, Emerald tried to get out of it, but Aunt Eva excused him from chores and convinced him to stay. Maxine, it turns out, had set up Emerald with Cara Bent on what amounted to a blind date, and as Emerald put it, "sparks flew from there. We contacted each other through the week by letters. And then in my senior year—Cara had graduated the year before me—we really fell deeply in love and we eloped and got married. Nobody knew it. We didn't live with each other. She said I want you to finish high school, and I said I want to too. So I went all the way through high school and graduated and told everybody at the end of graduation that I had gotten married to Cara."

There weren't many job opportunities around Hinton in the early fifties. Outside of farming, economic life revolved around a repair facility for steam locomotives. But "when the diesels came in," Emerald recalled, "everybody lost their jobs. Railroads was the thing there, you know. They lost their homes, and everything. It destroyed the town, because everybody depended on the locomotives."[1]

Following his father-in-law's advice, Emerald began a correspondence course to become a diesel mechanic. Everyone in Hinton hoped that a diesel repair center might replace the defunct steam facility, but the railroad soon chose a different community for its new operations. Emerald continued the course anyway, all the while, he explained, "working odd jobs until I got something better." A chicken factory opened nearby in 1953: "Went out and applied for it—no problem, got the job. OK, so you know, not ever having a first job, how do you dress? So I went to work that day in slacks, and nice shirt, shiny shoes. I remember walking in, the guy looked at me kind of funny, says, 'Well, we do have a rubber apron, and we got some rubber boots.' 'Huh? OK.' So they put me at a machine here with two big rubber wheels with kind of knobbies on them. They back this truck of chickens up to the door and they're cackling, they're hollering and carrying on. So they didn't cut their heads off. They stuck them some way and hung them up on a rack. And the first thing they did was come through a machine like mine—it was a lot larger, with big rubber drums with the knobs on them, just beating the heck out of those chickens, and they was still kicking and everything. My wife picked me up at lunch time. I had feathers, shit, and blood all over me, in my hair—I never even went back. I went home and took a shower and said, 'That's it! That's it!'"

Soon, Willa called from Detroit, where she had moved in 1950. She was working at Ex-Cell-O, an auto industry supplier that had converted to military production during the Korean War, and thought her brother might be able to get a job there too. Emerald immediately headed north and hired in. "Tell you the truth," he confessed, "I was a louse. I think everybody should know this. A country boy coming into the city is very difficult because you're not used to this hemmed in period of cement, nothing to do. I was very bored—I'd maybe take off from work two or three times a month or whatever, go back to West Virginia. And maybe not even go to work during the week. I just didn't care." He was able to keep his job, it seems, because work standards had become lax during the war: "We could get done in eight hours, leave, go home, but we could get done in four hours. It was very simple, to get this production out. That's all they wanted, a certain amount."

When the Korean War ended, Ex-Cell-O management demanded greater efficiency and veterans returned to reclaim their jobs. In addition, Emerald and Cara had a baby that September. After offering another flimsy excuse for missing work, Emerald recalled that "the foreman straightened me out. He just looked right through me, and says, 'You know what? I'm going to tell you something. I'm going to help you out one time. If you miss for any reason, here on out, anytime, you're fired.' Well, that kind of soaked into me. Somebody had to tell me. I had that responsibility, which I wasn't realizing, of a family. From that day on to this day, I respect responsibility." It never occurred to Emerald to consult with a UAW representative, who might have refused to help anyway since these problems were self-inflicted: "I never talked to a union person the whole time I was there. Didn't even know what it was!"

Emerald, whose friends called him "Neal," indeed became more conscientious. His foreman "come over about a month later and says, 'Neal, would you like a better job?' I said, 'Sure.' 'Well, you done pretty good. I think you're straightening out a little bit.' So I went to this department and I had to work on a machine with a little rag wheel, a buffing wheel—they thought it was too dangerous for a woman to do." Most of the employees in this department, including his supervisor, were women. "You had to buff these parts that had to be just precise because they're aircraft parts, you see. It was nice. Better job."

With more stable employment, Neal and his family settled into their one-room apartment: "I worked midnights. Just slept in the middle of the floor all day while Cara did her work all around me. The bed pulled out of the wall. It was very hard." The apartment was in a crowded and noisy part of the city, near several factories: "These people were pushing these cars up on the sidewalk, to get their parking place. I couldn't believe it." Neal often had to park his own car six blocks from home: "I got I'd say, altogether, about twelve tickets in Detroit for parking in 'No Parking' zones. Maybe parking in front of a crosswalk." It was not like West Virginia: "I'm used to wide open spaces, you know."

In 1954, the economy headed into recession, Neal was laid off, and he and his family returned to West Virginia. Fortunately, a new machine shop had opened near Hinton and he hired in right away, with some help from an aunt "that knew someone" and "said I needed a job. They made war things too. Explosive chambers. We made the chamber part." The shop was filled with mills and lathes: "They hired me as a core maker. That's where you take sand, and you put this mixture with it, and you make these cores"—the insides of the part you're trying to make—"and put them in the ovens and bake them. You make a mold out of sand, but you've got to have the part to lay in the sand to make the indentation, and then you put the two sides together, and then you melt the aluminum, or the brass, you pour in this, and it makes that part." Neal saw long-term potential in this job: "I remember Mr. Davis—he was the president—would come around and talk to us. He personally come to me—he said, 'Maybe you should start learning more about machinery and gauges and stuff.'" Mr. Davis clearly thought Neal could be a skilled tradesman. "And then all of a sudden they decided that they wanted to form a union. And of course I went along with everybody, and we met at the Commerce Building there. And then Mr. Davis—I guess he heard we was trying to form a union—he come out, and says, 'I don't really have anything against the union, but right now we're getting started, and we don't have enough contracts to pay the wages you want to be paid.' So everybody was talking about all of this, and I said, 'Maybe we should wait until he does get more business.' But they were set about their ways." The company threatened to close the factory if the workers unionized. "Sure enough," Neal remembered, the workers "voted for the union, they shut the doors the next day, and that was the end of that job."

Neal and Cara thought about staying in West Virginia. When they first moved to Detroit, she left a job she liked at a dance studio. She had also taught dance at local high schools and had received threatening phone calls for working at Lincoln, Hinton's segregated school for Black children.[2] "I always asked her," Neal reflected, "did I pull her away from what she really wanted to do?" But Cara was willing to move wherever necessary for Neal to find a job, especially since she could potentially teach dance anywhere.

A few months later, Willa convinced them to return to southeast Michigan. Willa and her husband had relocated to Willow Run, near Ypsilanti, about thirty-five miles west of Detroit. Willa's husband had worked at the GM Transmission Plant in Livonia, just west of Detroit, until an explosion destroyed it in August 1953.[3] GM shifted its transmission operations to a portion of the huge plant in Willow Run that had produced bombers during World War II and had more recently been used by Kaiser-Frazer, an upstart, unsuccessful auto company. Although many former Livonia transmission employees were unable or unwilling to transfer to Willow Run, some fifteen to twenty miles away, Willa and her husband made the move, with Willa leaving her position at Ex-Cell-O. Willow Run was hiring as the economy picked up in late 1954, so Willa again called Neal, who came north and was quickly hired.

"I operated a broach there," Neal explained. "It was a huge job. This machine has three broaches. They're long things with teeth on them that cuts internal teeth in this drum for the transmission, see? So that was good. No problems." But shortly after Neal took the position, Cara's aunt died in West Virginia. He sent a telegram to plant management informing them that he needed a week's leave for the funeral: "Up front, good worker, no problems there." On their way back, however, a car crashed into them when they slowed down for a truck: "It was a young kid. Here he come around that curve, man, didn't even see it.

Wham! Puts us right into the truck. The rear lights flew out all over my baby. Oh my goodness! And we couldn't get out of the car. The doors were jammed." It took well over a week to sort out the insurance issues and to get the car repaired. Neal tried to keep his supervisor informed of the situation via telegram. But when he returned, his foreman said, "'You know I should fire you Neal. I don't know where you've been.' 'Come on, I sent you a telegram.' 'What telegram?' He wanted me to prove that I sent a telegram. Now he could have been lying. I don't know. But I went down to the Western Union office and they had a copy." Neal produced it for his foreman, who said, "'Get to work' And that was the end of *that* ordeal." Still, given his unsteady work history and his dedication to change his ways, this was a troubling incident.

Neal remained wary of GM management. Little things gnawed at him, such as company rules that he considered petty. For example, everybody had a locker for personal items: "The lockers go about the length of that plant. Well your job might be a half mile away from the locker. People would cheat a little bit. They'll take their coat, and they'll take it to their job, and they'll put it down by the machine somewhere or something." That could save time when leaving at the end of a shift. "So one night they came through. They was on a jacket drive. They must have had a hundred jackets they picked up, mine included. We couldn't say nothing because we knew what the rule was: put it in the locker. They just gathered them up. Boy, come quitting time, they had all these hundred jackets. They was all mixed up man, everybody scrambling to get their jacket and get out of there. I think mine was a white one. It was totally dirty when I got it. It was a little uncomfortable, things like that."

Neal had heard good things about a nearby Ford plant, in Ypsilanti, and checked to see if they were hiring: "I'd keep coming and bug them every month or so." One day in 1956 they offered him a position, and he took it. Hedging his bets, he kept his job at GM and worked at both plants, which violated UAW rules but was difficult to discover. He appreciated having two incomes from auto work: "That was good money back then." But it also took a toll: "I worked GM days, Ford's afternoons. I had thirty minutes to get from one job to the other. Cara would be standing at the door with a lunch bag." She'd give him a kiss and he'd be off to the Ford plant, but after two months like that, he recalled, "I was getting very tired."

He had to choose one or the other, and it came down to management. Neal had nearly completed his diesel mechanic course, finally, and all that remained was two weeks in Chicago for "in-shop training." But his GM foreman wouldn't let him go. In contrast, his Ford foreman responded positively. "That's no problem," Neal remembered him saying. "You got it. You'll be a benefit to us, probably." Neal promptly quit his GM job and stuck with Ford: "I think they recognize you more as a person than General Motors does. Back then." Once again, it never occurred to him to check with a UAW representative about his rights at GM, although doing so could have been risky since he had been breaking union rules for months. He also never went to Chicago to finish the diesel mechanic course.

Neal enjoyed his job at Ford, inspecting parts during the production process. His decisions were binding, and he liked the authority: "You take a sample out of the finished product, and if anything is faulty, you reject the whole thing. Production has to go through it again—all of them. So that's a good job, you see?" The job also required additional training and expertise: "You had to read blueprints, you had to read mikes [measuring gauges], and you had to pass these tests to get it, you see, so education helps."

But nothing was constant: "There would be cutbacks, and I'd go and drive a Hi-Lo some, and there was times I went on production work." Neal also experienced numerous layoffs. Occasionally the family would head back to West Virginia during these downtimes. Indeed, one of their children was born there during a layoff. But back in Michigan, Cara got a job at Moray's Jewelers in Ypsilanti as well as part-time work at an Arthur Murray Dance Studio in nearby Ann Arbor. Her earnings helped the family survive when Neal was out of work. They both wanted her to get a job at Ford, but company policy at the time prohibited a husband and wife from working in the same plant.

Cara's earnings were particularly important after her parents gave the couple $800 for a down payment on a house in Ypsilanti. It was difficult to make their $76-a-month payment on their loan, backed by the Federal Housing Administration, especially during the 1958 recession, when Neal was laid off for a year: "I did every kind of job you can think of. Most of it was with a company putting up cyclone fences, and they didn't have power posthole diggers. Hand operated—and the soil in this country is hard rock clay. We dug those things all day long. Our hands got very calloused. The guy sent us out on a job, no money to buy gas, didn't pay us half the time. It was rough. It was really rough. But you had to have a job to pull in a few bucks or pennies, whatever you could."

Neal was thrilled when he finally received a recall notice from Ford: "Back on inspection. And you couldn't *ask* for a better job." Autonomy and dignity were crucial: "Say you had to go to the bathroom, you'd go to the bathroom." And inspection, unlike production work, offered a degree of power, "a little bit like being a policeman. You want a quality part out the door here, and if it's not good enough, it's no good." Things could get contentious: "Boy, the people on the line, when you reject their stuff, then they would get irritated. Everybody wanted to get done early or something and just do it and get done. That put you in the middle, because here I am picking on my brothers and sisters." Fellow union members could be disciplined if they were at fault for shoddy work. Foremen, it turns out, could also pressure him to ease up on his enforcement: "I may see my Inspection Foreman and Production Foreman were talking at the coffee machine and come over and say, 'OK, let it go.'" Management had the final say, even if the parts were defective. "I think the main point was get it out the door, whether it's good or bad," Neal recalled, and he took note of the lesson. "I just slacked up. I felt, 'well, if they bought this before, then I'm not going to be so hard on my brothers and sisters next time.' But I did the inspection the best that I could, and I always had the quality in my mind. I don't worry about a little piece here or there, as long as it's not a safety factor, OK? 'No, I wouldn't want that on my car.' So I would say, 'I would have that on my car, yeah.' Make that kind of decision."

In the 1970s, Neal became interested in local union affairs and successfully ran for a position on the shop committee. He continued to work for the local until he retired in the early 1990s, when Cara became ill. Cara had worked at the Ypsilanti Ford plant, after the company's policy changed, until her health deteriorated. Neal and Cara moved to the country and eventually opened an antiques store in the Irish Hills, about twenty miles southwest of Ypsilanti.

One of Neal and Cara's three daughters worked in an auto plant, on cleanup in the same Ford Ypsilanti plant where Neal spent much of his career. Their daughter Cara worked for a Ford dealership in Belleville, about ten miles east of Ypsilanti, and Sherry worked for a corrugated box company in Lambertville, about forty miles south of Ypsilanti on the Ohio border.

2

Elwin Brown
(1931–2010)

Elwin Brown's parents separated when he was around four years old. His father had arrived alone in Pontiac, Michigan, in 1926, having left St. Thomas, Ontario, after the local steam locomotive plant shut down. In Pontiac, he found work at the General Motors Truck and Bus plant. Elwin's mother had moved to Pontiac from Michigan's "Thumb"—a peninsula on the east side of the state that protruded into Lake Huron—leaving behind an extended family of farmers. The second of three children, Elwin was born in Pontiac in December 1931. The circumstances of his parents' breakup remained fuzzy: "I just remember going to my grandmother's farm, between Forester and McGregor in the Thumb, and staying for two or three years. I went up there and spent first and second grade. I just stayed with my aunt and uncle, and two uncles, and my grandmother." His older brother went with him. His younger sister stayed in Pontiac with family friends.

Elwin's dad continued to work in Pontiac, having moved from Truck and Bus to Pontiac Motor, while his mother lived in Port Huron, about fifty miles south of the farm and fifty-five miles northeast of Pontiac. Eventually, however, there weren't enough people left to run the farm that had become home for Elwin and his brother. The boys' uncle Cap took a job at a power plant in Marysville, their uncle Lee got a job in Port Huron, and their uncle Ernie enlisted in the Army. So Elwin and his brother moved back to Pontiac to live with the Willis family, which had kinship connections to their mother in a complicated way. This time their sister joined them.

Agricultural chores dominated Elwin's early years. On his grandmother's farm, there "wasn't a whole lot I could do. I was too young. But I used to carry water to the tractors, go get the cattle, bring them out for milking and stuff like that." After returning to Pontiac, "My job was to take care of the garden, which I didn't like to do all the time—all the weeding and hoeing and all that kind of stuff. And we raised a lot of our own vegetables, potatoes included. I was responsible for taking care of most of that. We also had chickens, and then we got some hogs, and I took care of the hogs, too. I had one sow out there that was my baby. When they got ready to take her to have her slaughtered, I had to coax her out of the trailer." Elwin helped a neighbor farm the fields at the end of the street, then watched after WWII as that cropland became a housing subdivision.

The neighborhood kids in Pontiac loved to play sports, especially baseball and football. There was "a vacant piece of land across the street," Elwin recalled, "and one of the neighbors there had a Ford tractor with a plow on it. We plowed out a spot for the infield, laid it all out. Put our own backstop up with chicken wire and everything. I was interested in baseball, but I was no good at it. My brother was a baseball player." Some sibling rivalry, some envy, and perhaps some pent-up aggression from living apart from their parents became apparent during these contests: "We played scrub football in the fall. We had plenty of kids, and I was good at football and my brother didn't like that because I'd tackle him. He'd kick me. Kicked me in the jaw."

While living in Pontiac with the Willises, Elwin and his siblings saw their dad "all the time." Their mom also visited frequently from Port Huron. Still, Elwin missed the pre-separation family trips to visit relatives in Canada, and he regretted that disruptions prevented him from becoming an Eagle Scout: "I was bumped around all my life and I didn't get a chance to. I probably would've if I had got a chance." Elwin recalled that he "had some good times" with the Willises, especially when he "went up north with them and helped them build a cabin near Lincoln, Michigan, on Trask Lake," in the northeastern Lower Peninsula. He also enjoyed singing in the church choir and watching planes take off and land at the local airfield: "I'd ride my bike out there and sit around all Sunday afternoon, hoping for a ride. And I'd get a few, too."

Most of Elwin's formal schooling took place in Pontiac. He especially liked industrial arts classes: "I had some problems with English that I had to take over, and I went to summer school one year to make up a couple credits I needed. I played football when I was in high school, except for my senior year. My senior year I was working, so I decided I'd stay working rather than play football. I worked at the Lincoln Junior High cafeteria. And then I also worked in the Pontiac Central High School cafeteria." Just before Elwin graduated, however, his dad and the Willises had a falling out, so the Brown brothers moved into an apartment together while their sister went to live with family friends. Despite what happened, Elwin remained close with the Willises: "We stayed in touch right up to the time that they both passed away. I was a pallbearer at both of their funerals."

In January 1951, Elwin was working part-time at a local print shop, using skills he developed at Pontiac High School: "I helped set up the school newspapers, football programs, basketball programs—I used to do all that. I used to run the Kluge for all the commencement exercises. The Kluge was an old flatbed press that was converted to an automatic. I was taught how to run it, and I was one of the main men to run it in my two years there."[1] At the print shop, Elwin produced "information cards for the fire department, stationery, envelopes and stuff like that." He loved the work, but he had limited hours and didn't make much money.

Elwin's dad participated in the union organizing drive at Pontiac Motor in the 1930s and served several terms as an alternate shop committeeman, helping to settle disputes in the plant. Elwin remembered him as a "strong union man," mainly because of his concern with "working conditions." Elwin's dad firmly believed that Elwin should abandon printing and become an autoworker, especially when jobs were available at Pontiac Motor in early 1951. His dad's message was blunt: "Get your ass over there and get yourself a job!" Elwin obeyed, and began in mid-February: "My first job was stacking cardboard in the parts warehouse. It was all right. Something to do." He also "picked parts" to be mailed to repair shops, and he checked parts for quality. But after three months he was laid off and ended up working at a friend's gas station. Three months later he was recalled to work at Pontiac Motor.

His job was at the Retail Store, which prepared cars for purchasers around the country who wanted to avoid expensive delivery charges. "People would just come by train or airplane to Pontiac, pick up the car," Elwin explained, and drive it home, wherever that was. "They had people come in as far away as Alaska for them." Elwin's first job at the Retail Store, however, posed some difficulties. He was supposed to fill gas tanks, siphon out five gallons from each one to make sure the fuel gauges worked, then drive the cars to a parking lot. But he had never driven a car: "I more or less learned to drive in there."

As much as he liked the Retail Store, Elwin's low seniority made him vulnerable during slack times, and after a year he was transferred to Plant 9 in the Pontiac Motor complex. "My job there was to inspect pin bearings on the crankshaft," an essential part in car motors. He used "a stamp gauge that was the size of the pin" and checked the pin bearings "to make sure they weren't out of round or anything, and you marked them up if they were" and sent them to the Repair Department. "It was a little hard, but not that bad. You picked the crankshaft off the conveyors, and they picked out a person that was pretty hefty and pretty muscular to do it because the crankshaft, at that time, was heavy. And you'd lay it on the bench and then you'd inspect the pin bearings. When you got done with it, you'd pick it up and roll it down a chute to a guy in back of you, facing you, and he inspected the main bearings." Elwin worked with three others, each of them inspecting every fourth crankshaft that came down the line: "You'd find several that were a little bit out of round—you got to remember, the machinery that they were using was mainly from World War II—then they'd get re-inspected and sent on their way."

Elwin was working at this inspection job when his Army draft notice arrived. He remembered the precise date: July 23, 1952. "I took sixteen weeks of heavy weapons infantry basic at Camp Breckenridge, Kentucky, in the 101st Airborne Division," he recalled with pride. "Nothing I couldn't handle. Some guys didn't like it too well. Sometimes they'd make you get out of bed and go running early in the morning. When you get in ranks, you better be standing tall and not fooling around." Elwin had no trouble with weapons training, even though his experience with guns had been limited to deer hunting with his brother: "I learned to fire everything from a .45 caliber pistol up to a 4.2 mortar, which included the 75 recoilless rifle [75mm—also called the M20], .50 caliber machine gun, .30 caliber machine gun, M-1 rifle, BAR [Browning Automatic Rifle], and how to throw hand grenades."

War was on, and after six months, he shipped out for Korea. First and foremost, Elwin emphasized, he was "a BAR man. That weapon will put out about five hundred rounds a minute, if you want to fire it that fast. I did do that one time. I went out on patrol one day as a support group, and the support group got in trouble. I put about twenty rounds of clips through that weapon inside of ten minutes." Once he was almost killed: "Outpost Harry was right beside where we was on the main line. I went out on patrol over Outpost Harry," about sixty miles northeast of Seoul. "The thing I remember most was I had my head a little too high in the trenches. The guys that were in the Outpost Harry said, 'Get your head down there! There's a sniper out there!' Well, I got my head down. No sooner I got my head down, *ding*!" A bullet hit his helmet. "That's one of the things I really remember about Korea."

Elwin was also proud that he was chosen to attend Non-Commissioned Officer (NCO) school while in Korea. His commanders noted his skill and leadership abilities, which he had also demonstrated as a boy: "I was in Boy Scouts. I went through the ranks—patrol leader, assistant patrol leader. In sports, I kept the spirit up." He didn't have the athletic skill, he said, to be "captain or anything, but I kept the guys going when they got down." After completing NCO training and becoming an assistant squad leader, Elwin and the soldiers he led were sent to relieve a division of South Korean troops during the 48-hour truce before the signing of the armistice. He hated that duty: "All we had to do was sit there and make sure nothing happened. And you'd just sit there in the foxhole or in the bunkers. That's all you done for forty-eight hours—and pull patrol or guard duty. You talk about a miserable forty-eight hours. I didn't think it'd ever end!" The "only consolation," he recalled, was that his squad's mail finally appeared: "They had lost it when I was in NCO school, when the company got hit real hard" and had to retreat. But out of the blue "they brought me a stack of mail."

Some letters were from Elwin's fiancé, Hilda. He had met his future wife while he was stationed at Camp Breckinridge in Kentucky. On weekend leave, he could go anywhere within a ninety-mile radius, and he chose Evansville, Indiana, a relatively bustling city about thirty miles northeast of the base. He stayed at the YMCA, "because it only cost you two or three bucks." While there he looked downtown for a church to attend: "Church was drilled into me, from the time I was a kid. First it was the Presbyterian Church, and then the Willises organized a community church, a non-denominational church. And that's where I went after that. It was just a religious upbringing. When I went in the service, it followed me." The Evansville pastor introduced him to a young woman—Hilda's sister. Elwin returned whenever he could, and he ended up dating Hilda: "I liked her better, anyway, and my wife and her sister still don't get along." Elwin and Hilda both enjoyed singing, especially in church, something they continued to do for years.

Elwin remained in Korea until May 1954, long after the July 1953 armistice, teaching troops how to use the Browning Automatic Rifle: "They also had alerts that the whole company would be called out on. The trucks would come and pick you up and you'd go. You wouldn't know if it was practice or real." For the most part, though, Elwin's post-armistice stint "was just a bivouac—camping." Eventually he had the choice of either four years on active or eight years on inactive reserve. He seriously considered re-enlisting, perhaps opting for a military career, but he became "disgusted" with the Army: "I had a bad experience in Korea with a captain. He was just on me, because another person in that unit, I got his rank instead of him. It's as simple as that." The captain sided with the one passed over for promotion, and made life miserable for Elwin, who got out by choosing inactive reserve.

Shortly after returning to the US, Elwin bought a new car, a '54 Chevrolet. He drove it to Evansville to see Hilda, he recalled, "and we got married the

18th day of June." For their honeymoon, the newlyweds traveled to Pontiac, and Hilda quickly "decided that she wanted to live in Evansville." Elwin agreed, hoping to re-enter the printing business, the profession he liked best: "I went down there and tried to find a job and couldn't. They had a couple big printing plants in Evansville. My father-in-law got me into them for interviews, but they weren't hiring." The nation was in a recession. After nearly three months, the couple moved back to Pontiac and utilized their fallback plan. Upon leaving active service, Elwin had ninety days "to hire back in on my old job" at Pontiac Motor "and hold my seniority. I hired in on the eighty-fifth day." Shortly after reclaiming his inspection job, however, and about the same time the couple learned that Hilda was pregnant, he received a layoff notice.

Even before this most recent setback, Elwin had thought about leaving Pontiac Motor: "I had an opportunity to go to work for Halliburton," in the oil and gas industry. Hilda accompanied him to his interview and they seriously discussed the possibility of a career switch, but in the end the likelihood of frequent relocations was too much of a drawback: "So we gave that up and I come back and went to work, and I got laid off." He and Hilda returned to Evansville: "We didn't have that much. We just packed everything up in the car and moved back down. We moved back in with her folks and stayed there." Elwin picked up odd jobs to provide a bit of income. When he received a recall notice from Pontiac Motor in the fall, he moved back to Michigan and stayed with his father and stepmother. Given their most recent experience with auto employment, Hilda remained in Evansville.

Work was relatively steady at Elwin's new job in Plant 9, "machining synchromesh flywheels" for transmissions: "I learned to run the whole line. I could run the drill press, I could run the balancer. I probably had it down pat in a couple weeks." With Elwin's situation apparently stabilized, Hilda joined him in early 1955: "And my daughter was born in May of that year. My one and only daughter. My one and only kid we've ever had."

Hilda had a difficult time adjusting to Pontiac: "She didn't have no *relatives* up here. No friends." Hilda was also taken aback by what seemed to be, by Evansville standards, relatively desegregated public accommodations and institutions: "Of course, I was raised in this area, so I was used to colored being in the school with me, and to getting along. Now when I met my wife, they hadn't integrated the schools in Evansville yet, as far as the upper grades go. You had a colored high school, two white high schools, plus the Catholic schools."[2] Buses also provided contrasts in race relations. Elwin explained to Hilda that Blacks "don't have to sit in the back of the bus here. I went to Evansville and rode the city bus there when I was going with my wife, go from town out to where she lived. I'd ride in the back of the bus. I didn't think anything of it. But they didn't do that down there. That's for the colored," Hilda told him. "She's a Southern gal." Elwin noted, though, that things changed over time: "My wife gets along with them. She has several colored friends now that she worked with at Crowley's," a department store. "They still get together." At the time, to ease Hilda's homesickness the Browns visited Evansville as often as they could, sometimes for extended stays.

When auto production slowed in mid-1956, Elwin was transferred to Plant 5, which rekindled ideas about leaving auto work: "Thought about being a policeman. Some job in government. But I never did do it. I kept with Pontiac." It helped that his new job in Plant 5, building rear end assemblies for Oldsmobiles and Pontiacs, was running full time. Still, it was never clear how long that would last, and even working full time, it was hard to make ends meet: "We lived from paycheck to paycheck. I can remember the apartment we lived in on Huron Street. I wondered if I was going to have enough gas to make it to payday." Despite living frugally, Elwin and Hilda were unable to create a financial cushion until the late 1960s. But everything was manageable compared to 1958: "I got laid off from March of '58 till November of '58. That's the longest period of time I was off." At first, he had no luck finding an alternate job, although he did claim unemployment pay. In August, just before those benefits expired, "the preacher's son asked me, 'Why don't you go caddying with me?' I caddied right up until the snow fell. That's when I got called back to work. Right in the nick of time."

During that 1958 layoff, the Browns had trouble keeping a roof over their heads, moving three times. A friend offered them space in his house, then asked them to leave, "because my daughter was making too much noise." In the middle of the baby boom, it was difficult to find landlords who would rent to families with children. Desperate, the Browns met a retired couple who wanted to sell their home. During the 1958 recession, however, the owners couldn't find a buyer but still wanted to travel, so they cut Elwin and Hilda a deal on rent if they would take care of the entire house. The real estate market remained grim when the owners returned, so Elwin offered to buy the property. He converted the upstairs into two rental units to help pay the mortgage, kept the downstairs for his family, and the Browns ended up living there for twenty-five years.

Still, nothing came easily at work in the late '50s and early '60s. After being recalled to Pontiac Motor in November 1958, Elwin ended up back in assembly, installing exhaust manifolds. It was "hard," he recalled, because of the angle at which the parts arrived on the line: "Made my back sore." He quickly put in a transfer request, hoping to return to the parts warehouse, where he had been working in early 1958. His request was granted, but only for a short time.

Business conditions slowed and he got transferred again and again. Once, he was put "on a machine running left-hand exhaust manifolds." He found it too repetitive, "but they found out I could do a lot of things so they pulled me off that machine and put me on other machines a lot of times. Put me on the right-hand side for a while sometimes, and sometimes I'd be on the intake manifold. I learned them all." He also worked on job setting, making sure everybody had the proper tools and parts, in the flywheel department: "Plus I had a drill press I had to change over. I had the balancers I had to take care of."

Eventually the company rewarded his aptitude and versatility with an invitation to enter the skilled trades. It was unusual for someone his age to get such a chance, but the economy picked up in 1963 and there was sudden demand for more skilled workers. With crucial help from a foreman who attended his church, Elwin entered the eight-year Employee in Training program, a chance of a lifetime: "I had some ups and downs when I was on hourly, but once I got on the trades, I never had any ups and downs anymore. More *ups* than downs." The best things about it, he emphasized, were "money and security. Because unless things went kaput all over, you had security in the job. You was working a lot when nobody else was." After his eight years in training, he received his journeyman's card. "I still got it on me," he noted, more than thirty years later, well after retirement. Elwin did well with his opportunities, but he also indirectly recognized that Black workers could not follow his path. "When the colored come into the plant, they were hired as sanitation, lower end," he explained, mainly as "chippers and sweepers," responsible for cleaning up metal debris that accumulated around the machines. Only gradually did Black workers gain access to the types of production jobs that allowed Elwin to demonstrate his abilities, and Black workers were not allowed to enter the skilled trades.

Yet stability did not come easily for Elwin. He battled through family trauma, gave up on a printing career, had his work career interrupted by military service, considered giving up on auto work several times, endured numerous layoffs and unwelcome job transfers, and had difficulty supporting and finding housing for his family, before finally benefiting from an inside connection to get him into the skilled trades. He was justifiably proud for having made it through tough times.

Elwin and Hilda recognized their daughter Sherry's interest in music and bought her a piano when she was eight. She eventually graduated with a degree in music from Western Michigan University and played the organ for various churches, especially for weddings and funerals. Elwin remained interested in airplanes, although it was too expensive to become a pilot, so he focused on experimental model aircraft. He took on a leadership role with a local model airplane organization after he retired from Pontiac Motor in 1985. He also called Bingo games at his American Legion Post. When Sherry's marriage ended and she was laid off from her job, she and her two sons moved in with Elwin and Hilda. Elwin loved this opportunity to connect with his grandsons. Perhaps his fondest memory was helping his older grandson complete the service requirement to become an Eagle Scout.

3

Paul Ross

(1925–2009)

"I never knew my dad," Paul Ross made clear. "I don't know where he come from, or where he went." Paul didn't see his mom much either, and his memories of her were not fond: "My mother told me don't take this bell apart on the tricycle. I did it anyhow, and she beat the hell out of me." Paul was born in Asheville, North Carolina, in 1925. Shortly afterward, his mother got a nursing job in Greensboro, 170 miles to the east, and eventually sent Paul to live with her mother in a town—Leaksville, later named Eden—about thirty miles north of her new home. "My grandmother more or less raised me," Paul explained. But it was hardly a warm and nurturing environment. His grandmother had married when she was eleven years old and had given birth to eleven children, several of whom still lived at home: "It was like a boarding house. Everybody and his brother lived there."

Paul's grandfather held jobs as a brick mason in the private sector and as a "revenue man," busting moonshiners for the federal government. Still, it was difficult to feed such a large extended family: "I used to sit down at the far end of the table, and after the prayer, whatever was in front you better get a good helping of it, because time that chicken got down to me, the only thing left was neck and feet! I grew up hungry. I was always hungry." Paul worked in his grandparents' garden and occasionally milked cows on an uncle's dairy farm. He saw his mother at best every three months, sometimes only twice a year. Whenever Paul got in trouble, his grandfather would "go get a switch off the tree" and whip him. In contrast, his cousins were merely scolded for their transgressions and were quickly comforted by their mothers, while his mom was far away.

School didn't go much better: "It seemed like I spent about five years in the fifth grade. I even spent two years in the first grade. They didn't learn me enough, so I had to stay back a little bit more." Discipline was an issue: "I used to start in the back of the class, way in the back, and before the year was up, I was sitting next to the teacher and looking at the class, sitting next to her desk. I must have been a son of a gun. But I didn't get much education. I wouldn't give you a plug nickel for my childhood."

When Paul was around twelve, his mother married a man from Michigan: "A Yankee, a northerner. How he got down in Carolina, I don't know." His mom moved to South Lyon, Michigan to live with her husband, who worked in the foundry at Pontiac Motor, thirty miles to the northeast. About a year later, his mom and stepdad sent word that Paul could join them. His grandmother accompanied him on the train, but no one was there to greet them at the station in Detroit, so they slept on a bench. Paul's mother later claimed that she had tried to find them but couldn't. Paul took off the next morning without telling his grandmother: "I got out there and hitchhiked down Grand River to Farmington, which is 10 Mile Road, and goes into South Lyon. And I got on 10 Mile Road, and I was eating apples all the way," from the orchards along the way. Finally, "some woman picked me up in a Model A and took me into South Lyon." Meanwhile, his grandmother had stayed in Detroit, "waiting for my mother." When his mom, stepdad, and grandmother arrived in South Lyon, he was waiting on the front porch. It was a relatively new house on ten acres of land, surrounded by farms.

For Paul, life in Michigan was only a marginal improvement: "When I come up here, they didn't cotton to hillbillies too well." School still went poorly. Paul remembered digging potatoes on nearby farms for a dollar a day, mowing the ten acres surrounding his stepdad's house—no power mowers back then—and hunting: "I used to go out there and lay on a fencerow, and I'd shoot a pheasant in the head with one shot, .22, and we'd eat that." Occasionally his stepdad would take him out to practice with a shotgun, but those were the highlights in South Lyon. "One thing led to another," Paul remarked, cryptically. "We never got along, you know, me and my stepdad."

A couple of years later, in 1940, Paul lied about his age and signed on at a Civilian Conservation Corps (CCC) camp near Crescent Lake, between South Lyon and Pontiac. The CCC was a federal government program during the Great Depression that put young men to work on projects such as planting trees and building recreation facilities. CCC recruits were supposed to be eighteen, but at fifteen Paul was big for his age and nobody checked. He remained despondent, some sixty years later, at his mother's indifference. Her response to his enlistment was, "Who cares?" CCC officials soon transferred him to their East Tawas camp on Lake Huron, 180 miles north of Detroit, where, he quipped, he served as "'latrine sergeant.' Nobody wanted that job! Taking care of the latrine, and then take care of the boiler at night." As for his fellow CCC members, "they all went to the forest to plant trees, or whatever the hell they did. I stayed home, stayed in the camp, you know, keep my nails clean."

Around nine months later, Paul was sent to the CCC camp in Lake Gogebic, Michigan, in the Upper Peninsula, some 550 miles from South Lyon. Still on nighttime boiler watch and daytime latrine duty, he had laundry service added to his list of responsibilities. With access to laundry facilities, he made extra money on the side, much of which he spent in Hurley, Wisconsin, a border town about forty miles away, where "beer was a nickel a glass" and a dollar could get you a session at a "house of repute." Paul said he didn't like it all that much: "You're young, and you're away from home." But it wasn't at all clear where he might have felt more grounded: "I didn't get along at home too good." Paul remained in the CCC for a year, until the summer of 1941: "You're supposed to take six months, but they can give you an extra six." Then he returned to South Lyon.

Auto plants checked his age and wouldn't hire a sixteen-year-old. The Army also rejected him for being too young. But in October, he successfully joined the Navy. It took some doing. He and three friends set out for California on a road trip: "So we got to Oklahoma, and blew out some tires. We'd steal tires at night and keep going. But then pretty soon we got down to about Texas, New Mexico, we blew a rod. And we got on the bus and went on into L.A." At that point, two of his friends headed back to Michigan while Paul and the fourth in the group headed for San Diego: "I had to do something. Not much education. Just illiterate running around there loose. So I got down there and I told them I'd sign up for thirty years. I'm tired of starving." In a telegram, Paul's mother lied about his age, claiming that he was seventeen, so he ended up on what was called a "minority cruise." He would be eligible for discharge when he turned twenty-one.

"I only spent about two weeks in boot camp," Paul recalled. "And most of that was in the dentist's chair. Never shot a gun the whole time. What they needed was people on them ships. What they needed was a strong back to haul stuff." During that brief training period, he occasionally wondered if he had made the right decision. But then he'd "go down to Marine basic training next door to the Navy base training station. I'd go over and watch them Marines, and believe me, man, when I come out of there, I said, 'Whew! Am I glad I didn't go in no Marines.'" Instead, he ended up on a supply ship heading for the naval base at Pearl Harbor, in Hawaii: "We let off the material, then we come back on the cargo ship." Three days later, when his ship was approaching San Diego, the crew heard the news about the Japanese attack.

Now at war, the Navy assigned Paul to the *U.S.S. Idaho*, a battleship commissioned shortly after World War I. There were several months of training maneuvers off the San Diego coast. But the highlight of this period, Paul claimed, was dancing with movie stars Bette Davis and Ida Lupino while on shore leave. In October 1942, the Navy scheduled the *Idaho* for serious upgrading: "We had to get fitted for war, so we went to Bremerton, Washington for three months. I think it rained every day up there. They put what they call torpedo bumpers around our ship and all that stuff." In April 1943, the *Idaho* participated in the campaign to dislodge Japanese forces from the Aleutian Islands in Alaska. "Took Attu and Kiska away from the Japanese," Paul said, although enemy forces had left before U.S. troops arrived. In late 1943, after their Alaskan operations, Paul and the *Idaho* were deployed to the areas of fiercest fighting in the Pacific: "We went to the Gilbert Islands, that's Makin and Tarawa. We become a bombardment group, the old battleships. We bombed the islands before they landed. We sat out there in the atolls and bombed them for days in and days out." Next, the *Idaho* participated in the successful assault on the Marshall Islands. Then, Paul recalled, "we went up to Saipan, which is the Marianas. And we sat there in Saipan, bombarding that. We had what they call Kingfishers—planes—on our ship. They would go over and spot guns, and we would bombard them. Saipan was very, very hard to take. They was entrenched there quite big. They had the guns embedded in the mountains."

At first, Paul was on the ship deck, but then a friend convinced him to join the "black gang," the crew that worked below deck with the boilers, turbine, refrigeration, and water desalinization units. It amounted to a crash course in engineering and machine repair for him as the crew kept the ship running. Boilers needed relatively salt-free water, as did humans, and providing ample supplies became Paul's primary duty: "Water for the boilers, it had to be pure, but as drinking water we let it be salty, 0.7 percent. You couldn't taste it." Work, however, was never all-consuming for Paul. Between the Marshall and Marianas campaigns, the ship and crew spent some time in Australia, where he quickly fell in love with a woman who, he said, looked like the movie star Laraine Day. They were headed for marriage, he insisted, but he shipped out and the romance ended.

Long before fighting ended in the Pacific, Paul successfully transferred back to the United States: "I wanted to get home before the war was over." He was stationed at Mare Island, near San Francisco, where he encountered, for the first time, a military unit consisting of women—he remembered them as WACS, members of the Women's Army Corps, but they might have been WAVES, Women Accepted for Voluntary Emergency Service: "We was marching, struggling along, and here comes this 'hup two' crowd, and it was WACs, marching along. They could put us to shame." It reminded him of scenes at sea: "When I was on board ship, on the *Idaho*, there ain't a day didn't go by they didn't have those Marines up on that deck going hup two, hup two, hup two. I said, 'Are you crazy?'"

Paul earned a leave, so he headed cross-country to Pontiac, where his mother had moved. "I think I found about every woman I could find," he bragged, "In them days, it was something. I was doing good." He also took an unauthorized trip to North Carolina to visit his grandmother. He managed to avoid the military Shore Patrol until he was back in Michigan, where he was supposed to be: "I had all the paperwork. You got your ID and your leave papers, and they didn't bother you after that. That was all legal there—well, I mean I was shady legal. I didn't get caught."

Upon his return, Paul was sent to Boston to serve on a ship that "carried Marine raiders, 180 Marines. We worked with the invasion forces." But first they had to get the ship and crew battle-ready, which included a cruise to Bermuda, passage through the Panama Canal, and a stop at Pearl Harbor before heading to the Philippines. Although he missed the Iwo Jima campaign, his ship was involved with the final stages of the Okinawa assault. Once again, Paul was stationed below deck, this time maintaining the steam boilers to generate electricity. He was also close with the guy serving as the "jack o' the dust," who was in charge of the food supplies. Together they traded extra food for shots of liquor, which were provided to the Marines after dangerous missions. The Marines coveted fresh-baked bread: "What we would do is trade them a half of a loaf and a quarter pound of butter for two shots—and we got them suckers lined up like that. Went on a binge." Legendary poker games also took place below deck, all while the ship's guns bombarded Okinawa in advance of the landing.

Paul noted that his former ship, the *Idaho*, also participated in the shelling of Okinawa. "Should have stayed on that son of a bitch," he insisted, with hints of truth and sarcasm. "I had it easy. Ice cream every day." On his new ship, he said, "you had more work to do." Yet all had not been easy for the *Idaho*. That ship suffered serious hits during kamikaze attacks: "They did a lot of damage. I could see a lot of that stuff. The worst thing that we had going around out in the sea was having these hospital ships. We didn't want them nowhere around us. They was lit up like a Christmas tree." He remembered as well sitting on deck and seeing "a big flame come up at the horizon, out in the ocean, somewhere. That was them 'Kaiser Coffins,'" small aircraft carriers named for Henry Kaiser, the industrialist whose company produced them. "They held about fifteen, twenty planes maybe. They called them coffins. They was very thin."

The fear of kamikazes intensified after troops landed ashore: "We went on picket duty after they invaded. Out in the ocean. We had to be out there on the outline to radio when they was coming this way. They'd come over by the hundreds." Once his ship was hit: "We had to go back to the States for repairs. They was still fighting on the beach. So we went back to LA, to San Pedro—we had Navy docks there—to get fixed. We stayed there twenty-two days. You talk about getting messed up. With that Hilton Hotel on 6th Street, we had a suite of rooms, and we run like crazy, man." Once repaired, the ship headed back to the Pacific theater, but "three days out of San Pedro, the war was over. That was it!"

Instead of heading toward defeated Japan, Paul's ship went to Haiphong, in Vietnam: "The dock was full of Japanese," who had occupied Vietnam during the war. "All they did was take baths and have a stick to beat each other in case somebody got mad. But they was all surrendered then." Ignoring orders, Paul and some friends bribed the guard on night duty and explored the city: "Me and my two buddies got a rickshaw. On one side of the street was French, and the other side was the Nationalist [Chinese] troops." The atmosphere was tense and dangerous: "We just wore dungarees. We didn't even wear our white hat. Some of them thought we was Spanish sailors or something like that. But we was American." If he had made a false move, or showed a gun, he suspected, "they would have shot me full of holes. And you wasn't even supposed to be on the beach to start with. The Navy would have said, 'Good riddance!'" His ship remained in Vietnam for several months, the crew assisting the transition from wartime conditions to what turned out to be the return of French colonial rule, thwarting Vietnamese dreams of independence.

From there, the American ship headed to the Chinese coast, where it spent another few months. Once again, Paul and his compatriots snuck ashore, this time trading Pabst Blue Ribbon beer for food and sex: "They unloaded shit-loads of that stuff over there. Of course, I took care of the cooler aboard the ship—refrigeration. Finally got caught one time over there. They was going to throw us in the brig, but we didn't have no brig." Instead, he explained, "they started registers. We had to check in every half hour." That system was hardly foolproof. At night, Paul said, "they'd put some boatswain or something" on duty, someone less than diligent, and "down that gangplank we'd go, down into the night, come back before daylight." Paul and his partners also took advantage of the postwar turmoil and sold food from the ship's stores to the desperate Chinese: "We went to Shanghai and the Yangtze River there, and we were sitting in dock, and we were selling oranges, potatoes, eggs, everything off of the back of the ship, which you wasn't supposed to be doing." After another stint in Haiphong, where Paul and his coworkers continued their black-market operations, they headed back to California: "I got discharged there."

Paul returned to Pontiac: "Thumbed a ride back." It was 1947, and he quickly landed a job at the Baldwin Rubber plant: "I worked mostly midnights. The old and the ugly, they all work days. Young kids work at night. What you did was make rubber mats for cars, and they made tires and tubes and all kinds of electric wire, for housing and stuff like that. Anything you'd wrap in rubber." Before long, however, the United Rubber Workers local at his plant went on strike, and he had little desire to wait it out, "so I went to Fisher Body," also in Pontiac.[1] He stayed there for seven or eight months, working on door assembly. It was a hard job, and Paul didn't like it. "I'm above that work stuff," he said, half-jokingly.

One day he went to Pontiac Motor and was hired for a position in nickel plating. Immediately, he "went back to Fisher Body and quit. I just up and left. Didn't worry about it." The two main tasks in his new department were stripping and plating, involving vats of either harsh chemicals or metal solutions, for creating the shiny metal exteriors on bumpers and other car parts. Stripping the metal parts required careful monitoring: "You had to be right there, stuff was coming through, you had to handle it." Plating, however, was a bit more relaxed: "You just did it on the time. You hear the gong, you go get the stuff out, put new stuff in." Although there were production quotas, the pace was not as relentless as his door assembly job at Fisher Body: "You could take your time." Eventually, Paul found a niche, preparing parts to be dipped in the various solutions: "You rack material to go into metal plate to be plated. It would be copper first, then nickel, and then chrome." He worked in the nickel plate department for about four years, while living with his mother and stepfather, until he was laid off in 1952.

Unsure how long the layoff would last, Paul asked his foreman if his experience as a mechanic in the Navy might make him eligible for a skilled trades apprenticeship. His boss thought it would be a good idea: "So I went down and got in the pipe gang. I went in as a trainee. I think it was only eight or nine of us. And then it was three years training on the job." This was an accelerated program, a year less than the usual four, which credited him for his previous work maintaining boilers and pipes on Navy ships. He got the position just in time. When there was a boom in civilian auto production in early 1953, auto companies rushed to increase the number of skilled tradesmen and offered fast-track apprenticeships to many people with far more experience and scholastic aptitude than Paul: "Thank God I got in before them. I never would have made that apprenticeship. I didn't have enough education to be dog beans at that time." But his program was hardly a breeze. "I had a hell of a time," he recalled. Foremen "used to get on our back." They'd ride the trainees and threaten them with demotion: "Hey, you're out of here, boy! Back to production!" Nevertheless, he survived and became a journeyman: "After that, you could do what you want to."

An African American autoworker at the time, however, would never have had the opportunity to learn various trades in the Navy and would never have been considered for the accelerated program that took Paul. Black workers, Paul noted, had been limited to "menial jobs, the sweeping, the cleaning, stuff like that," in support of the white skilled tradesmen. Paul compared it to what he had observed in the service: "There was no Black people in the Navy. We had a few on board that old battleship—officers' orderlies, that was it." Over the course of Paul's career, he recalled, Black workers gained entry into the skilled trades, "and they worked out good." But there was plenty of resistance from the white tradesmen. Some of his coworkers would say, "What we going to do is send that Black guy back to Africa, and we going to put a white guy, a hillbilly, under each arm and send him back."

Shortly after finishing his training program, Paul got married. He met his future wife, Sally, at the Oakland County Boat Club, where he and a friend often went sailing: "We had a 21-foot little sailboat. It always flopped over." Sally was a secretary at a law office in Pontiac, and the couple had five children together, beginning in 1954. Financially, Paul recalled, "it was rough. We didn't make much money in them days." He didn't offer many details about his family life: "You lived in a house, go to work every day. Waterford School system. Had one of them '57 Chevrolet station wagons. Wore that thing out." All they were doing, he remembered, was "staying alive. I think our biggest day was on Friday, going to McDonald's. That was it."

Life for Paul tended to revolve around work—he said that Sally cited excessive overtime when she sought a divorce after twenty-seven years of marriage—and the Elks Lodge, where he enjoyed hanging out with coworkers from Pontiac Motor. "Friendship," he said, is what the Elks meant to him. Much of their talk revolved around various dramas in the workplace, often involving bosses they did not like. Remembering one new foreman, Paul remarked, "First thing he did was spit on my shoe." Then there was the infamous boss they called Dooby: "He was all right when he was foreman, but when he made General Foreman, he became a nightmare. He didn't like me to start with." Dooby insisted that the maintenance crew be at their work sites with toolboxes beside them the moment their shifts started, which was difficult to do when the time clock was in the basement and jobs on any particular day might be far from that spot. Dooby didn't care, Paul said, and issued numerous disciplinary write-ups. "Dooby was a son of a bitch," Paul ranted. "We went to a baseball game one time, down at Tiger Stadium, and we come by White Chapel. Dooby was buried in there. He had a massive stroke or something. He was fairly young too. So we stopped the bus at the cemetery and relieved ourselves on his grave." Perhaps part of the extreme response was management's indifference to safety. Repairs and maintenance were required in all kinds of dangerous places: "We had 8-inch pipes, 6-inch pipes. Used to have 40-foot ladders you run up with a big wrench. You fall and you're dead! We lost a lot of people in that pipe gang."

In the mid-1950s, Paul gained extra income from a gambling ring he ran in his department: "What I did is run a check pool. Everybody gets a check once a week—in them days they paid you by check—and you had a number on it." Workers in the pool picked their best five numbers, as if they were a playing a hand of cards: "Everybody that wanted to play, they'd pay a dollar, and whoever got the best poker hand won the money," minus Paul's cut. At times, he remembered, "we had about 300 people in that sucker. I took care of the books." Each payday, Paul determined the winner: "Pay them off, and then start next Wednesday, start picking up the check pool again. Worked that way for months, years. I made my car payments and stuff on that." Then, in the late '50s, his General Foreman transferred him to another department, after refusing Paul's offer of payoffs from the gambling pool to let him stay.

Many years later at annual UAW retiree picnics, Paul held court at a table on the edge of the festivities, offering wisecracks and commentary on events, past and present. He also had numerous photo albums filled with pictures of himself with celebrities. His fellow retirees called him "The Senator," perhaps for his freely offered opinions and filibustering ways. But it had been a long struggle from being an abused and neglected kid in North Carolina to a retired skilled tradesman with a pension. He owed it all, he said, to the United Auto Workers: "If it wasn't for the UAW, I'd be dog beans, nothing! Everything we got, we owe to the union. If there hadn't been that union, I wouldn't have lasted at that place. There would have been a lot of us gone. They just look at you crossway and you're out of there."

Unlike many of his fellow skilled tradesmen, he never begrudged the wage and benefit compression, especially in the 1950s, that reduced the economic distance between themselves and production workers.[2] Maybe, he said, "we should have had a better this, or better retirement. In other words, if you're the lowest, you still get the same retirement, stuff like that. There wasn't that much difference in the pay, either." But, he reasoned, "they got to live too, you know. Ain't no free lunch out there."

Beginning in the mid-'60s, Paul spent time as a union benefits representative, handling disputes over pensions, unemployment pay, and health insurance. He didn't recall those duties with great enthusiasm, but he appreciated that he had been appointed by regional UAW officials because they thought he would do a good job. He was married a second time, for twenty years, until his wife died in 1998, about ten years after he retired. "Marriage is good," he reflected. "I think if you ain't married, it's a useless life, really. I enjoyed it. I used to holler, 'I'm nothing but a slave around this house!' I wish I was a slave again. Now my life isn't meaningful." Most of his former world was gone. By the early 2000s, Pontiac Motor was virtually extinct and the local Elks Lodge had lost three-quarters of its membership. There were still nearly 8,000 Pontiac Motor retirees, but many of them, he said, were struggling: "Some of them are living on food stamps—a lot of them. It's taking every dime I make today to live, but I'm better off than a lot of them."

4

Margaret Beaudry
(1925–)

People learned not to tangle with Margaret Beaudry. Barely five-feet tall, she challenged foremen, a superintendent, the FBI, and any number of boorish coworkers: "I demanded respect. And if you didn't give me no respect, because of the way I was brought up, I *demanded* it. I made a big deal out of it." Margaret Hill was born in December 1925 in tiny Chatham, Michigan, a rural crossroads in the state's Upper Peninsula with "a bar, and a restaurant, and a gas station, and a post office." Her parents were mostly Finnish, with some Italian heritage on her mother's side. She was the sixth of twelve children—eight boys and four girls—and the third sister. "When I bring my mother's name up, I cry," Margaret said, with tears. "She was wonderful. And didn't have no life, really. But, oh, we loved our mother very much. My mother was such a wonderful mother that she made each one of us think they were her favorite without letting the other one know it." Although Margaret also loved her father, she rarely saw him: "He worked in heavy equipment. Construction. So he used to get his jobs out of state. There were times he was away from home and the job was over with, but he didn't have money to come home."

Margaret's mother made do with limited resources: "I had a good life. But poor. Talk about being poor! I came from *poor* family, but we had so much love that we didn't even think nothing of it." The Hill family "didn't have no telephone. Didn't have no electric lights, either. No indoor bathroom. We had kerosene. And I remember when we got our first gas lamp. Was that wonderful!

It was like electric lights. I mean, it really brightened up the place. But other than that, we didn't even use candles." Her mother was afraid they'd burn the house down. "Sometimes my mom would say, 'well now kids, if your dad don't get home tonight or in the morning, I don't know what I'm going to have for you to eat tomorrow.' And I'd say, 'Well ma, you don't have to worry about me because I'm invited to my girlfriend's house. So you can eat my share.' My mother went without many times." Most people in the area, Margaret recalled, "were very proud. They didn't want to ask for help. But boy, my mother used to say, 'It is a *sin* to have so much pride that you won't ask for help when you have children's mouths to feed.' So she *did* go and try and get help when my dad was away for so long." At age nine, Margaret began contributing to the family's finances with her first babysitting job. On occasion, Margaret's dad tried to convince the family to move to a different state. But neither mom nor kids would consider it. Chatham is what they knew, they had relatives in the area—"piles of them"—and, as Margaret conceded, "we didn't know any better."

Staying put required pitching in during the long, cold winters in the Upper Peninsula: "We had wood stoves. That's how we heated our place. My God, some of the mornings we'd wake up and we couldn't get out of the house because it would be a big, big storm, you know. And then we used to have to help dig the wood out from underneath the snow banks." Delivery trucks dumped "big chunks" of wood near the main road, "and we all took turns with my mother to saw them" so they'd fit in the stove.

Margaret enjoyed school and was a good student—there were twelve in her graduating class—but a summer program had a lasting impact on her: "It was for the children that didn't have nothing. There was this one fellow, our first recreational leader. He was college educated, and he made up programs. We had horseshoe tournaments, and we used to go swimming, and we used to take tap dancing lessons, and I always sang." Margaret also remembered that a lady from the nearest city, Marquette, offered tap dancing lessons at her school on Saturdays: "Me and my brothers and sisters couldn't afford none of those things. But I used to go with my girlfriend when she took the lessons and I could watch. I learned, I came back home, and I taught all the other girls." Margaret also participated in entertainment programs at a nearby nursing home: "It was a beautiful place. Most of the people up there were Finnish and these were people that had a different accent and could hardly speak English. I used to go there and sing for those older people, and dance." These experiences sparked Margaret's imagination: "I used to dream that I was going to be in show business. Of course, that didn't pan out." Nevertheless, singing and dancing became lifelong passions.

As a teenager, Margaret longed to escape small-town life: "What is my life going to be like? It was not going to be in Chatham. It was *definitely* going to be away." In 1935, when Margaret was ten, her oldest sister led an exodus: "She was married, and of course jobs were not available then." Her sister's husband got a job at Pontiac Motor, then helped Margaret's brother George land a construction job in the Pontiac area. When Margaret was fifteen, she spent the summer in Pontiac with her brother: "I just lied my age, and I got a job." It was at Scrib's Drive-Inn, a popular local restaurant. After this taste of city life, Margaret returned to Chatham for school: "Oh God, I hated it. I hated it. I said, 'Well I'm not staying here.'" She might have stayed for a boyfriend, several years older, named Marvin Beaudry. She met him when she snuck out to hear her brother Frank sing with a band. Marvin "was very nice. But he didn't know I was as young as I was." The Japanese attack on Pearl Harbor, however, motivated Marvin to enlist in the Army Air Corps, and "because he wasn't there, I didn't want to be there." After finishing the school year, Margaret left for Pontiac with no intention of returning.

Back in Pontiac, Margaret found a job at Neisner's, a dime store: "I worked in the stock room. I was the helper for the lady that was the main manager. And it just so happened that we became very good friends because she was from the Soo"—a nickname for Sault Ste. Marie, Michigan—"and that's in the Upper Peninsula. Her husband was in secret service, and she's a lot older than me. She could've been my mother, you know. We had an apartment together in a doctor's house, and she taught me everything about the business."

But Margaret wanted to be near Marvin, so she bought a bus ticket to Dodge City, Kansas, where he was stationed. "Can you believe it?" she laughed. "I was sixteen years old!" The heat and humidity of a Kansas summer almost did her in. "I'm going back home!" she insisted to Marvin. "But anyway, we got married there. When I went, I knew I was going to get married." But by Kansas law, she had to be eighteen to consent to be married. "I had to lie my age. I didn't want to lie." And she got nervous at the last minute, asking Marvin to go ahead and get married without her. "He says, 'You fool! I can't get married by myself! You got to come with me!' Oh, we laughed about that *so* much." In Dodge City, Margaret found a job at a Woolworth's store, working in the stockroom and helping to produce souvenirs for "Boot Hill," a "Wild West" tourist attraction in town.

When Marvin was shipped overseas, Margaret returned to Pontiac and resumed her job at Neisner's. She also applied at GM Truck and Coach, which most locals called "Yellow Cab," a plant that had converted to military production. Defense work paid much better than Neisner's, for sure, but Margaret insisted that patriotism was a major factor: "I just was so into the war, because my brothers were all in there, too. I felt like I was doing something for my husband and my brothers." To get the GM job, Margaret recalled, "I lied my age. And they hired me and they told me to come in to work the next day," with documentation. "I never did get my birth certificate. They asked me a couple times for it, and I said, 'Oh, it's on its way.'" Neisner's supported Margaret's decision, offering her part-time work. For a while, she had three jobs, full-time on days at Yellow Cab, then until 9:00 at Neisner's, followed by an hour or so at the Triple X, "a hamburger joint," where she worked for free dinners: "I was busy, but that was because I was married. I couldn't go with the single crowd, so I said, 'What else can I do but work?' And it was kind of social activity for me."

Margaret's job at Yellow Cab began with a crash course on tool use: "It was a program you had to be in for six weeks where they taught you how to use a screwdriver and an electric gun. And then a hammer and pliers, because I didn't know how to use those kind of tools. I was a girl. I just knew how to wash dishes and iron and stuff like that." She excelled in training: "They took me out of the class before my six weeks was up. They put me on the job because I learned fast, I guess." That first job involved installing spark plugs and wires on trucks. Then she was moved around: "I never did the same job. That was hard, because you'd think, 'Oh, this is a pretty good job.' But they'd come and get you, put you on another job. I suppose they figured if something happened to somebody and they needed somebody on that job, they wanted you to know every job." No matter the specific responsibility, "that work on the truck line was hard. Oh god, getting in and out of those trucks and putting parts in under the dashboard. You had to use those heavy machines that would shake you, and it was dangerous. I mean, you'd bump your head and everything! And then we are taking somebody to first aid all the time. I was a woman. I didn't want to get hurt like that, you know? I felt like that was a man's job, but I wanted that job."

War work definitely had its pluses: "I couldn't believe that I was getting that much money. Good money! A lot better than nine dollars a week!" But there were downsides as well: "The men that were working there, they didn't treat us nice. They called us names. And you had to learn to let it go by. We were Rosie the Riveters. 'Hey Rosie!' They called all of us Rosie. I didn't care. It didn't bother me. But it did upset some people. They didn't like us women being in there." A particular incident stood out: "This one guy used to come through and maybe he was flirting with me. I don't know, but I was married and that's the way I was brought up. I didn't pay any attention to other men. This guy used to go all over and check the work. He used to come by and he'd say something to me and I ignored him. My job was taking the carburetors off of a motor that came from a block test." She had to pour out any gasoline that remained after the test and box the carburetors for shipment overseas. "And this one day, I was bending over and he patted me. Whoa boy! I mean, I blew! And *I really* got mad! I pushed him. And the boss came over and told me that that was not right, and I said, 'Well, you better tell him that what *he* did was *wrong*!' I was mad. And he said, 'Well I'll take care of it.' But he says, 'Don't you do that. That's against our rules and regulations.'" The perpetrator was indeed scolded, Margaret remembered, "and the next day he came through and boy, he stayed clear of me. But I happened to be in his way one day. He said, 'Get out of the way, you little piss willy!'" So instead of dumping the leftover gasoline into a tub, Margaret poured it "on his shiny shoes. Oh, man! Did he ever get mad." The General Foreman confronted her, and she hollered, "I'm not going to take that!"

The General Foreman let it go, and he was impressed: "We got to talking about it, as friends. Come to find out, he was from Marquette," a town in the Upper Peninsula, about thirty miles from Chatham. "He said, 'Where are you from with such a temper?' Well, it appeared to be a temper because, see, I was a tiny little thing there, for god's sake! Anyway, we became real good friends. His name was Jack Johnson." As for the offending coworker, "it was really funny because a long time later, I goes to my sister's house, and there's this guy that did that. And my sister and brother-in-law introduced me to him. And we recognized each other. He said, 'You mean this is your sister?!' He says, '*Wow*! I know her.' He says, 'Well, you're like night and day.' Because I had such a temper and my sister was so easygoing." Margaret's brother-in-law "laughed his head off. He remembered me telling him about this incident at work and he had got a big kick out of it to think I fought back. My brother-in-law thought that was great. But he never realized it was one of his friends." There were "a couple more incidents like that, which I had to fight. So I had respect there. You could always tell how a man treated you if his wife worked. If his wife worked, he treated you nice. But if his wife didn't work, he didn't treat you nice." A woman being harassed, the logic went, was probably someone else's wife, and could be your own wife in a different department. Yet some of the sexism was structural. For example, it bothered Margaret that her sister wasn't given respect commensurate with her duties: "She was a foreman, but she didn't have the title because she was a woman and they wouldn't give a woman that title. But she did the job."

Margaret was soon assigned to a new job, preparing motors to ship overseas for amphibious military vehicles, DUKWs (pronounced "Ducks"): "We had to work *every* day. Not a day off." Because of that grind, she didn't end many days at the Triple X, but she still worked evenings at Neisner's: "Every night when I'd leave Yellow Cab. I'd get off the bus downtown and then I'd go to Neisner's. I knew the manager and he really liked me and I knew the district manager, too. And I used to like to go and visit him. They almost became my friends, you know. And then I knew all the girls that worked there, too." There was more camaraderie at the dime store than on the DUKW line, where they "didn't have any time to make friends because it was constant work."

Margaret always did her best, but on one occasion government authorities investigated her for possible sabotage. She had been transferred to a new job, disconnecting water pumps from motors and boxing them separately for shipment overseas. A crucial step involved tapping a wooden plug into an opening in each water pump to prevent anything from entering. Margaret recalled that she filled her "apron pockets full of wooden plugs, and I had a hammer. I had to take that wooden plug and put it in the hole of the water pump and give it a tap. And I did that I don't know how many days. I was a good worker. I really put out work." But some plugs were undersized and fell into the pumps when tapped. Not understanding that this was a problem, Margaret carried on: "I just put another one on the top. That happened several times. But I never thought nothing of it. I never reported it. I was dumb when it comes to stuff like that. I'm a girl. I'm not a man. I didn't have no sense when it came to stuff like this." She was also only seventeen years old. About six months later, "I get called to the office. And my General Foreman says, 'Margaret, the FBI is here and they want to talk to you.' I said, 'Why?!' He said, 'I don't know, but we'll find out, because I have to go with you.' So, these FBI guys are in there, but I'm young and dumb, don't know any better. I wasn't scared. I said, 'Well what did I do?' I says, 'I didn't do nothing wrong.' So they started questioning me about the job I did. It was kind of weird. Why are they asking me questions like this? And you know they just kept harping and harping and harping at the same questions over and over again! My General Foreman was there, but that's because he liked me. So anyway, I got mad. I said, 'Well what the *hell*'—and I said 'hell'—'is going on here?!' And I even apologized for my language. 'I want to know what's going on and let's get to the point! *What have I done*?!' And they asked me about the water pump again."

Margaret learned that in Europe, some DUKW motors had overheated because of small wooden plugs blocking their water pumps from the inside. Stamps on each shipment led investigators to her, so she became a sabotage suspect: "Ooh, then I hit the ceiling! I said, 'I got six brothers in the service and one husband, and many, many friends!' I gave my brothers' names and where I thought they were, and where my husband was. I said, 'I'm here to help them out!' You know, I was mad. And Jack Johnson, oh god, he got nervous.

And he said, 'Calm down, Margaret.'" Apparently satisfied, the FBI agents sent Margaret back to her job. But she "felt just terrible" about the malfunctioning pumps: "And I told Jack, 'I don't want to go on that job no more.' I says, 'Could you give me another job?' Because he knew I didn't do that on purpose. Didn't make sense." She understood that the FBI agents "were doing their job." But she worried about her reputation, for good reason. Her sister reported hearing rumors right away about what happened.

Margaret worked for the remainder of the war, still filling in wherever necessary. Everyone celebrated when Germany surrendered: "We got the news in the plant. Oh god, I took my gloves off, I took my apron, I went home. I know I wasn't supposed to, but I did. I was so happy. I went to first aid and got a pass and said I was sick and I had to go home." Many others left as well. "Of course, I went back to work the next day. I got called to the office. They accused me of starting a whole shoot and caboodle of everybody walking off their job! They thought I was a leader, I guess. Maybe I was too mouthy. I just wanted to know more about it. Everybody was out of the buildings, the stores and everything! They were all over the streets! And they were building a big bonfire in the middle of Huron and Saginaw. Everybody was so happy, and hugging each other and everything."

Margaret wanted to keep her manufacturing job: "But I also knew that when the war was ended, we might not get a job. because the men that were over there, they had to come back to their jobs." Whether or not Margaret would remain at Yellow Cab, however, became a moot point. After returning briefly on furlough from the European theater, Marvin had been redeployed to the Pacific. Then after Japan surrendered, he was sent to Spokane, Washington. Margaret was determined to move there as soon as possible. She left Yellow Cab, reunited with Marvin, and found a job separating whites from yolks at an egg factory: "It was *easy*." At Yellow Cab, by comparison, "you hurt your hands on everything. You had scratches and stuff all over you." Before long, Marvin received orders to be discharged from Ft. Wayne, Indiana: "He didn't have to go to the Pacific, so we were able to travel together to Fort Wayne. We took a bus from there to Pontiac, and then from Pontiac we went to the Upper Peninsula. And I left ties here at Pontiac. I never went back to the Yellow Cab."

The Beaudrys thought they would re-establish roots in the Upper Peninsula, in Marvin's home town, Munising, about twenty miles northeast of Chatham: "We bought a house up there." Marvin went into business as a painter, and in June 1946 they had a daughter. Margaret became a homemaker, but she felt frustrated: "I didn't do anything. I just stayed home." Although she liked caring for her child, she would have preferred "to work to help out. But jobs weren't that easy to get up there." Painting jobs also "got slack" during the 1949 recession, so Margaret suggested that Marvin look for work in Pontiac. She recalled telling him, "You could go and stay with my sister and apply for jobs at all the factories, and then I'll come down. And you can come and get me." As it turned out, Marvin was hired right away at Pontiac Motor. His experience as a painter opened doors. Besides his recent work for his own business, he had done similar jobs for his father and during the war he had painted insignias on military aircraft. With these credentials, he obtained his journeyman's card as a skilled tradesman without having to go through an apprenticeship. Margaret was thrilled: "We rented out the house that we had in Munising, and my dad took all the other stuff. Then my husband came and got us."

Glad to be back in Pontiac, Margaret stayed home with her daughter for another year while longing to work outside the house. She returned to Neisner's in 1952, when her daughter was in first grade: "I always went back there." Then in 1953, the auto industry boomed again, and she "got word that they were hiring women at Pontiac Motor. So me and another friend decided that we were going to take off from work the next day. And you wouldn't believe it. She got hired and I didn't! This was in January. And so I asked another friend of mine in May, I says, 'I think they threw my application away. I'm going back.' Because I knew they were hiring. And I'm not hearing nothing! So she said she would like to go. It was kind of chilly and kind of rainy that day. We were in line at 4:00 in the morning. And she never got called, but I did. I got called this time. So I got hired in on May 11th of 1953. Oh, I was happy." Marvin, however, was not so pleased: "He didn't really want me to work," even at Neisner's. "But he knew that the money helped." Margaret fibbed a bit to smooth the transition, suggesting that she wouldn't stay on the job for long: "I said, 'I'll just use all my money and we'll get a brand new car. And then I'll quit.' Oh, that sounded good to him." It helped that Margaret and Marvin usually worked on different shifts, so there was always a parent around to care for their daughter. As backup, Margaret's brother and her sister-in-law, who stayed home full-time, lived nearby and were willing to babysit as necessary. Margaret was impressed that Marvin looked after their daughter in the evenings, when she was at work, and assumed other duties usually left to moms: "I mean, he curled my daughter's hair. She must've been a good kid because she just sat there and it took him an hour to do her hair when I was gone to work. Of course, my husband was a perfectionist, so it was done right!"

At Pontiac Motor, Margaret was assigned to Plant 8, on the body line in final assembly: "Oh god, what a job! Whew! But we had committeemen then. I used them, too! They were there whenever I needed them, because they didn't treat us nice! You had to have somebody on your job before you went to the bathroom. You got to go to the bathroom, don't you? Yeah, but they only had one person. You wait until your turn came. I didn't wait sometimes. I'd just leave the job. But see, when I worked on a job, I would get it done so fast that I would be ahead. So I'd get ahead of myself and then I'd take off and I'd go across the railroad tracks to the bathroom. But I'd also tell a friend, 'keep an eye,' you know. So I never did do anything wrong. But of course, the *boss* didn't think that was right. I don't think he liked me. Tell you the truth, I used to mock him. He acted like he was a big wheel. He was a General Foreman. I don't think he *ever* did work production." Once he issued a warning to Margaret about her bathroom breaks, so she immediately called her union committeeman: "They were on my side. But they could only do so much. They had to kind of smooth it for you." She was grateful. Without such interventions, she conceded, "I would've never lasted. Because I couldn't stand that when nobody respected me. My mother taught us to respect another human being. But they were not respecting *me*. And I just was a fighter."

Margaret applied her principles of respect and fairness when engaging with African American coworkers: "I got along good with them. I never had no problems with Black people, *ever*. I always said, I wished all white people were as good as the ones I was involved with. There's a lot of white people that are prejudiced. But this one Black girl, she said that she finds that Black people are more prejudiced than the white. And I said, 'Well why would you say that?' She says, 'Well when I talk and get too friendly with a white person, there's always a Black one that's there telling me, you're whitey.'" Margaret saw race in terms of personal characteristics and relationships. "They're not all alike, see? Just like the white people aren't all alike. But maybe when it came down to the nitty gritty, maybe the Black man would turn against me. I don't know. But I wouldn't do that. I would stick up for the one that's right. I was never prejudiced. It's odd that some of my best friends are, and I don't like it." It was more difficult to spot other forms of discrimination. For example, Neisner's was targeted by the National Association for the Advancement of Colored People for employment discrimination in the 1950s.[1] Margaret's safety net was unavailable to African Americans.

Any hint of coercion rubbed Margaret the wrong way. Once she felt pressured by her foreman to contribute to the United Way: "They used to kind of get feathers in their hats if they could get everybody to donate a certain amount of their wages. I said, 'I'll give to the United Way in my own way, not through you.'" Retribution came quickly: "Oh, he really got hostile. He says, 'We'll see about that! I'm your boss!' Was he ever awful to me. He put me from one job to the next." Margaret called her union representative, "and of course, the committeeman says he has no right to do that." Ultimately, upper management agreed, and a company official apologized to her. She would not accept it, however, unless the offending foreman delivered the apology in person: "The committeeman's just sitting there. Now he's not sticking his nose in." The General Foreman pleaded with her: "'What do you want us to do? Do you want us to put him in the middle of the street and throw stones at him?'" She asked to have a meeting with R. M. Critchfield, the General Manager of GM's Pontiac Motor Division: "That's the big top man, you know. Nobody ever asked for that. But I did. And that committeeman, he loved it because I wasn't scared. But I wasn't no rebel. I wanted respect and I wanted them to treat me as nice as I treated them." Although she never met with Critchfield, she did get an apology from her foreman, and she made sure that everybody in her department knew how the case was settled: "They could tell by the way he treated me. He was there, saying, 'Hello, how are you?' and everything." From then on, she emphasized, he was "nice as pie."

Still, work on the body line was difficult and relentless. Margaret was in charge of "fuses, bulbs, and all kinds of little things to wire the car." The wires attached to a harness, which she had to install. Fifty-four cars per hour passed by her, and Margaret was responsible for wiring a third of them: "It was really, really hard." As soon as she finished one car, she restocked parts and another harness and the next car "was right here." She slid into the front seat to do her job, and "wore out a pair of pants every day." It got so expensive that she wrapped company-issued aprons around her trousers. That way, only the aprons were ruined. The harnesses contained numerous wires, each of which had to be screwed into connections with appropriate fuses. Workers had to put their initials on the car body so the company could assign blame in case of error. Margaret hoped to transfer as soon as she could: "That'll kill you, that Plant 8. The only job I would've liked in Plant 8 was to drive the car off the line. And you really had to have high seniority to do that."

Near the end of the 1955 production boom, Pontiac cut back in Plant 8 and Margaret was transferred out of final assembly. Fortunately for her, she had worked at Pontiac Motor just long enough to stay employed: "I went to *every* plant there was. I was transferred because they go according to seniority." Fortunately, though, she "never went back to Plant 8." At first she moved to Plant 7, operating small presses that made parts. She was amazed at the intricacy of the process. A piece of metal entered a line and was passed from press to press, each one refining the shape as it gradually became the desired part. Margaret helped produce headlights, control arms, and flywheels. Despite the massive machines in the room, the work itself "wasn't heavy." But it was dangerous: "You could get your fingers taken off. If you followed safety rules, you wouldn't have to worry, but there was several people that lost their hands, and if a new woman came in she got the hardest job every time."

Prolonged reductions in car assemblies eventually meant cutbacks in parts production as well. Barely escaping layoff again, Margaret was sent to Plant 9 to install spark plugs on a circular line called the merry-go-round: "I didn't have no say about where they put me. I was just lucky I had a job. And the union didn't have anything to say about it, either. The only time a union rep could do anything about what job you got would be if it was a hindrance to your health, like maybe the fumes or something." Sometime in late 1956 or early 1957, production woes at Pontiac finally caught up with Margaret and she was laid off for nearly a year: "There was a lot of other people that got laid off when I did, too."

A sister who worked at Community National Bank helped get Margaret hired there in the bookkeeping department. Margaret also took occasional shifts at Neisner's. She worried that her layoff might last so long that she would have to hire in from scratch at Pontiac Motor. Yet she also enjoyed her job at the bank and management seemed to like her: "They treated me so good there." Marvin, however, pressured her to quit work altogether: "It was many, many, many disputes about that." Margaret prevailed, but unlike at work, she tended to win through passive aggressiveness, not quitting, but not telling the truth about her long-term intentions. That evasion strategy was tested when she received a recall notice from the plant: "I didn't have to go, but I wanted the check." Auto work paid much more than bookkeeping or Neisner's: "Oh, lots. It wasn't even a comparison. At Pontiac Motor, I made almost as much as my husband. The only reason I didn't make as much as him is because he was on skilled trades, and I wasn't." She went straight to the plant and hired in: "I didn't tell my husband that I went back." When she finally told Marvin, she said only that Pontiac Motor had called her back, not that she had already returned to work there. He told her, as usual, that he didn't want her to work at all. She just kept going to the plant and thinking to herself, "why would I even *consider* not?"

Back at Pontiac Motor, Margaret discovered that several men had been recalled before women with higher seniority, including her. "So what am I doing? Back the first day and I'm already calling the committeeman." An investigation proved Margaret correct, and her committeeman said that if she signed a grievance, she would qualify for back pay. But she had concerns: "What about the ones that didn't get called back that got more seniority than me? He says,

'If they do sign the grievance, the highest seniority on the grievance *will* get the pay.'" Although Margaret encouraged all of her women coworkers to join the grievance, she was disappointed to find that "every single one of them said no, they didn't want to sign the grievance. So it was mine alone. See, women are like that. They just figure, 'Well I'm glad to be back.' They didn't realize that they were giving up their *rights*."

Management retaliated by placing Margaret on some of the worst jobs in the plant. Pointing to a spot above her elbow, she exclaimed, "They gave me a job that I had to actually put my hands in oil all the way up to here!" There was no stability: "Every day it was a different job. So you don't really get a chance to *learn* the job. Oh, they were awful. I called the committeeman all the time. I thought, 'I'll be a mosquito on your back. You'll want to get rid of me.' It just went on, maybe about four, five weeks. I wouldn't give." She was pleased that her committeeman supported her. The company wanted her to settle for two weeks of pay, far less than the six weeks she had lost: "I said, 'No, I want the whole.' And the committeeman says, 'It's up to you, Margaret. I'm on your side, no matter what you choose.'"

Eventually, the superintendent asked for a meeting with her in his office: "I says, 'Tell him to come down here. And the committeeman looked at me and laughed. And I say, 'If he wants to meet me, I'm on the job.' I said, 'Make him do what I want!' That's how I felt, because he's giving me the runaround and they didn't do me right by hiring these other people in there when they got less seniority than me. And they were men. So anyway, the superintendent did come down and he met me on the job. And the committeeman was there, too, and my foreman was there. And I wasn't mean about it, but I just *demanded* my rights." She reminded the superintendent that the facts completely supported her: "He was kind of stupid. I wouldn't give an inch." Her committeeman later told her that the superintendent "had to meet that girl," that he "had her pictured like she was a real big lady, with red hair," and that he was amazed to find out "what a little, tiny thing she was." Margaret was satisfied because she got all of her back pay. No one else signed the grievance.

That incident inspired her to become a union committeewoman: "I'm going to watch out for the women, because I think women do need a woman to fight for them." She was disappointed again, however, to find that few of her women coworkers supported her: "They were not happy for me at all. They kind of were, 'Who does she think she is?' I *know* that's how they felt." Margaret believed that a number of those women privately backed her and "knew I was fighting for them, but they just didn't want to take no chances." She figured there were only about four "fighters," at least against management, out of the thirty women in her department. As for the others, "you know who they fought against? Their own fellow employee." It wasn't the crusade she had hoped to lead. "'It's women like me that are fighting for all these rights and you're getting the benefits,'" she insisted to her coworkers, "'and I'm getting the dirty end of the stick.' But I didn't care, because I was fighting for myself, too."

Most of the cases she worked on as a committeewoman were routine: "It would be if a person was switched from one job to another that they had been doing and why did they give it to another person? And you usually ironed it out. They got their job back." Or perhaps "the calls would be because the boss wouldn't give a person a day off, like for a vacation day. And then you could just talk and dicker with them." Perhaps her most memorable case involved a male employee who got free food from vending machines by using slugs instead of coins. After he was caught, Margaret explained, "He called me, and I told him, 'I'm a staunch union member. I'm your committeeman, but that's a federal offense.'" She refused to represent him, "and ooh he was mad. He really swore at me and everything. But I told him right out, I'm for the worker but you are doing something wrong." There weren't many cases of discrimination against women in her department while she was a committeewoman: "Everything was fine. I don't know if the company knew that I was going to fight for the women or not."

After six months as a union representative, during which she also worked her regular job, Margaret was ready to move on. Pontiac Motor was opening a new facility, Plant 15, which was the new site for the small press jobs she had enjoyed during her time in Plant 7: "I liked Plant 15. It was clean and they had nice restrooms. It was better." But she had also been under pressure to give up the union position: "I really resigned because of my husband. He didn't really like me mingling, all the men and the women calling. I thought it would make our relationship better if I got out of that department. So it was really personal for me."

Margaret enjoyed her work in Plant 15, although there were still frequent layoffs. Each time she "went back to work for Neisner's. It was so easy to get back there because there was always somebody there that I still knew." The 1958 recession caused a longer layoff, although she returned to work sooner than many others in the plant. As always, Neisner's offered her shifts, and fortunately, Marvin wasn't laid off at all: "He painted all the show cars. He was that good."

Eventually, Margaret was hired for an inspection job in Plant 15. "Reliability," she called it. The company "didn't want me in it. They didn't want women in it. But I fought to get into it. That's a good job. My committeeman said, 'It's not easy—mental, but it's not hard.' I said, 'I'd love it.' So he said, 'Why don't you put in for it?' Well, I did. But I never got it and never got it." Persistence paid off, however, and inspection turned out to be her favorite job as an autoworker. As promised, it was a mental challenge, not very physical, but with plenty of responsibility. She liked her work so much that she never considered staying home when her second and third children, both boys, were born in 1962 and 1965. She and Marvin continued to work separate shifts and took charge of child care when home. She didn't have enough seniority to ensure a job on days, but Marvin did, so she usually worked evenings. Their daughter was also old enough by then to look after her little brothers a bit. And there was a "lady across the street" who would stay with the young ones for an hour or two if necessary. If things worked well, Margaret would start her shift "around 3:00 or 4:00 in the afternoon," when Marvin would be "on his way home. We would pass each other. And my kids were on their way home from school."

Margaret loved her work and her family. She was grateful to General Motors for hiring her and to the UAW for standing up for her. "Where would I be if there was no union?" she wondered. "I wouldn't be getting this good pension. I wouldn't be getting these medical benefits." Also important, Margaret's karaoke machine was a highlight at retiree picnics, where she sang her favorite tunes.

5

Joe Woods
(1927–2020)

"If I'd have lived and stayed in Alabama, I would have been gone," Joe Woods insisted. "Shoot, I would have either been in prison or been dead." Joe was born in 1927 in Hale County, Alabama, on the east side of the Black Warrior River, about seventy miles southwest of Birmingham and a hundred miles northwest of Montgomery. He was the third child, after his two older sisters, with a younger brother to follow. His paternal grandparents owned the land on which Joe's parents and many others in the extended family lived: "We had a little house, off from my grandmother's house." His family had never been sharecroppers, although they had been renters. It was an important distinction. Black sharecroppers were beholden to white landowners for everything, from housing and tools to food and clothing, accumulating debts throughout the year, sometimes for generations, and always subject to eviction and homelessness. Since relatives owned the land that the Woods family lived on, they had more leverage than sharecroppers in negotiating the terms on which they rented land to farm. Indeed, a number of African-American families in Hale County had bought land after the Civil War to make freedom meaningful and gain a measure of control over their lives. Still, whether landowners, renters, or sharecroppers, Black Alabamians could always be the targets of arbitrary punishments and savage violence inflicted by white people.[1]

When Joe was seven, a feud between his mother and her mother-in-law resulted in a move across the river to Greene County: "I can remember what

I carried. I had my daddy's shotgun across my shoulder." Hoping to create the same kind of family system on the west side of the river, Joe's dad and uncle bought nineteen acres of land along the edge of the river: "That's what all of them lived on. Then they would rent land from other people to raise cotton, corn, and stuff." Joe marveled at the river, but also understood that it posed risks: "That river was wide. Boats and things were running up and down it." After heavy rains, though, "the water used to come all the way up on the side of the house. We were that close on the river. And we had to put our cows way out on the hills, where the water wouldn't get them. We'd put our chickens in the crib where the corn was. We'd put our hogs on the back porch!" Eventually, Joe's family acquired enough land that they could rent some of it to Black families.

Joe was needed in the fields by age eleven, when he "learned how to plow a mule." But he "just couldn't pick cotton. I figured one time I was going to pick 100 pounds of cotton if it killed me. I did get 100 pounds of cotton that day. And, shoot, I ain't picked no cotton since." There were plenty of other chores: "We had two pecan orchards on our place. And we never had to buy nothing but some flour and sugar, because we raised our own hogs, and chickens. We raised our own cows. We killed hogs and smoked that ham and stuff. We didn't have no Frigidaire freezer to put no meat in. Hang it up out there in the smokehouse." To Joe, processing meat beat working in the cotton fields.

Joe remembered how the New Deal's Agricultural Adjustment Act (AAA) affected his family: "The government stopped the people from planting so much cotton. You had to cut that cotton up. You couldn't plant no more cotton." Federal officials hoped to reduce supplies of crops and thereby raise prices, thereby boosting farmers' incomes. To the Woods family, however, it looked arbitrary: "Big farmers, they could do what they wanted. But we couldn't." The AAA also sought to raise prices for livestock by reducing supplies. Government officials would "give you so much money for each cow" that had to be killed. Once Joe helped his father fool the authorities: "We had a bull, see. I told my daddy, said, 'Hide that bull in the woods!' And he did."

The family found ways to supplement their income: "We used to fish in the river." Joe and his dad would set up multiple fishing lines with hooks: "And then you'd put baits on it. Then you stretch it out, and you'd put a sinker on it. And then you'd go out further, and you'd put another sinker on it. Then when you get to the end, then you put a sinker on that end. And you'd drop it in the river. And about twelve o'clock, we'd go over there, check it, got a fish on it. And my daddy used to make a little old container he'd put the fish in, let it stay in the water under the tree where it was cool until Saturday morning. And then

Saturday morning, he would get the fish—it would be fresh fish, and they'd still be alive and everything—and take the fish to town and sell it. Catfish." It was popular and sold out quickly. It was a long way to town, though, and Joe only went on rare occasions: "We lived way out in the country, see. My grandmother or granddaddy, they had a mule and a wagon and they would go in with the wagon. We didn't know what light bread was. When mama would bring us some light bread" from town, "we thought we had something."

Stories circulated among African Americans in the area about the injustices they faced and occasional triumphs. The case of Richard Webb was legendary. Webb was a sharecropper who refused to play by the landowners' rules: "The way [a landlord] would do you, if you was working for him, they would be loaning you money for this, and loaning you that, and at the end of the year they were supposed to be getting half of what you got. But then you got to start right back getting money from him again, see. And you never get out of the hole." Webb, however, picked his cotton, had it ginned in town, then sold it somewhere else, away from his plantation, and brought cash back to his landlord to settle his debts. The next day, the landlord "sent some guy down there to tell him he had to move." But instead of leaving, the story went, Webb "turned around and taken the money and bought the place from him." If true, such a happy ending was rare, as plenty of other cases turned out badly. For example, one of Joe's grandfathers spent time in jail for selling the cotton he grew to the buyer of his choice. Another time, a neighbor hoped that taking his cotton across the river would provide cover for obtaining a more beneficial sale price. But word traveled quickly: "Oh, he went to jail, and they put him in prison for a couple of years. Another guy they put in there too, for a couple of years. That's the way they done him." Everyone knew that any of those incidents could have easily resulted in death. "The stuff that we went through," Joe said, shaking his head.[2]

As a teenager, Joe had some tense interactions with a nearby white plantation owner. Joe was seeing a young woman who lived on that plantation. The landowner "had bought a Ford tractor, and he wanted me to live on their place, and work for him. I'm going to drive the tractor, and do plowing and stuff, and the girl I'd marry was going to be working for him and his wife, and I'm supposed to be eating out of their kitchen. And he's going to tell me what to do. I told him, 'No!' I'm staying with my own folk right there. I told him, 'If I marry a woman, she'll go where I want to go. I ain't eating out of your kitchen, and nobody else's.' He said I couldn't come to see the girl if I didn't do it like that. I said, 'Now if her mama and her daddy tell me I can't come to see her,' I said, 'fine and dandy. But you can't tell me.'" Joe won the verbal exchange, yet he also didn't see that girlfriend again "for over thirty years." He did, however, continue to see the plantation owner: "He'd come by and see me sitting on my own porch and wanted to know did I want to go to work for him. I told him I was looking for somebody to work for me! He didn't like it." That kind of response to a white person could be dangerous and was part of the reason why Joe figured he'd be dead or in prison if he had stayed in Alabama.

Joe recalled that his mother "didn't do much" during these years, explaining that "she was sick most of the time. Stomach problem. Sometimes my mother would get out of bed, she would cook for us, you know, that's all she could do. She had dinner on time. When she was sick, she didn't do no working in the fields, but she made sure we did!" As memories unfolded, however, Joe mentioned that his mother "put up peaches, apples, and pears." In addition, after the men killed the hogs she'd "take that and grind it up and make sausages." She also "made her own cornbread and biscuits" and shared her secrets: "My mother learned me how to cook. Homemade biscuits. I cook cornbread. Shoot, I make my own peach cobbler if I want to." Joe's mother also handled the garden: "Good Friday, Easter, mom would plant her garden. Everything on Good Friday. And that stuff grows." Joe's mother also encouraged education. He attended the local school for Black children, which went through sixth grade and required "a five-mile walk each way." After that, there were no alternatives nearby, so he moved fifty miles away to Tuscaloosa to live with an aunt and go to school.

While in Tuscaloosa, Joe worked part-time at a hotel restaurant: "They had me busing dishes and all that kind of stuff." The owners, a white couple, treated their Black workers poorly: "That lady, oh she thought she was 'Miss Ann.' Oh man, you talk about prejudiced. And her husband, he was something else." The two frequently hit employees: "She grabbed a guy and then slapped him. And man, I looked at her, and I just shook. I was about seventeen or eighteen." Another day, after her husband did the same, Joe said to her in private, "'Look, he ain't got no business pulling an old bald man up, slapping him, and talking to him like that.' I said, 'We're all human beings. He better be glad that it wasn't on me that he was slapping, because you know what, I'd drill his butt all over that place.' But he never said nothing to me." Joe had taken a huge risk to speak up: "I sure did! I looked at it like this. You don't go through this life but once. I figured like this—if I'm right, then that's it. I stood up, oh yeah. I ain't had no cheek to turn. If I did, the Good Book didn't say what to turn after you slap the other one." But he had to leave Tuscaloosa: "See, that's why I tell you I couldn't have stayed down there."

While Joe was away, wartime opportunities motivated his father to move to Pontiac, Michigan, where he was hired to work in the Pontiac Motor foundry.

So when the school year ended, it was up to Joe to run the farm: "My dad told the peoples to show me what to do, what plow to use. And not a person come and told me nothing. The only thing I did, I went by the way I had saw him do it." He resented the lack of help from relatives and neighbors, but he was proud that he managed things mostly on his own, along with his mother and sisters: "My sisters were going to school in Bessemer," just southwest of Birmingham. "They would come in the summer and help us on the farm until school started again. So we did all right. We baled enough cotton to pay the rent." It helped that his dad sent money from Michigan.

Despite his success on the farm, Joe would have gone north if he could have afforded to get there. He had no interest in exploring opportunities in the segregated steel industry around Birmingham. Instead, he worked odd jobs that frequently involved aggravating circumstances. Once when he was cutting trees, his boss paid him less than his partner on a two-man saw. "He said it was because I was a boy," and the guy Joe worked with "was a man—I wasn't worth as much as him. But I was doing the same thing. I'm on one side of the tree pulling the saw, and he's on the other side." Other jobs offered lower wages because of race: "If me and you were working together, you was white and I was black, I should deserve the same amount of money that you get. That's just the way I felt." In early 1946, three months into a UAW strike against General Motors, Joe's dad "come home to stay," or so he thought.[3] "After the strike was over, he changed his mind." He had "done got himself adjusted" to Pontiac and headed north, no longer wanting to live in Alabama. Joe reluctantly stayed behind for another year. But in the spring of 1947, he recalled, "I was plowing the mule, and my mother come to the field and called me and told me, said 'Your daddy sent you fare!' I said 'Whoo!' Just like that. In the middle of the field!" The envelope contained fifty dollars in cash, enough for a ticket to Pontiac. Soon he was on a bus to Bessemer to meet up with his sister and her husband for the journey north. In Pontiac, Joe's dad met them at the station and took them to various employment offices. One of those stops was "Pontiac Motors, and they hired me the same day. That was on May 7 of '47."

Joe learned quickly, however, that he had not left segregation behind: "They put all the Blacks in Plant 6, in the foundry. And if you got in the main plant, you got a job on sanitation." African Americans, Joe noted, "didn't get no production jobs, unless it was a job that didn't nobody want." Of the two options for Black workers, he preferred sanitation: "I was blessed that I didn't get in the foundry. I got in the main plant as a chipper and a sweeper. I couldn't have stayed in the foundry. I would have quit." His father was disappointed: "He wanted me to work in the foundry, because he was in there."

Joe told himself he "was going to work two weeks, and see how I liked it. I hadn't ever been in no plant." He learned that chipping and sweeping were important tasks. Presses, which were machines that stamped out auto parts from metal, also produced lots of scrap, called "chips," that varied in size from specks to quite large and could be stuck in machines or strewn around the floor. To clean up the debris, chippers used a shovel and a fork, the fork for the largest pieces and the shovel for what could be more easily scooped. Sweepers then came along and took care of whatever remained. Joe put the chips in a wagon and hauled them to a hopper. A truck hauled the metal from the hopper to the foundry where it could be melted and reused.

It seemed straightforward enough, but the workload—five presses "to sweep and chip"—was too much. By the time Joe finished chipping the last one, "the first machine down here filled up again." There was no time to sweep before starting the next round of chipping. The work was also dangerous. "A lot of chips was flying on the floor," he explained, and he could get hit if he was "too close around. I had to be careful." Joe fell behind, he said, and his foreman "done put me in the office, and he was going to fire me and put another guy on my job." To Joe's surprise, a union committeeman came to his defense, arguing that the job was excessive for one person. In the end, Joe said, the foreman "put me back to work. He didn't say no more. And put somebody over there to sweep, to help me out." This incident contributed to Joe's strong support for the UAW. He estimated that the company tried without success to fire him "three or four times" that way.

A higher-level supervisor arranged for Joe to be transferred to the night shift, away from that foreman: "That was the best move I made. We didn't have a supervisor on third shift." The chippers and sweepers received detailed orders each night, but without direct supervision they adjusted those plans depending on how things developed. "If the machine repair want you all to do something for them," Joe explained, "you all do it," instead of what was on the list. Joe's crew largely controlled what they did and when they did it: "There was five of us on midnights. We had one General Foreman who wanted to know what we were doing, and we wouldn't tell him. We had that man running all around, trying to find us." Often, the chippers and sweepers completed their official duties fairly quickly: "Shoot, we'd go to sleep. See, we had it made then." There was another advantage to being a chipper or sweeper: "Every year they'd go down for model change, but by you being in sanitation, we didn't get laid off." The machine modifications generated plenty of debris, "so we'd have to be in there cleaning up." Nevertheless, they were still subject to the vagaries of auto employment: "If we got laid off, we'd be off for a couple of weeks, and draw unemployment and stuff."

Those early years in Pontiac tested Joe's priorities. His mother and younger brother made the move north in 1948 and the family needed a bigger place than the apartment he shared with his father: "In '49, I had saved up enough money, with my daddy, to put a down payment on a house. I made sure my mom and dad had them a house." He remembered talking with a white coworker who expected him to be more interested in buying a new car: "I said, 'I'm not going to buy no car to park in somebody else's driveway.' He looked at me and said I'm crazy. He said, 'You don't hear colored people talk like that.'" But after saving for the home, Joe noted, "I bought myself a '48 Chevrolet. See you can do things if you got your mind on it." That same coworker teased him: "'Oh, you got you a car now. You can get any kind of woman you want.' I said, 'No. I ain't looking at that.'" The two struck up a friendship: "He was up there with sanitation too, but he was a truck driver, driving chips and stuff. Now that was one white guy—I can't ask for a guy no better than him. He was in my corner. He would tell his foreman about how they was treating me, and he would always back me up a hundred percent. When I saw what he was doing, hey, I kind of changed my attitude. I see everybody ain't the same. The way he was treating me and everything, I seen then he wasn't the type of guy that some of the rest of them was."

A lot of white people in the plant, Joe emphasized, "was really 'Southern.' Oh man, they was prejudiced. Shoot, they would be watching me, and they would run behind my back, and do things, mess my job up or something. They was trying to get me fired, see, because I wasn't the type that would do like they wanted." They wanted Joe "to get them some Black girls—said they'll get me a white one." Joe refused, emphatically: "They found out how I was, then they changed. I didn't have no more problem with them." Some of his Black coworkers told him, "Man, you're crazy. You don't talk to white people like that." Joe responded, "'They put their pants on just like me. They sit down and shit just like me. They ain't no more than me.' They looked at me and said I'm crazy, and maybe I was. Maybe I was."

Although Joe didn't cater to his white coworkers' fantasies, he enjoyed nightlife in Pontiac: "I never did drink, but I'd go to dances. I'd go with guys that drank, and I'd go to clubs with them." He had sworn off alcohol after a bad experience with homemade peach brandy back in Alabama: "Man, I got so drunk I couldn't even see nothing." But he enjoyed the dating scene: "Oh man, if one girl wasn't ready, then I'd go to another one. If I pull up to your house, blow the horn, and you didn't come out, I'm gone."

He balanced his nightlife with devout Christianity. He and his family were Baptists, and back in Alabama there was "a mourners' bench. All of the sinners, they'd go to church and sit on the mourners' bench up front." He remembered how hard he and his sister Ella prayed, and the time that she "got up, and just went out on the floor. And all of the sisters and mothers was all around us, singing and praying and shouting. I was going to pick her up, and mama said, 'Nope. Let her lay there. The Lord will pick her up.'" Once when he was about ten, Joe asked the Lord for a sign that he was on the right path, and "all of a sudden, I just started burning all in here, and my eyes come open, and it looked like everything got bright. Just lit up, everything lit up." As an adult, Joe remained religious, but he also maintained that "everything the Good Lord put on this Earth, he made it, it was good, and he put it here for us to enjoy ourself with. We should be able to enjoy our life as best we can." That could include gambling and alcohol use, he determined, if kept in moderation. Those who "get to drinking and get drunk and everything else, they put everything ahead of the Good Lord." Although Joe rarely had to work on Sundays, others did and missed church. His pastor and congregation, however, would "never condemn anybody for working" on a Sunday. "You've got a family to take care of."

Shortly after the Korean War began, Joe was transferred to Plant 14, the "Gun Plant," where "they were putting new machines in." He worked closely with skilled tradesmen who dismantled, checked, and reassembled the equipment: "After I'd get through cleaning the parts off for them, I would help them put the machine together." He performed these tasks as competently as those who had been through apprenticeships. One outside contractor observed him in action, Joe remembered, and told the supervisor, "I don't see why y'all want to hold him back. He do just as good a job as the rest of the men." Joe realized he had the ability to become a skilled tradesman: "But see, they wouldn't have no Blacks on skilled trades." Unlike his approach to individuals who spoke or acted offensively, Joe wasn't sure how to fight against this job barrier. He was convinced, however, that the company chose who entered apprenticeships and that the union fought for more inclusiveness, even though white skilled tradesmen at the time, also union members, often strongly opposed breaking that color barrier. Desegregation came more quickly on production jobs, which Joe recognized after three years in the Army: "When I went in service, I was a machine cleaner. When I come out, I wound up on production. Before that you couldn't do that. They'd hire somebody off the street and put him in there. Walter Reuther changed the contract where any job come open in our department, they had to go by seniority." This strengthened Joe's loyalty to the UAW.

Joe received his draft notice in 1952, and along with thousands of other inductees he was sent to Fort Leonard Wood, Missouri. Most of Joe's memories of basic training involved racially charged interactions. Once on a free weekend, Joe and a few white soldiers headed to Springfield, the nearest town, almost a hundred miles away. The white guys were from Pennsylvania and New Jersey and didn't understand local racial customs. When they arrived at the Springfield bus station, Joe remembered, everyone in the group used the same restroom, labeled "White": "We all come on out of the bathroom, and I see everybody standing there looking." He and his traveling companions went to hotel after hotel, but at each stop they were told that no rooms were available. Finally, a proprietor told them the truth. As Joe recalled, the owner pointed to the white soldiers and said, "Well you all can stay here but he can't. I didn't make the law, but that's the law down here." Joe's fellow soldiers stood up for him. One of them said, "'We're in the service together. We take a train together. We sit down and we eat together. And pretty soon we'll be fighting together overseas.' Yeah, that was a white guy who was helping." The hotel owner directed Joe to a place in the country with cabins for Black travelers. The white guys said, "'Well if he goes, we go too.' So we all got in a cab and went out there." The night life was "jumping" in the cabins, and the white soldiers enjoyed it but found it strange that they could stay in that Black establishment while Joe was forbidden from white hotels. Back in Springfield, the group couldn't eat together at restaurants or sit together at the movies: "Nobody would eat a thing until we got back to the bus station. That's a mess, ain't it? People just don't realize what a person goes through on some things." The segregation they experienced, however, was not much different from what Joe faced in Michigan at white-owned establishments: "Shoot, I couldn't even go in a bar here in Pontiac."

Back on the base, Joe recalled returning to his barracks one time after "driving around all day, all night, for two days" as part of his training. His white bunkmates from Texas were playing loud "hillbilly music": "I hadn't had no rest, no sleep, no nothing, and I was tired." One of the white guys hassled him, and Joe snapped: "Anybody from Texas don't show me shit!" They jawed back at him, and finally Joe threw the record player on the floor: "Nobody said a word. And it was just two of us Blacks in there. All the rest of them were white, and all of those from Texas. They ain't bothered me no more, you know, and we all got along together." It helped that the record player still worked. One time, the Texans even gave Joe some money when he was short on cash. Still, Joe much preferred his brief stay in Pittsburg, California, east of San Francisco, his point of departure for Korea: "Shoot, man, we was having a ball. We'd go out to Oakland and cruise out there. I didn't drink, but we'd have a nice time. Then we'd go to 'Frisco. We'd have a ball out there. And you didn't know no color."

Korea was a different world: "When I got over there, they didn't even have gear for me to eat out of. I had to borrow some of the guys' gear. Finally, they got something for me to eat out of, and finally I got a tent. It was a lot of times cold! I know one thing—I didn't see nothing over there fitting to fight for but hills and rice paddies. You didn't know who was who. You didn't know who was the North and who was the South." Joe's duties included engineering support for construction of an airfield (K-14, known as Gimpo Air Base) west of Seoul and various bridge projects: "I wound up in a job there guarding the airstrip. I could make two trips a night, carried the guards out there on the airstrip. One time I put canned goods on the manifold so they'd be hot when I got ready to eat! But I was running back and forth, back and forth, twice a night changing guards. And sometimes I had to haul water and stuff for the mess hall." As part of the motor pool, he also delivered supplies to combat troops, just miles from enemy lines, and he could get stranded. Once he hunkered down in a cemetery: "They started dropping bombs on us, and we had foxholes dug in the graves." Although Joe survived unscathed, shell fragments struck the soldier next to him. The night before the armistice was signed was the worst, "because we was in a horseshoe, and they could close in on us anytime they wanted. Bombs there all over the place. That was when I almost got shot, and I could feel the wind of those bullets above my head."

In addition, there were racist aggravations, for example a lieutenant who kept calling Joe "boy": "I ain't never stopped walking. He wanted that 'boy' to come. I looked around and said, 'What he want? He ain't calling me.' I looked on the ground, looked all around. He says, 'What you looking for?' I said, 'I'm looking for that boy.' I said, 'Look, I'm not no boy.' I said, "If I'm a boy, send me back to the States where the boys is at.' I said, 'I didn't ask to come in here. Uncle Sam drafted me and he didn't want no boys. He wanted me.' He didn't say nothing. I said, 'Now if you don't know my name, you call me soldier, GI, Private, or whatever, because I ain't no boy.' You know he never said that no more." After the armistice was signed, Joe was sent to Guam. He hated the heat, but he worked on a new airstrip and appreciated being in an integrated crew.

In 1955, Joe returned to Pontiac Motor after his discharge from the military and ended up "on the block line." It was a production job, previously off limits to Black workers, but it wasn't satisfying: "All I was doing was checking the bore numbers and sizes, make sure everything was correct. You could just sit up there and go to sleep. I stayed there until they started laying off." That was most likely when auto sales sagged after the 1955 boom.[4] Joe avoided some of the layoffs, however, because his seniority dated to 1947 and had accrued while in the military. But his workload increased. To cut costs, Pontiac Motor tried to squeeze more production out of each employee. Joe was assigned to two jobs, on separate lines, and was told to run from one to another whenever there was a lull. Joe successfully challenged his duties on a technicality: "The rules said, no running in the shop." He told the foreman, "'If I'm going to run over there, and run back over here, I'll be breaking the shop rules.' He couldn't say nothing because he knew I was right."

Joe used his GI benefits to enroll in welding classes: "I could do heliarc welding. I could do arc welding. I learned all that stuff at school. The hardest job for welding I could do was aluminum. And I learned how to do aluminum welding." His skills didn't matter: "I went and put in for welding. I couldn't get it. They wouldn't let me in." He was bitter: "I asked them what the heck I went overseas and crawled on my knees and my belly for and dodged bullets for, and come back here and can't even get nothing. I said, 'I ain't got a thing here to protect. The only thing I'm protecting over there is what y'all got.'"

Joe was also trying to figure out his personal life: "When I got out of the service and come home, things weren't like it was. I had to start all over again. The first thing I said, I wasn't going to run around like I did. I didn't know what a bed was until I got in the Army. Before I got out, I said I was going to cut all that. So I did. I said I was going to get married so I wouldn't be running around like I had been doing. And I did." He met his future wife when she stopped by the house he shared with his parents: "She was out selling stuff, going door to door, selling some kind of cologne." She got him involved in politics: "She had me going out, trying to get people to join the Democrat Party, getting them to go to meetings for that, and who to vote for, who'd you be campaigning for. I did all that stuff." He worked for candidates at the local, state, and national levels, "even up to the president." But he didn't enjoy it and eventually "bagged out on some of that stuff."

Joe was deeply affected by discrimination he encountered when searching for a home. He looked at a couple possibilities outside the city. One was in nearby Auburn Hills, but "they told me they didn't sell houses to Blacks out there." Another was on lakefront property in suburban Waterford. When the seller "found out what I was, he come and told me the house was sold, see? So that cut that out." Joe tried to get a Veterans Administration loan to build a brick house, because he didn't like "the little things they were throwing up" on Pontiac's south side, where most African Americans lived: "They told me they wasn't building no brick homes for Black folks. I said, 'Why?' He said, 'Well, ain't nobody been requesting them.' I said, 'Yes there is. I'm asking for one!'" Joe got nowhere: "That's when I blew my top! I told him, 'Man, you mean to tell me that you cannot build me a brick home and you're building them for the whites, but you can't build them for the Blacks?' I said, 'What the hell did I go overseas and fight for then?'" Amid this frustration, Joe and his wife divorced after three years of marriage.

Fortunately for Joe, he had advanced to a position in engine repair. It wasn't welding, and it wasn't a brick house, but it was a higher-level job that had previously been for whites only. He benefited from his time with skilled tradesmen in the gun plant: "If I had a motor, and I figured it wasn't no good, wasn't no need for me working on it because it was scrap. I wouldn't bother. I could hear a motor running and I could tell you exactly what was wrong, and I would fix it." The General Foreman doubted Joe's ability: "He watched everything I did. So I got a motor down there, and I tore that motor down, and when I found what was wrong with it, I fixed it, and I just hung it on the line." Joe didn't bother to test it, which infuriated the General Foreman. "I said, 'No, I ain't going to check it to see if it's all right, because I fixed it right.' And you know, he followed that motor all the way up, and I'm down there working on another motor. Finally, he come down there and told me, 'You was right. It is all right.' I said, 'That's what I told you.' You know, he never followed me no more."

During the 1958 recession, when Pontiac Motor ran one shift at best, Joe had just enough seniority to claim a job on the production line. But his foreman knew how good his repair work was and arranged for him to be moved back on that job and had a repairman with greater seniority take the production position. To avoid a grievance, the company paid repairman's wages to Joe's replacement.

While officially working his engine repair job, Joe also served twenty-seven years as a union committeeman. In reality, the union position became full-time. As a committeeman, Joe advocated for greater racial, gender, and ethnic diversity in all departments: "They had it set up, a bunch of whites working together, a bunch of Blacks working together, a bunch of Mexicans. And during that time, see, people carried racist stuff and all that mess in the shop." He recalled a typical plea for integration he would make to foremen: "'The Blacks over here be talking about the 'whites this,' and the whites be talking about the 'Blacks this.' I said, 'Let them get in there and get together, and talk, and mingle together, and then they can understand one another. You'll see things will be quieted down a whole lot.'" Joe maintained that he was proved right, at least in the departments that tried it.

Other plants in the Pontiac Motor complex continued to discriminate, however, so there was significant variation. To Joe, perhaps the best evidence that workers began to see themselves simply as workers came when a fight broke out between a white guy and a Black guy as they left the plant: "A bunch of whites was standing here, and Blacks all around, and wouldn't nobody help either one. Let them two jokers fight themselves out—a Black guy and a white guy. Man, they was duking like the devil. And finally the Black guy stopped. He pulled the white guy up and said, 'Man, that's enough!' He said, 'I ain't hitting you no more. Let's quit.' And they shook hands, they hugged one another, walked right on by." Joe was certain that in earlier times the incident would have provoked a racial brawl. But this time, everybody, Black and white, "just stood around and made sure nobody got involved."

Joe took pride in knowing the union contract inside and out and fighting as hard as possible for fellow workers as long as they were honest with him. He would be a bulldog if he believed in the case enough to write a formal grievance. Typical issues he dealt with included heavy workloads, overbearing supervisors, ignoring seniority in recalls and layoffs, and unfairness with transfers, reprimands, suspensions, or discharges. He had a reputation for refusing to "horse trade" with management to resolve a grievance at the expense of fairness: "See, you had some committeemen that was crooked." The number of complaints and grievances varied, and some committeemen spent their shifts at the bar, compromising their authority. Joe emphasized that he was always in the plant and visible, which in his view gave him greater credibility. Once, when workers complained about the heat in their department and company officials ignored them, Joe turned the air conditioning off in the superintendent's office and listened to the whining. Soon the company installed fans for the workers: "When I argued something, I knowed what I was talking about!" At one point in the early 1970s, Joe represented a worker who was reprimanded for missing time, it turned out, while participating in a school bus bombing in Pontiac as a member of the Ku Klux Klan.[5] Joe insisted that because he was a union representative, he defended the Klan member regardless of politics. Besides, he said, the Klansman was good at his auto job.

When not in his official UAW role, Joe had his greatest impact in one-on-one verbal challenges: "If I got something on my mind, I'm going to tell you, whether you like it or not. I'm like this—I watches things, and if I see you ain't right, I don't bother with you. If you ain't right, or if you're prejudiced, or all that kind of stuff, I won't have nothing to do with you." Still, he had faith in the power of moral clarity: "Eventually, you're going to lay that prejudice aside." He had seen it happen. "You know when they killed that kid in Mississippi," referring to the 1955 murder of fourteen-year-old Emmett Till, "I never seen so much reaction." White and Black workers alike "couldn't see why people would stoop that low. And when they killed Martin Luther King, one of the white guys I hated, he walked down the aisle, and he saw me and just fell down on his knees, started crying. He said, 'Joe, that man, he wasn't just for you all. He was for all of us. He helped me too. We was poor people—they treated us the same way they treated you down in Mississippi.'" Although Joe knew better about that supposed equivalence, he maintained hope that people could find common ground.

6

Les "Lucky" Coleman

(1922–2013)

It took a community to raise Les Coleman. He was born in 1922 in Mooreville, Michigan, a rural crossroads about fifty miles southwest of Detroit: "I was the last one of twelve children—in the second family." Les's father had seven children with his first wife. After she died, he remarried and had five more. When Les was a year old, his family moved a few miles northeast to Ypsilanti: "I didn't really know my father too well. When I knew him last, he worked for the city of Ypsilanti, cleaning streets." Les's dad died in 1933, in the depths of the Great Depression. About that time, the family lost their house because they couldn't afford the taxes: "Then we moved to an apartment over a meat market in Old Town of Ypsilanti. And there again, we weren't able to pay our monthly rent for a long time. I think we owed them money when we left."

Several years before these hardships, Les got his first job: "I sold papers on the street corner from the time I was six or seven until I graduated from high school. I stood on the street corner, and I got home probably 11:00 at night. I was working on my own, mostly. I had a lady boss, and she kept track of me. Each night when I got done, I had to go to this lady and pay her for the papers I sold." He kept the rest of the money, he said, "but most of the time I didn't have too much left, because I had regular people who didn't want to pay until the end of the week. A lot of times I'd go home with a nickel or a dime after selling papers for 5 or 6 hours." Many residents looked after him: "The mayor of Ypsilanti always come down and bought a paper from me." And "the people in the stores in Ypsilanti took care of me. If I needed a haircut, the barber I sold papers to would get me up on a chair and cut my hair. And when I needed shoes, the shoe store fellow would set me down and give me a pair of shoes. Ypsilanti was good to me." Other shopkeepers helped Les learn financial lessons: "I sold papers to the man who sold bikes, and he trusted me. I put a dollar down and 25 cents a week to pay for my bike." Les didn't want to disappoint the store owner. Owing money "made you thrifty," he explained. "You saved that 25 cents. You had to pay that bill."

To young Les Coleman, "Ypsilanti was a metropolis. I mean all kinds of people. Fridays and Saturday nights the streets were loaded with people. The Salvation Army had their little band on the corner of Michigan Avenue and Washington Street. And they used to come out there every Saturday night and sing and play, and tell people to believe in Christ. One of my brothers was involved in that for a short time. He would get up there and sing, and play an instrument." But much of Les's childhood was during the Depression: "We had quite a few people in Ypsilanti that were very poor. I mean they lived from Day 1 to Day 2. You'd find them in the doorway sleeping. The police would go around and check all these things. I don't know where they'd tell them to go, but the police were very strict about seeing that they weren't on the street."

The Colemans could easily have been on the street, but the large family created a safety net together. A sister from his dad's first marriage and her husband rented a house that was also big enough for Les's mom and his siblings from the second marriage. Two of his brothers had fairly steady work. One took over their late father's Ypsilanti street-sweeping job and another got a position with the federal Works Progress Administration. Everybody pooled resources to buy groceries. Les's mother took care of the children, generations of them, since some of his oldest half-siblings were in their thirties at the time and had kids of their own.

In April 1941, Les traveled to the Ford Rouge Plant in Dearborn during the UAW's campaign that finally won recognition and a contract from the staunchly anti-union company. It was entertainment for many residents of Ypsilanti, but it was also of local significance since Ford had opened a parts plant there in the 1930s: "We went around to the [Rouge] plant. People were driving around there all the time, just seeing the strikers and seeing what was going on down there. They kept saying that Ford wasn't going to give in, that all those people were fired. This is before I even had an inkling that I'd ever get a job at Ford's."

Despite disruptions, distractions, and late nights, Les graduated from high school that year and accepted an offer from Ford for the company's four-year skilled trades apprenticeship program. Because he wasn't yet 21, his mom had to give her permission. The training was rigorous, including "algebra, geometry, trigonometry, and metallurgy." In addition, "you worked all the while you were an apprentice." Ford assigned him to its new Ypsilanti parts plant, where he learned to operate equipment like shapers and milling machines: "A foreman would set you up on a machine. In the beginning, he checked up on you a little bit until they could trust you. They had leaders, also, that would come around and check out what you're doing. And if you got into trouble, the leader would come over and get you straightened out." After the Pearl Harbor attack, many more apprentices were hired. Some already had useful experience: "I had a friend whose dad had a jobbing shop on the side, and he'd come in there and he could run anything. But I didn't even fix my bicycle, so it was kind of tough for me to get started." Yet Les never considered quitting, "because that was my livelihood."

The skilled trades program was a mixture of hijinks and somber duty during these years. Once, a prankster put a Coke bottle full of water in Les's pocket: "You pull it out, and all the water still comes out of it. Your whole leg is all wet!" Les didn't seek revenge, he said, "because if you tried to get him back, he'd be planning something even better." Another time somebody emptied the contents of a firecracker into a fellow worker's pipe tobacco: "This guy's pipe blew right out of his mouth! Interesting things that go on in the plant, you know." Eventually, one of the foremen sat the apprentices down for a serious talk. Les remembered him saying, "I have two boys over there fighting. You guys are in here safe and sound. I want you to get your work done, and keep your nose to the grindstone, because I'm going to be watching you."

Because the skilled trades were considered essential for the war effort, Les was exempt from the draft. Instead, he focused on his apprenticeship. The Ypsilanti plant had converted to producing parts for military vehicles: "I was on the bench, making dies and building fixtures. I actually took care of a line—the dies and the welding fixtures, which would get all out of shape. That whole line was part of my responsibility." He took pride in the results of his efforts: "The finished thing, to see it work, it's like conquering something. You got your fixture going. It did what it was supposed to do, or your die performed what it was supposed to do. It's exhilarating. You know, you feel great. 'I *did* that. I *did* that!'"

Some people in the plant were helpful, and some weren't. Les recalled that one time when working on a starter, "This tube needed to be bent, so of course I went to the engineer and asked him if he had any ideas. And he says, 'No that's why we gave it to you. You've got the job. Do it!' So then I had to go to a quality control engineer, and I said, 'Is there any way that we can get some fluid that will fit in this pipe and freeze in there so we can bend the pipe?' And he come up with it right away, and so that's what we went and did. And the job was completed." Les tried to stay on the good side of crucial coworkers. A welder, for example, "could really mess you up if you needed something welded and he wouldn't do it." Les was willing to pitch in whenever skilled work was necessary: "When I was a die maker, I did my die work, and sometimes I'd have to do machine repair. It was just sort of a help thing." If machine repair had a backlog of work on weekends, for example, he'd join them. There were also financial incentives: "I wanted the overtime. I needed the money."

Les, known to family and friends as "Lucky," became increasingly involved with his local union. He had attended many meetings: "There's always somebody had a gripe, and they'd start arguing about their gripe. 'The company should do this,' and 'The company should do that.' Mostly what they did is find out what was going on." Les's interest and levelheadedness caught the attention of local UAW officials and fellow workers, who recommended that he run for the shop committee. "I worked all over the plant, and I got to know lots of people," he explained, accounting for his support. "I wasn't trying to *get* anybody or anything. I just thought that maybe I could do a good job representing the people."

Les won in a plantwide election and attended a union camp—FDR-CIO, named for President Franklin Delano Roosevelt and the Congress of Industrial Organizations—in Port Huron, Michigan, for training.[1] "They told how you had to give and take. They'd give you a specific question of this man being picked on, or something like that, and what do you do? And the foreman says, 'He isn't keeping up with his production.' You go through what you have to do to satisfy both the company and the man too." Les threw himself into this job, which was full-time: "It was enjoyable, because you'd go talk to the people who had the problem, and lots of times just by talking to the foreman, and talking to the person, you could get it settled." Other times the problems proved thornier: "One particular time, the line went down and the people had a *legitimate* reason for not working on the line." The company "had run the line up too fast. That was it. These people said, 'We can't keep up!' So they all stopped working. We talked to management, and we said, 'Well let's go back to where the time study had been prior to the speedup, and start over again and re-study this line.' And management would have nothing to do with it." So Les performed his own study: "I got a time watch and timed it out." The company refused to share its own time-study data: "I tried to compare them, but they wouldn't give me theirs to look at." Eventually, management "did slow the line down somewhat. They did increase the production, but they didn't increase it as much."

Les remained skeptical of company time studies. He remembered that "they had time-study people all over the place," observing every working motion in hopes of achieving ultimate efficiency. "They'd stand by the line, and sometimes they'd say, 'they reached further than they had to, and therefore it was an inherent delay,'" which would result in higher production quotas. "It was quite amazing how they'd do all that, you know. They would set up the study and then the time-study man would go back, and he'd figure it all out, and say how much could be done." There was no discussion with workers about the results: "They wouldn't know it until they jacked up the line and they'd start running." That was usually when Les the committeeman would be called in: "'They're running that line faster than they should.' You heard that all the time." Still, workers had different sensibilities about whether or not to file charges. "They'd say yes or no," Les explained. "'No, I don't want to get my boss mad,' or 'Yes, I'll sign a grievance on that.' You can see where these people could be pinpointed out if they signed grievances against the company and everybody else on the line says, 'Oh, we can do it.'"

Les proceeded only if the case had "merit" and affected workers understood they might not win. If they chose to go forward, he emphasized, "I'd write the grievance to the best of my ability" and pursue it as far as the shop committee thought reasonable, possibly all the way to the Ford arbitration umpire, who had the final say: "You don't take every case to the umpire. You try to settle it within the plant. If it was an emergency, we'd go right to the management right now and get it settled." Les enjoyed this challenge: "I like talking to people and feeling a part of the organization. It'd give you a sense that you're *doing* something for people." After a single three-year term, however, he lost his bid for re-election: "No problem there. I went back to the tool room, and about a year after I went back to work, they offered me a foreman's job."

In 1951, the former shop committeeman indeed became a foreman, a position he held for three years, overseeing a production line: "I thought I was doing one great job. I had a good record as far as getting the productivity of it. Of course it would go up and down, but you come across the middle where the center line was supposed to be, and my people were just above that." He thought he had good relationships with most of the workers he supervised. He bristled, however, at company policies about dealing with workers: "They said, 'Don't have anything to do with them outside of the plant.' 'Don't do this.' 'Don't do that.' I said, 'You're crazy. That isn't the way you do it.'" It turned out that Les didn't associate much outside work with those he managed, "but just the fact that they told me I couldn't made me mad. And I didn't feel that that was right either, because I'd bowl with them, you know. I mean, what kind of crap is that?!"

Les had persistent difficulties with higher-ranking managers: "My boss was a guy I had bowled with, and I had done everything with." Nevertheless, "when it came to being your boss, he was kind of difficult. He was always messing around with my job." Les took pride in his ability to solve problems and keep production flowing. "I had a timing plan," he explained. As an example of his boss's meddling, he recounted an instance involving tumblers, which contained "polishing rocks," or "grit," to smooth the edges on newly stamped parts: "We had three tumblers, and this line over here wanted certain parts. This line over here wanted certain parts. And I couldn't do all of them at the same time, but I'd do a few of these and a few of these, and keep all the lines going as best I could." It took "a long time to tumble parts," he emphasized, so foremen had to plan ahead to stay on schedule. Les's boss, however, often undermined those plans. Les recalled checking on the state of certain parts, "and I'd find that there's none in there. They'd been dumped out and something else had been put in there." As a result, a production line would have to stop: "I asked the guy that's doing the tumbling for me, I say, 'Why did you take those out?' 'Your boss told me to take them out!'" The same boss who sabotaged the schedule would then scold Les for failing to meet production goals, leading Les to conclude: "I just can't take this anymore."

There were two "last straws." One involved a machine that punched out different sizes, progressively smaller, of fiber parts: "When you got down to the smallest ones, probably half of those were scrap. And we'd get in there and we'd pull that out." One day, however, Les's boss demanded that more of those faulty parts be saved: "Well it was impossible to do that, and I told him that." The other came at the end of a shift, when one of the men Les supervised forgot to put away a piece of equipment after staying a few minutes overtime to make sure a crucial machine was in working order when the next crew arrived: "My boss came down, 'I want you to reprimand that guy! Reprimand him! He left that block there! He wasn't supposed to leave that block there!'" After Les responded sharply—"You can go to hell!"—his boss pushed for formal punishment. "I had to think about it a while," Les explained, then "turned in my resignation."

Years earlier, even before Les served as a union committeeman, his marriage had reached a breaking point. His wife "did a little bit of everything. She sold Avon Products and Sarah Coventry jewelry. She worked for a day or two at Bell Telephone. She didn't like it." The sales jobs allowed her to be home with the couple's two children while Les was at work. But other times she tended to be gone: "I don't know where." After separating and several attempts at reconciliation, the couple divorced in 1951. Les received custody of the children: "My mother stayed with me then and took care of the kids and kept me on the straight and narrow. I didn't do much besides go to work and take care of my kids, because my mother went to church every night. So I would have my kids all evening long." His former in-laws also helped out: "I was like a son to them, I guess, because they treated me really nice. I was still friendly with all her family."

While at FDR-CIO camp, Les met a librarian named Marilyn Heeley, who was a graduate of Oberlin College and the Western Reserve Library School in Cleveland. Les recalled that a fellow union trainee "introduced me to her, and so we started playing ping pong together. Later on, she needed a ride to her home, which was in Roseville, and the guys I was with give her a ride. So we went in, and we had some pecan pie and some coffee." Les's matchmaker saw chemistry developing and recommended that Marilyn take Les home to Ypsilanti, about fifty miles away: "She said, 'Sure! I will.' And I stayed around a while, and we talked. Found out a little more about each other. So she brought me all the way to Ypsi, and drove back to Roseville by herself." Marilyn, Les said, "kept coming back about every other weekend to see me. She met my family, my mother and my kids." She had been married, but had no children. "Once in a while," Les traveled to Roseville, but he usually had to take care of his children so couldn't be away. Les and Marilyn were married in early 1954. "Our first child was actually a little ahead of time," he laughed.

Despite having a skilled tradesman as primary breadwinner, the Colemans struggled to make ends meet: "It was really kind of rough. Skilled tradesmen, they're making more, but I don't recall ever having a lot of money. I didn't buy any extras or anything. All my money went for clothes for the kids, school, things like that. It was quite a few years before I started living fairly comfortably. Probably in the '70s." Marilyn took several years off to raise the two children she had with Les, and, during the week, Les's two other children, who stayed with their mother on weekends. Les's mother continued to live with the family and help out with the child care, which was especially valuable later in the '50s when Marilyn got a job at the Ypsilanti Public Library: "My second wife and my mother were just real close." For his part, Les worked as much overtime as possible and also held a number of second jobs, "at night, maybe work five hours, whenever I could."

Within a year of starting a family with Marilyn, Les quit his foreman position and returned to the tool room: "I was transferred right back in to my leader's job. It wasn't hard. I knew what I had to do. But who do you suppose came over and wanted a job done because he had a business on the outside and he wanted a part made?" It was the boss who had tormented him when he was a foreman. "Put his hand on my back, and says 'Lucky, I got to have this part.' I felt like hitting him right in the mouth. But I made him a part, and got him out of the way. I thought, well, if I've got to eat this a little bit, I will. I could have just as easy grabbed a hammer and hit him, but I didn't."

Les's responsibilities included developing technological innovations, called automation, that eliminated production bottlenecks and jobs. It was challenging work and tested his abilities, but it also had its downside: "When automation first came in, I thought, well this is a thing of the future. I felt sympathetic towards those people that would be put out of work if we did the automation. But I *knew* that this was coming. A lot of us were against it, because of the fact that it was putting all our people out of work. And if you're in the union, your heart is with these people!" It was often "a gradual process," Les noted, with only a few people displaced at any one time. On the other hand, "in some places, at the Rouge, there are probably whole departments that was put out of whack. They were always bringing in new machines that automated, moving people out."[2]

Much of his job, however, involved routine repairs and replacements from normal use: "I just worked anyplace where a die broke down. We were always taking care of presses that were broke down—put new dies in, or new parts in, rebuilding the dies, or something." Les took pride in his accomplishments, including developing a technique that allowed him to repair a die in fifteen minutes instead of the usual half hour. He also served as a liaison with suppliers to resolve problems at the source: "I went to the company that built the fixtures and made sure that their parts were right before we brought in the new machines. Even though I was just hourly, they sent me to these companies. I was a leader, I guess."

Les always tried to do what he thought was right. Shortly after he returned to the tool room, an emergency arose while the plant ran overtime on a Sunday: "This young man was asked to go up in a crane, which was shorted out. He was a machine repairman. He wasn't an electrician or anything. And they wanted him to do some kind of work up there where that crane was—it had stopped, part way on the track. He wouldn't do it because he says, 'I've got five kids. I don't want to get electrocuted. I don't know anything about that electrical thing up there.' So they fired him." When the company held firm, Les and other skilled tradesmen called an unauthorized "wildcat" strike, left the plant, and gathered across the river: "The whole skilled trades were there. We all walked off." Because wildcat strikes violated the contract, Ford fired everyone who participated, including Les. Three hours later, the company relented and allowed the skilled workers back in the plant. Union officials had argued successfully that the contract allowed strikes over safety issues. Under different circumstances, however, any of them could have lost their jobs for good. Most importantly, Ford rehired the machine repairman who refused to risk his life atop the crane: "That's what we were after. That's what we went out for."

The 1958 recession also jeopardized Les's career. His layoff was relatively short, several weeks, but he was forced again to find alternative work. This time he found a skilled position at an outside "jobbing shop" and he later landed a job at the Argus Camera Company in Ann Arbor, where he worked twelve-hour shifts until he was recalled by Ford. Despite these interruptions, he remained devoted to his job at Ford, his family, and his local union. He was a leader in every community campaign in the plant, especially the Red Feather, which later became the United Way, and Red Cross blood drives. As he recalled with pride, "I was always involved in something of that nature, besides working in the plant."

Les marveled at the success of his children and grandchildren. One of his daughters was "pretty high up in General Motors," his son worked for the State of Florida, another daughter taught school in Ohio, and a third daughter worked for a doctor in a medical practice. He had grandchildren graduate from a variety of schools, including Michigan State University, Eastern Michigan University, the University of Toledo, and the University of Michigan. "I'm just so proud of them," he said, knowing how far he and his family had come from the streets of downtown Ypsilanti during the Great Depression.

7

Gene Johnson

(1925–2012)

Overcoming adversity was something that Gene Johnson mastered. It could be said that adversity ran in his family: "My grandmother on my dad's side died about three, four days after my dad was born, and my grandpa, I guess, felt helpless to raise a baby. And he took off on his own and he was an old photographer—went all over the country riding a bike, taking pictures, kids on their horses and everything." Gene's father, William, was raised by his maternal grandparents just north of Greenville, Missouri, in the foothills of the Ozark Mountains. The fifth of seven children, Gene was born there in 1925. Greenville was a railroad town: "They had a roundhouse there for where the trains turn around. And a train machine shop where they repaired boxcars." That and logging provided most of the opportunities for Gene's father to make a living. Gene's mother, Bertha, also grew up in Greenville. Her father, a train engineer, was blinded by steam from a locomotive, an incentive for her to marry young, which she did at age fifteen, to Gene's father, who was twenty. Their wedding provoked controversy. Gene explained that the couple "run off to get married" by a relative, Ben Eads, who was a Baptist preacher, and the father of the bride "had the sheriff out looking for them all night long." Family lore had it that "when they found them, they was already married. My grandpa threatened to shoot old Ben Eads!"

Although tensions eased over time, the local economy took multiple hits in the early years of the Great Depression: "They shut down the roundhouse and the timber ran out." In 1929, William looked for work in Michigan and landed a job in Pontiac, but "when everything fell to the bottom" there, he returned to Missouri. Back in Greenville, Gene's dad "just done like anybody else—he done anything to make a living," without much success. Running out of options, Gene's parents moved the family in the early '30s to Bernie, Missouri, about fifty miles to the southeast. They thought they could survive as farm laborers near Bernie. Farming was next to impossible near Greenville: "It ain't nothing but hills over there. Even a sheep almost falls down trying to stand up."

Bernie was a tough, small town, for whites only. Streets were unnamed, because everybody knew you and where you lived. Plenty of residents worked as hired help in nearby cotton fields. When he was still six or seven, Gene recalled, he "was picking cotton with a little old tow sack. And I'd fill that full of cotton." He eventually became an accomplished picker. When he was ten, Gene emphasized, he started "working as a *man*." At that point, his dad asked the farmer, "'What do I get for the kid?'" The farmer replied, "'Whatever I give you guys if he can do the work, if he can keep up.' Well my mother seen that I kept up a row just like they did. Now from that day on, I worked, and I worked my you-know-what off." Everyone in the family helped out in the fields. Cotton farmers hired workers by the "truckloads," Gene explained. "It was almost like migrant workers, but we wasn't migrant. We were citizens of the town." The Johnson family worked many different farms: "We could get through with one patch, and another farmer would need some workers." Despite the widespread demand for labor, landowners never competed with each other by offering higher wages: "Oh no. No. No. No. No. No. I guess they figured you would be glad to get that dollar a day. Well, we were! I done work like that 'til I was sixteen."

Gene offered a description of work in a cotton field: "Picking cotton's hard, but if the stalks is high enough, you can hide yourself—especially if you're a kid, you can lay down on your side and rest for a little, once in a while." With chopping cotton, however, "there's no breaks at all." It involved thinning plants to about five inches apart when they were "about two inches high. And the sun's just blistering out in the field, and at the end of the row you turn around and come back another row, quarter mile long row. And out in the middle of them fields, when the humidity was high it felt 110, 115 degrees. All day long. Sun just burning down on you. No shade trees at all. And in the summertime, a day can be twelve, fourteen hours of sunshine. You work from sunup to sundown. One dollar a day. A dollar a day. You got your head down and leaning down all the time. I think that's the reason why a lot of them old timers is hunchbacked. I remember *all* these things." There were no drinking fountains out in the fields:

"The farmer, probably be his kid or his wife, would bring us water. And they had this big, old, gallon pickle jug. And they had a gunny sack wired around it to keep it cold as possible." Usually the jug was offered first to the older men, each with "a big old cud" of chewing tobacco "at the back of his jaw. When they brought that jug to you, you'd have to blow away the dregs and you drank. You didn't question it. Hell, you was thirsty!" There were also poisonous snakes in the fields, "water moccasins galore." Gene was used to people recoiling at these stories: "I'm saying it just like it was, and I ain't cutting any corners anywhere, and I'm trying not to be embarrassed about it. That's the way it was. That *is* the way it was."

For long stretches each year there was no work in cotton fields, and there weren't many jobs to be had around Bernie: "If there was any industry in a town ten or twenty miles up the road, you can bet your bottom dollar that everybody in that county had the job already. Any *decent* jobs." For a while, Gene's dad, William, had a job with the New Deal's Works Progress Administration, draining wetlands in what was known as "Swampeast Missouri." He could also count on several weeks of work after the picking season at the local cotton gin. Everybody, including Gene, was expected to contribute during the cotton "off season": "There was five widow womans in that town and they all bootlegged whiskey, but they didn't pay no tax on it. And the law winked at them because they already had their husbands in jail. They knew they either had to let them go ahead and sell it or pay for raising their kids." Every afternoon, Gene recalled, he'd "come home from school and go through the back alleys and find whiskey bottles," then "hide them under them little storage sheds that the merchants had out there." On the weekends, he'd take his "wagon and go down and get them" and "haul them across the railroad tracks" to the bootlegging women. "I got a penny apiece out of the whiskey bottles. I could play pool all day long with what I got out of them whiskey bottles. It was two and a half cents a cue." Everything earned in the fields "went for food" and other necessities.

The Johnsons eventually entered the bootlegging market directly with their "home brew. I could make it blindfolded right now." They started with "clear bottles, from Spiegel out of Chicago. Spiegel catalog. And plain copper caps. And we had a crimper. Dad would fill it up 'til about maybe a half an inch or an inch from the top" and "would leave it set about twelve days. Then he'd put a half a teaspoonful of sugar in it. That'd help it ferment quicker. Leave it set another three days. Fifteen days altogether." On Saturday mornings, Gene, his father, and another brother would stand "down on the street selling it. Me and my brother, we'd have our shirts blossomed out like this and all the wet bottles of home brew in there. We sold it for fifteen cents a bottle." That was significantly cheaper than the taxed alcohol sold at the local drugstore, and "just about everybody down there drank." Gene had no qualms about their enterprise, because it helped the family survive: "Heck no, it wasn't legal! The statute of limitations would protect me! I don't care."

The family also made money by helping neighbors stock up on firewood: "Wintertime come, there ain't nothing then but cutting wood. We had them old two-man cross-cut saws. I'd get on one end, my brother would get on the other end, saw them trees down." They'd burn the unusable brush: "Kerosene was pretty cheap then, four cents a gallon. But of course, four cents was hard to get, too. We didn't pour it on real heavily." After sawing the logs from twelve to fourteen feet long, they'd load them into their '36 Chevy truck and haul them home to cut them into lengths that were appropriate, once split, for wood cooking stoves, which almost everybody in the area used. If the logs had "big knots" in them that "wouldn't split, or couldn't split, why, we sold them, too, for the people who put them in what they call big can heaters, for heat. People didn't have furnaces then."

The Johnsons engaged in these activities with heavy hearts. The family's oldest child, Calvin, died of pneumonia in 1931, when he was fourteen years old. Gene was six at the time: "It tore Mom and Dad all to pieces. That was their oldest son. My dad used to make me feel bad—he didn't *mean* to—and I know he made the other kids feel bad, too, always talking about Calvin being the favorite. From a kid's point of view, you're wondering, 'Well where do I stand?' I *know* that he didn't mean anything by it, but they was so attached to my older brother, and lost him, and I understand that." Gene had fond memories of Calvin. With their middle brother, Harvey, they used to perform with their dad: "We was all musical. And we'd go out and play for square dances out on the old farms. And he'd play 'til three or four o'clock in the morning, fighting, drinking moonshine. I was just a kid, but I remember all that. We played guitars. My dad played fiddle." Gene also remembered that Calvin used "to take me piggy-back to Sunday school. We only lived about two blocks from the General Baptist church. But mom and dad, they didn't go to church."

Gene's memories of Calvin's death and funeral remained powerful: "When he died, this is the indelible impression. I'm not trying to use fancy words. They come in there, guys from the funeral home, with the little gurney, with four wheels on it, picked him up out of the bed. He was as stiff as a board. And I still see that. And they laid him on the little gurney, right in front of me. And I remember saying to my older brother, Harvey—I had no concept of life and death—'Harvey why is he letting them do him that way? Why is he letting them put him on that?' Probably affected me more than it did anybody else. I remember being in the car and seeing the truck, open back of that truck, seeing the casket and going up to the cemetery. I remember that real well. Maybe other people are able to *forget*. But I'll tell you what, I haven't forgot any of it."[1]

Despite limited resources, the Johnson family was known for its generosity during the Depression: "We had a big garden. Back in those days a lot of hobos rode the rails, because this is the Depression. They were just going all over like a crossword puzzle trying to get a job." The train stopped right near the Johnson home, and their garden: "Them hobos—they'd be six or eight in them boxcars—they'd be sitting in the door hanging their feet off, and they'd run over to that turnip patch, start pulling them turnips up, and go on back to the boxcar." Rather than protect his crop, Gene's dad "increased his turnip patch. I never will forget that. Dad was compassionate. And when I was a little kid the hobos come to the door and ask if there was any work they could do. Dad turned around to mom and said, 'Berthie, save a place at the table!' He did that all the time. And mom would fix the old boy something to eat."

School wasn't the highest priority in the Johnson family, especially if attendance conflicted with paid work: "I passed usually with a C or C+. But the reason why was because I missed three or four months of school every year. Because I *had* to work the fields. There wasn't no such thing as a truant officer. Kids had to work back then." There were about twenty children in each grade, two grades to a room: "In eighth grade, we got to go down to the big time, the high school. The last year I went to school there was eighth grade, and then I started high school in the ninth grade. And then I quit. I didn't go the full way."

Some children in town attended school regularly, and the rest took notice. In Bernie, Gene explained, "there was only two classes of people—people that had it and the people that didn't have it. And the people that didn't have it had to kiss the other people's you-know-what to get anything. The ones that didn't have anything didn't have *anything*, period. Had to work for every scrap that they got. But you still had your merchants—they was the so-called high elite—and their families. And three or four kids would have their new bikes and stuff like that, that you would wish you had one, but you couldn't."

Racial dynamics in town were also strained: "You've heard the old saying that you got to be out of town before the sun goes down on you? Well that was the attitude there of that town."[2] Bernie had no Black residents, except for a few domestic servants in the wealthy neighborhood. African Americans "lived out in the country." Rarely did Blacks and whites work side-by-side in cotton fields. Smaller landowners tended to hire poor whites for field work, while most Blacks were sharecroppers on larger plantations. Those large landowners "furnished them little huts. They called them houses, but they was huts." Considering only material existence, Gene insisted, poor whites and poor blacks "were equal. We didn't have no more than they did. All we knew is just that guy's a different color than we was and hell, he done the same thing we did and it was hard for him to get enough to eat just like it was for us."

World War II changed the economics of the region. Shortly after the Pearl Harbor attack, the federal government funded construction of a military airfield a few miles south of Bernie. Gene drove to check it out, "and man there was just a string of cars on both sides of the road. Everybody was trying to get a job. About the second week I got hired, and boy I was doing all right. It was sixty-five and a half cents an hour. Can you imagine going from a dollar a day, fourteen hours a day to sixty-five and a half cents an hour?" Gene hauled cement in a wheelbarrow: "I hadn't never done a job like that. I was tired and I was breaking my back, and one guy come up and said, 'Son, let me show you how to do that.' I was just setting the wheelbarrow down, and they'd just fill it plum full, right up to the brim. He said, 'Hold them handles up, and they can't put so much cement in it.' I appreciated that." Gene noted that these were union jobs: "They charged me fifty cents a month. Kept it out of my check." He never minded joining the union, he said, and neither did his coworkers: "Absolutely not. They'd think you'd lost your mind and was ready for the mental asylum."

After the airfield was done in late 1942, Gene found a job repairing tracks on a railroad "section gang." He was seventeen, the youngest guy the crew had ever hired, he said, "and they paid me seventy-four cents an hour." It was hard work: "Hottest place you can be in the summertime, and the coldest place you can be in wintertime. They had these little handcarts—they'd ride real slowly on it watching for spikes up," and if they found one, they'd "take turns swinging that old spike in—after a while you drive that old spike down." Rail traffic was so important that the section gang covered their entire four-mile route every day, lifting the handcart off the tracks to avoid oncoming trains. The hardest job was replacing rails: "We used to unload these big creosote ties—ten-by-ten cross ties—out of the boxcars." Each one weighed about a hundred twenty pounds: "Hey, I was seventeen, but I could do anything back in them days."

After a few months on the section gang, Gene headed for Pontiac, Michigan. It was 1943 and he had just turned eighteen. He lived with "an aunt up here, my mother's sister." He also "had a sister up here, and a couple of cousins." His uncle worked at Pontiac Motor and got him a job there on material handling. His responsibility was "stacking ring gear housings on a pallet." He did that, over and over, for five or six months. Then he got a job as an "inside power truck driver, hauling pallets" and putting them on "big freight trucks." The pallets held various parts, such as piston liners, rocker arms, and valves, that Pontiac Motor manufactured and shipped to assembly plants across the country. When asked how these jobs compared with working in cotton fields, Gene was emphatic: "Oh, hell, it was a snap, man, it was a snap!" Referring to Pontiac Motor, he insisted that "the worst job they *got* can't even compare to chopping cotton." By contrast, auto work "was heaven! That was paradise. Only got ninety-nine cents an hour, but still, I'm talking about from sixty-five and a half, to seventy-four, to ninety-nine. I'm going up, see?"

Most of Gene's coworkers were also from the south: "Like me, got tired of being down there, come up here and got a job. Shoot, you could go up to these local bars and half of the people in there was from Arkansas, Missouri, or Tennessee, somewhere like that. They called us hillbillies. At first we resented it, but later on we almost got proud of it, to be honest with you. We wouldn't back off. And if anybody started trouble, they knew there's five or six they're going to have to whip. It wasn't right, but I mean, that's the way it was."

A lot of his coworkers were also young, but hardly any were Black: "There was a few, but not too many in that department." However, "a lot of women were driving power trucks. You wouldn't think they would. Women was welding—a lot of welders. They had a job just about for any woman there. Had almost as many women as they did men. But I noticed there was no women on any skilled trades."

Gene remembered being solidly pro-union from his first day on the job: "I've always thought it was good, because I guess I had sense enough to realize that people wasn't being treated right, from where I came from. So that was my attitude right there. Anything that would better the people that had to work every day to make a living, yeah, I was for it. Yup. Absolutely." That sentiment, he said, was common among transplanted southerners: "They was so glad to get a better improvement in life that, naturally, they was for the union."[3] They also listened to the plant's old-timers, who educated the newcomers about the way things had been. A couple of examples stood out for Gene. Before the union, if the line shut down for any reason, workers had to punch off the clock and wait without pay until production resumed: "Then when you went back to work you punched back in. And you bought your own gloves, you bought your own aprons, or anything else that you needed."

After about a year in Pontiac, Gene was drafted and reported to Jefferson Barracks, just south of St. Louis, Missouri: "When my training was over, I thought I was going be shipped overseas or somewhere else, but instead they sent me to clerical school. Administrative school, they called it." It astonished him, given his weak academic credentials: "They thought I'd be good at it. They assigned me to the W.D.P.C., War Department Personnel Center, in St. Louis, where all the records was of all the Army GIs." He still expected to be shipped closer to combat, especially when he was transferred to Fort Lewis, near Tacoma, Washington: "But instead I got in this accident." It was a collision between a cargo truck and, of all things, an ambulance: "Crushed my hand and hurt my back. That cost me fourteen months in Madigan General Hospital."[4]

While Gene was healing, the war ended and demobilization began: "They discharged me there, and I come home. I went back to Pontiac Motor and got my job back." Several months later, he married a woman, Agnes, who also grew up in Missouri, about sixty miles west of Bernie. He had met her briefly at a church revival, "what they call a Brush Arbor meeting," just outside Bernie, but he met her "*seriously*" in Pontiac, a year before he was drafted. Gene explained that a friend "introduced me to two girls, and one of them was Agnes. And we hit it off just like that. In fact, I took her home that night." Their wedding was on February 13, 1946. "I didn't even have sense enough to wait another day, make it Valentine's Day," he laughed.

It took time for the couple to figure out how to make the relationship work: "We fought for three years and finally got there. And we had six beautiful kids." Their oldest child, however, had been born the year before they were married, which was controversial at the time: "Now, I've been honest on all this stuff. People are going to read between the lines and compare dates and stuff like that. Me and my wife wasn't married then. Now these are the little things that I might would have been reluctant to mention, but I'm not. It's just a part of my life. I suppose that most people could tell the same story if they'd be honest."

Gene strained the marriage that first year by deciding to re-enlist in the Army: "How could a guy who was fourteen months in the hospital re-enlist?" He and a sergeant challenged each other to re-up. "We were both drinking," Gene explained. The recruiter was willing to accept Gene's friend, but not Gene unless he signed a waiver forfeiting rights to future disability payments because of his injuries while previously in the service. He signed, and resumed his military career. It meant that his family relocated to Fort Campbell, Kentucky, leaving Pontiac behind and many relatives who had moved there. Gene preferred to focus on the positives: "I don't know what these people seen in me at all. But anyhow, they seen something. They cleared me for access to secret material." Not bad for a "cotton picker," he thought.

Gene was given significant responsibilities, including printing and handling "special transfer orders, troop movement orders, court martial orders and memorandums, letters of commendations, and general transfers." It was all highly confidential information: "That's where the clearance has to come in. I'd have to stay there with my blinds pulled down in my office until every piece of paper" was accounted for. "We had a little incinerator out the back. I'd have to go out there and stand there until every backing of the stencil—because, you know, there's print through the backing—every inch of that was burned. A lot of times I didn't get home until 1:00 in the morning." Gene found this work interesting and challenging—"never was a dull moment"—and he also developed a competition with a younger brother, who joined the Navy in 1948: "We was just playing tit for tat on promotions, see who could outdo the other one."

On leave, he occasionally returned to Bernie: "The chief of police was a buddy of mine that I went to school with. And we were real good friends. I'd be in civilian clothes, on a weekend pass." One time his friend appeared concerned, telling Gene, "'There have been three guys down here two different times asking me questions.' He thought I had deserted." It turns out, Gene explained, that military officials had asked many people in town, including all of his former teachers, "personal questions about my character." People in Bernie stood by him, and Gene was proud that he passed the security requirements.

By the early 1950s, Gene and Agnes had four children, and the oldest, Ronny, developed a strange, crippling disorder: "When he started in school, he was six years old. Didn't have no kindergarten. He was running out of the yard, catching the bus. For two or three days he would fall before he'd get to the bus. So we knew something was wrong. We took him to the hospital there, Fort Campbell Hospital, and they diagnosed him." It turned out that Ronny had Legg-Calvé-Perthes disease, which affects the blood flow to hip joints.[5] "I'd never heard of it before. And they said he *likely* would not walk again. But said there is a possibility. So the prescription was for him to stay off his feet. No medication or anything, no shots, just stay off his feet and watch him."

With the Korean War in its second year, there was a continuing demand for troops to replace those whose tours of duty were ending, and Gene realized that he might be assigned to go overseas. When considering re-enlistment in 1952, he learned that his superiors already "had pulled me off of two overseas orders." By rights, then, he should have been in Korea. Instead, he had been printing lists of draftees and reassigned military personnel. Should he rejoin and risk deployment to Korea? He remembered telling his boss, who wanted him to stay, that he couldn't leave his wife alone with four children. Ronny required lots of care: "We had to carry him from the car to the bathroom to the dining table. Had to carry him everywhere. Am I going to leave my wife with that and three other kids?" What "if something happens, and I'm gone overseas?"

It was a question based in part on another traumatic experience. A couple years earlier, Gene explained, a daughter, Sheila, contracted spinal meningitis, "and my commander had got me relieved from duty to arrange a funeral for her. They thought it had already hit the vital parts of her brain and everything else." But there was still a sliver of hope: "I went in the next day to visit her, and the doctor asked me to notice if she does things like she used to do. I had a little pocket comb. She'd always take that comb of mine and comb my hair. And she always wouldn't eat a bite unless I'd eat a bite first. And all a sudden she done just those things. Told her doctor about that. He said, 'Well, I think we might be wrong.' Said, 'She might pull out.'" Gene and Agnes held out hope, "saying out loud, 'Lord, if you'll only get her out of here, we'll do anything.'" It seemed odd, he emphasized, because "we wasn't religious then." Sheila survived, "with the only effects is she's deaf in one ear." With all this in mind, Gene left the service and conceded eventual defeat to his brother in their military promotion competition. Gene emphasized, however, that he "outranked him at that time."

The Johnsons returned to Pontiac, but "Pontiac Motor wasn't hiring then. The federal law stated that they must give you your job back. But if there's no job openings, they don't have to give you the job." They just couldn't "hire somebody else off the street" before recalling you. Instead, Gene drove a taxicab: "And buddy, that was work." He developed a strategy that focused on short rides: "I tried to make a hundred runs a day at the average of fifty cents a run. Some would be sixty, some would be eighty, some would be thirty cents. I wanted to stay close to where I'd drive around the house every once in a while to check on the kids, because all of them wasn't in school." His approach to the job made sense, but it wasn't lucrative. The split with the cab company was "fifty-fifty. So if I made a hundred runs a day at fifty cents a run, that gives me fifty dollars total in my little cigar box. And I get twenty-five dollars of that. I had to pay half the gas, and you burn a lot of gas. I wound up with about fifteen dollars a day. Now, that was twelve hours a day. They only had two shifts driving the cab: 6:00 to 6:00 in the evening and 6:00 in the evening to 6:00 in the morning."

Agnes had her hands full and did not work outside the house: "She was a housewife. She stayed home with the kids. All of them believed in this old cliché down South, you know, the man brings in the bacon. That to me doesn't mean that the man is Lord and Taj Mahal and all of this stuff. It just means that he's got a duty to do and so does the wife. And that's the way we operated." He knew that she was working really hard, especially with Ronny unable to walk and Sheila's hearing disability: "I wouldn't have traded jobs with her at all."

After eight months with no recall from Pontiac Motor, the Johnsons returned to Missouri, possibly for good. They settled outside of Doniphan, Agnes's home town, and occasionally attended church with Agnes's parents: "We wasn't religious yet. We wasn't atheist either." One night in "February of '53," Gene explained, members of the church youth group, including Agnes's younger brother, "come to our house, knocked on the door. It was cold. So we opened the door and invited them in. They asked us if they could pray for Ronny." Gene remembered thinking, "'Well, what's it going to hurt?' I said, 'Sure.' So they started praying and praying." This went on for a while, until the leader of the group turned to Gene and Agnes and asked them to leave: "Said, 'We got a feeling there's non-believers in here.' So I looked at my wife. She looked at me. Well, it doesn't matter whether you actually believe or don't believe. You ain't going to take a chance of spoiling a good thing. So we agreed to go out in the car. Remember this is in February. We sit out there for about, I guess, twenty-five, thirty minutes. And man, they was really pouring it on in the house, praying. And so they called us back in. When we walked back in there, Ronny was standing up, right beside the bed."

Gene knew there would always be skeptics: "I don't care whether they believe it or not. I know it happened. So I didn't take him back to the doctor no more, because it'd be telling God that I didn't believe that it happened." Ronny became stronger and began to walk: "One morning he was sitting up on the side of his bed and one leg of his pajamas was up. It happened to be the leg where we noticed it was getting smaller on account of that disease. But the leg was the same size as the other. I'm sitting here saying it and I'm telling you the truth." It turns out that Legg-Calvé-Perthes disease can resolve on its own. Nevertheless, there was no doubt in Gene's mind that prayer and divine intervention had restored Ronny's health.

The rest of the family's stay in Missouri proved less than miraculous. Gene had not grown up on a farm, yet it seemed odd, perhaps mocking, when people in Doniphan spoke of him, from Bernie, as some sort of city slicker. He thought he'd try selling milk and butter, so he bought a cow with his military payments, built a stable, and hoped for the best. But the cow had damaged udders and wouldn't allow herself to be milked: "Couldn't touch her at all. You get scars, where the calf had bit, sucking on the cow." Everybody in Doniphan knew about it: "The joke was going around there about Carl Parson's son-in-law, didn't know anything about farming. Well, that made me so mad, I told everybody about the dirty deal he pulled. And you know what he done? He come up on Sunday at church to my father-in-law and said, 'Tell your son-in-law to bring that cow back and I'll give him his money back.'" It was still an embarrassing episode, although maybe not as humiliating as his attempt to raise hens: "I bought a whole lot of chickens. Pullets and a couple of roosters. Going to have my own eggs and home-frying chicken and all that stuff. My brothers-in-law helped me build chicken coops. Put nests in there and everything. But I wasn't getting no eggs." He tried to trick the chickens by buying "artificial eggs to help the hens lay" and relatively expensive food to encourage more egg production. "Not an egg. Nothing." One day, Agnes saw one of their daughters making mud pies with yellow yolks inside them and asked where the eggs came from. She pointed to a nearby brush pile. "I went out there, and I bet you there was eight or nine dozen eggs in there." The hens hadn't used the coops at all. At that point, Gene quit farming and prepared to move back to Pontiac. As for Agnes: "Oh yeah, she was tired of it, too." Driving a cab was better than anything they tried in Missouri.

When they returned, the auto industry was booming and Pontiac Motor was hiring again: "I went back on April 4th, 1953."[6] His job was on "a big broaching machine, broaching the steering knuckles," which attached to a car's suspension. The knuckles were made at the foundry, he explained, "and you had to forge off the excess material" until each part met specifications. This involved mostly loading parts on the machine and pushing buttons, and Gene mastered it "in about four or five hours." It was better than driving a cab: "I got to take home more money and I didn't have to spend twelve hours on the job." His bosses, he recalled, "were pretty good to me. But of course, they had no reason not to be. I done my job." Still, he remembered that during his first time at Pontiac Motor his bosses "were pushy. And they'd always remind you that if you didn't like your job, there's somebody lined up waiting for your job. I resented it, of course, but you still have to do the job or quit." It helped that his broaching machine was elevated, "up on a platform, about six or seven foot from the floor line, pretty much by myself." A foreman couldn't "just come up and start talking to me."

Gene eventually moved to a different job, but not for long, because in August 1953 an explosion at a General Motors transmission factory in Livonia, Michigan halted production at Pontiac Motor.[7] "So I just went back to driving the cab. Drove for probably about ten weeks." Unemployment compensation was minimal: "I didn't bother to sign up, even though I didn't make much money driving the cab."

Sometime around November, Pontiac Motor recalled Gene to a job in the heavy press department. "We was pressing hoods, fenders, bumpers, and fender skirts," some of the biggest parts of a car. Large pieces of steel approached the press, Gene would insert them, and the molds on the top and bottom of the press would shape the metal into a rough version of the desired part: "We made as many as 4800 bumpers a day. I'd say seven or eight presses on the line." The first would "press the shape of it, the other press would trim off a little bit of it, another press would trim off some more of it. Then there'd be another procedure that punched little holes in them where they can fit it on the bumper, with the screws. And on down, till you hung them on the overhead conveyor that takes them over to the nickel plate room. When they go in nickel plate and come out, they're finished bumpers. Then they go to the assembly line. Everything worked right and no breakdowns, 4800 was easy. Wasn't no problem."

Yet there were drawbacks: "That was a line job. That was a every-minute job. I mean, you only got off the job when you got relief or the line broke down for a few minutes or something like that." It was also "hot in the summertime and cold in the wintertime, because didn't have no built-in heat and cooling condition at that time." In addition, it was physically tough: "Ohhh, those bumpers weighed sixty, seventy pounds." And it was loud: "The conveyors was all metal. And it would just echo the noise. I lost all my hearing in my left ear, and about half of it in my right ear. You better believe it was noisy. I talk loud. And that's an albatross for me because there's the old saying, the first impression is the lasting impression. Some people I have met, I talked loud to them and they think I'm aggressive. But the reason why I'm talking loud is because it was so noisy that you'd have to put your mouth right up against somebody's ear to make them hear you. After twenty-eight, thirty years like that, you know, you're in the habit of talking loud."

Heavy presses were also dangerous: "We had several guys in there that had an arm off and a hand off, stuff like that. But I don't know if it was their fault. I think it was carelessness on the worker. Also, I think it was negligence of duty for the supervisors." For example, workers were supposed to insert and remove parts with tongs, not their hands: "But maybe they wouldn't even come back and check and see if that guy's using tongs, which I think they would be obligated to, to prevent accidents. And a lot of times those presses would double trip. That means go up and come back down before you push the button again. If you happened to have your hand in there, too bad." Each pressing took only a few seconds, so damage happened quickly. Body parts had no chance: "Big bumper presses and hood presses, they shake the floor for several hundred feet around."

All in all, Gene concluded, heavy presses "was just a job." He did appreciate that "if you done your job and everybody else cooperated, you didn't have no problems." But he objected to how foremen manipulated the speed of production: "They'd bring a new man in. Of course he's anxious to get a job. It's a good job. He probably hadn't had no better job, especially if it's somebody from down south coming up here, a little bit scared of not doing exactly what he's told to do, and he wants to make a good impression. It was a practice to put him on the lead press. You know why? He's going to bust his butt. And everybody else down the line has to keep up with him. They played that game all the time." The more experienced workers, Gene said, would "talk to the guy," but "it wouldn't do no good. Here the guy was concerned about his job, and we *really* didn't *blame* him. It was just that he was being brainwashed, and being used. He was being used to *push* us." If the others down the line worked more slowly, the parts would "pile up behind and then the foreman come get on you, for not keeping up."

There were occasional time studies to set official production speeds: "Timekeepers that come down and time you, how you do this part, how long it take you to do this part and that part. And then they'd set the rate per hour. I'll tell you how you felt. You felt intimidated. Somebody looking over your shoulder, watching over you. I tried not to bust the record. And everybody else that had any sense would, too. It's not that you're not trying to do your job or you want to throw a monkey wrench in anything. It's just that you're getting tired of being pushed, and it's like any other place, they're always trying to increase production. And if you go along with them, who *knows* how high the production is going to be after a while? What are they going to do, hold a contest to see who can stand the longest before they fall? That's the way I looked at it. If the superintendent was pushing for more parts, more production—which they would do—they'd send time studies up again, see if they can't get a few more, maybe ten or fifteen more an hour."

In 1954, Agnes's parents moved to Pontiac "and they was pretty religious. We'd go to Sunday school and take the kids." But Gene and Agnes were just going through the motions. Still, they went one night to a church revival meeting: "Special pastor invited. I remember his name. Reverend Jason Felder. When there's something connected like this that's important, you never forget. And his last remark was, 'Did you forget your promises to God?' And I know that my wife—it must've hit her the same way it did me—because when they had a call to go to the altar, we both went." They remembered the prayers of the youth group in Missouri, how Ronny had healed, their own prayers for Sheila, and how they hadn't followed through on their promises. That night they pledged their lives to God: "You might think I'm a religious freak, but I'm not. You might think I'm a fanatic, but I'm not. I'm no better than anybody else. But I do believe in God. I believe in church. I believe in the Holy Spirit. I believe in all of that."

From that point forward, Gene emphasized, religion "was our life, going to church, going to Sunday school, going to prayer meeting. It was a Holiness church. It wasn't Pentecostal. You use the word Holiness, most people think

Pentecostal, but it wasn't Pentecostal. No, they didn't talk in tongues or anything like that." Sunday was the most important day of the week for the Johnson family. Sunday school in the morning, followed by regular church services, then youth service in the early evening, and another "preaching service" after that. There were often church meals in between. During the week there would be youth groups and prayer meetings, "and we were there, too. It was pretty much a way of life. We got into it full."

It was a huge change for Gene, who until his conversion still played music at bars and enjoyed going out drinking and dancing with Agnes. Gene recalled that they would occasionally run into their friends from their former lives and be asked, "'What do you do now for *fun*?' We said, 'We're busy, we're satisfied. We have lots of fun. We got lots of friends.' That's all we'd tell them. That's all we *needed* to tell them. We were happy." Still, there was something wistful in Gene's memories about performing in the "hillbilly" bars: "I played ordinary, rough, hole-in-the-wall, country-western songs. And then when I joined the church, I didn't go to those places no more. I played in the church orchestra. And it was just like playing two different instruments—the old straight-line country song music and square dance music and then playing our church hymns." Softly, he said, "but it didn't take long, get right into it. And I enjoyed that."

The family took vacations as well: "My kids have been to more places by the time they were six years old, than most adults do all their life. We traveled every time we got laid off. Used to get laid off for a whole season, twelve weeks. We'd go down to Missouri sometimes for the whole layoff time. And we'd go up north, up here to the sand dunes" in northern Michigan. "And then we'd go out to my brother's house in Las Vegas. Then we had some friends south of San Bernardino, California and we'd go out there. Shoot, we went just about everywhere. We'd go to Florida. I had a sister in Florida. We traveled all over the country."

At Pontiac Motor, Gene continued to press parts throughout the mid-1950s. There were indeed all sorts of layoffs—"furloughs," he called them. But the 1958 recession was the harshest: "Just about everybody was laid off. I was laid off for eleven months." As usual, he went back to driving a cab. This time, however, he found it worthwhile to draw unemployment compensation, despite reductions because of his taxi earnings. He even collected Supplemental Unemployment Benefits, which had been won in the 1955 contract, although he remembered that it "wasn't very much at all—$12.60 or something like that, supplemental pay."

When he was finally recalled, because of his relatively low seniority it was to the foundry: "I grinded the stupid blocks that come down the line. There's excess steel or iron on them. You just grind it down, smooth it down, knock off the big chunks with the chisel and hammer, and then take your overhead grinder and grind it and smooth it down." The job had annoying dangers: "I don't know how many times I went to the first aid there with pieces of metal in my eye. And it'll rust, that cast iron—turn your eyeball red." Protective glasses didn't help, because metal specks would "get underneath. They had more visitors in that first aid on foundry than they did anywhere else in Pontiac Motor." The foundry "was dirtier and hotter" than his heavy press job. Because Pontiac was slowly recalling employees, there were more white men than usual in the foundry and quite a few white women, some of whom had been with the company since World War II.

Eventually, assembly-line output increased and the foundry operated seven days a week to provide enough parts. But since his religious conversion, Gene had refused to work on Sundays. His supervisors in heavy presses had respected his convictions, even though by contract he was supposed to report to work if jobs were running: "They always went along with me because they could always pick up a guy in my place to work Sunday." His substitutes were "tickled that I wouldn't work Sunday. They'd get more hours." One Saturday in the foundry, however, when told he had to work the following day, Gene replied that he would be in church. The General Foreman approached him: "'Johnson,' he said, 'I'll see you tomorrow.' And I said, 'No, you won't see me tomorrow, Larry.' They didn't know nothing about my past. 'Well,' he said, 'if you don't come in *tomorrow*, you don't come in *Monday*.' I said, 'I intend to be here Monday.' So we left it that way." When Gene reported to the foundry on Monday, his foreman asked, "'What are you doing here?' I said, 'I came to work.' He said, 'Well I told you, you needn't a come in today if you didn't work yesterday.' We argued and argued, and finally I called the committeeman."

The company questioned whether or not Gene had really been at church: "They asked me what church I go to and what my pastor's name was. They questioned my pastor. They questioned my Sunday school superintendent. It was mainly because they didn't want nobody breaking their policy. They told me right then and there that the policy was that if the full department was scheduled, I was expected to come in, and they couldn't afford to make any special limitations for me. I kind of understand that. But yet, I didn't want to go against my policy either."

Gene was allowed to work until his case was resolved. He was by no means certain which way it would go: "I expected to be fired. I expected to be looking for another job somewhere, to be honest. I was ready to go. I had talked it over with my wife and everybody. All the people at church knew about it. I had everybody praying for it." The union shop committee worked hard to protect his job, even if doing so meant violating the contract. Fortunately, as Gene recalled, his explanations checked out and the superintendent said, "'Don't require him—don't even ask him to work on Sunday.' And, man, I was really relieved. I didn't want to quit my job. All my kids was still home then. And that was a paramount situation that I won."

Gene was grateful for the development of Pontiac's "Wide Track" cars in 1959, which proved popular with the public and got him "back to my home plant." But things had changed since he was last in heavy presses: "The whole department had different lines," and "you would be liable to do any job on that line. If your line was broke down, you could go to any other line in that department, or any other department if another foreman needed you. I've even went over to the other plants. Repair Plant, 16. Just short term. Maybe one day." He adapted, and he never worked a Sunday. For that, he was known to coworkers as "The Preacher." Gene wavered a bit from his most devout days, especially after Agnes died in the early 1990s: "I go up to the casinos, gamble. I didn't used to gamble. I've strayed away a little bit, but I won't stay away." His children, he said, were "not overly religious. They go to church on Easters and Christmas." Ronny joined the Army's 82nd Airborne Division and parachuted from planes—"A kid who wasn't supposed to walk no more join the 82nd Airborne Division!" In the early 2000s, Ronny owned a lounge in Tennessee. "Needless to say," Gene remarked, "he's still not religious." Sheila spent time at the Flint School for the Deaf and learned to read lips: "Everything's fine with her. She's ordinary. She's just like me or you or anybody else. And she can hear you if you happen to be on the side where her ear is not affected." Gene continued as a member of his church orchestra, and he played competitive softball well into his 50s: "I've had a hard life in certain portions of it, but I've had a very good life in other portions of it. So I can't complain. I don't complain. I've never had no great, high summit expectations of my accomplishments, but I've accomplished what I *needed* to. I'm satisfied. It was a rough life. It was tough. I don't say it's the worst life that anybody could ever have, but I'll tell you what, I haven't seen anything any worse. Maybe it's because I'm expressing myself and I'm *remembering* too much."

8

Dorothy Sackle
(1917–2015)

Dorothy Sackle shook her head when reflecting on her life: "How did I ever survive all this?" Born in 1917 on the east side of Detroit, she was the second child in the Kudrycki family. Her father had arrived in the United States from Poland in 1904, when he was sixteen, and her mother was the daughter of German immigrants. Dorothy figured that her parents must have met at a dance. Before having children, Dorothy's mother worked in a local cigar factory, which some family members considered scandalous. She stayed home after Dorothy's older sister was born. Dorothy's father found work in a Ford plant: "He was a core-maker, whatever is a core-maker." It was tough foundry work, it turns out, essential for creating components of cars, but at the time all Dorothy knew is that "he worked with some kind of fire" and "was pretty tired when he came home. He must've been paid pretty good because when I was eight years old they bought a house on Marion," also on the east side of the city. The Kudryckis were moving up in the world. Dorothy noticed, she recalled, "because I went on the railing, and my father says, 'Don't be such a wild Indian. This is a nice neighborhood!'" In the mid-1930s, however, tragedy struck. The family lost one nine-month-old child to diphtheria and another at age thirteen to a heart ailment. Then Dorothy's mother died of pneumonia in 1937 and her father suffered a fatal heart attack a year later.

Before the calamities mounted, Dorothy enjoyed her weekly trips to the corner grocer to pay the family's bills: "They would give us a little bag of candy,

Mary Janes and Squirrels." She had cousins in the neighborhood and they'd often play together: "We put the ironing board down, and that was our slide. And we'd have so much fun." When she was ten or eleven, she and her brother "peddled papers" out of their "little red wagon." Sometimes they ate their profits: "We'd have ice cream."

Like most families, the Kudryckis cut back during the Depression. Dorothy remembered that her father "had money in the bank, and the banks closed." That was followed by intermittent employment, at best, at Ford: "For Christmas, God, if you got a pair of roller skates, that was it. Maybe an orange and an apple. You didn't know any better and you thought this was wonderful." She was adamant on one issue: "I never went hungry, that's for sure." On the dreamier side, she remembered going to a friend's home, where "Grace's father would kiss her mother on the neck, and I thought, oh, when I get married, I want a husband like that!" More practically, Dorothy and her sister found jobs. Dorothy worked after school and on weekends for Kresge's, a dime store, in downtown Detroit. The work was "fast and furious," she recalled, especially during the Easter season, when candy sales soared. She remembered a particularly busy day: "When I came home, I was crawling on my knees. My mother said, 'You see why you have to get an education. Because you don't want to work for thirty-five cents an hour.' So that's why I finished high school." Dorothy hoped to become a secretary. But in the mid-1930s, she explained, "I couldn't get an office job, so I went to work in the factory at Plymouth Motor."

It took some persistence to get the Plymouth job. After an initial rejection, Dorothy recalled, her mother insisted that she "keep going every day. They'll get tired of seeing you." The plant was on Lynch Road, "quite a ways from where we lived, but I went every day until they hired me." Once in the plant, she quickly learned her responsibilities, despite little familiarity with cars or machines. One task involved using steel wool to prepare a surface for painting and "spraying it with a whatchamacallit." Women did the preparation, and men did the painting. On another job, she dipped wires into a vat of hot acid, pulled them out, and shook them off. It was part of the "solder pop" process, in which workers "would put solder on these little doohickeys at the end of the wire. You were only allowed six months on that job," a sign that its dangers were somewhat recognized at the time. Dorothy also spent time installing felt strips around various parts: "I had a lot of jobs, now that I think of it!"

She had "women supervisors," which was "very nice. They weren't pushing you or anything." One of her bosses allowed workers to double their official ten-minute breaks, during which they'd socialize in the restroom: "You got to know the women." Once Dorothy fell asleep during her break but she didn't get in trouble, "because everybody used to kind of doze off, you know." If possible, the women covered for each other; otherwise, they'd coax exhausted coworkers back into action.

Dorothy became involved, grudgingly, in the UAW's 1937 sit-down strike wave that organized Chrysler plants, including the Lynch Road facility: "Some of the men sat in the factory because there was a strike. I didn't, because I was a woman. But the men did. We had to bring them something to eat, in the factory." At the time, she said, she was lukewarm about unionization: "I was pissed off because I didn't like my five dollars taken out of my pay" for monthly dues. "I resented it." Besides, she had relatively nice bosses. She helped support the cause anyway: "They were doing a good thing, you know. They were taking a stand. They wanted the union to come in there and make things easier, probably for the men, where the lines were going too fast." Attitudes toward the organizing campaign varied among the women in her department: "Some of them liked it and some of them didn't. It all depends on how hard your job was."

Dorothy's responses to workplace conflicts were complicated by the dramatic changes in her family situation. She was especially despondent that her mother died before her wedding. She had mixed feelings, however, about her father's death. It bothered her that he had remarried fairly quickly after her mother passed. He had also never accompanied the family to church and had always been remote: "He was good to us. He never beat us or anything," but "he wasn't affectionate." Dorothy recalled that when his body was available for viewing at the family home, "somebody said to me, 'Well kiss your father goodbye.' And I said, 'I didn't kiss him when he was living. I'm not going to kiss him now!'"

A year later, she gave birth to her first child. She had met her future husband at a Polish dance, having gone there with her friend Grace for the polkas, food, and romantic possibilities. At the time, Dorothy recalled, he was looking for a job, "so I told him to come to Plymouth Motor. And he got hired in, so we both worked at Plymouth." Expenses mounted with a child, which contributed to her resentment of UAW dues: "I guess we needed the money when I first got married and I was pregnant." She kept her job while expecting, and her coworkers "even threw me a little baby shower." That lenient boss also helped, because Dorothy often felt sick and fatigued from pregnancy complications: "I weighed like two hundred, because I was filled with water. I thought it was my turn to die." Both mother and child survived, and after her daughter, Patricia, was born, Dorothy stopped working outside the home for a couple of years.

Her second child, David, was born in 1941, and sometime after the Pearl Harbor attack that December, she returned to the Plymouth Plant. She was motivated partly by wartime patriotism. "You were helping out," she emphasized, but her family also "probably needed the money." Dorothy's new job was on the midnight shift. "I was working on pistons," she laughed. "Whatever pistons are! They're nice and shiny." She inspected them for possible defects, often metal nubs. Others filed them smooth before sending them to final inspection. Even though she was good at her job, Dorothy lacked confidence. During final inspection, she recalled, "my head would go down and the inspectors would laugh because they would see my head go down." She was occasionally assigned to other jobs, none of them difficult to learn, for example on crankshafts, which were "really, really heavy," and on gun parts, which were "real oily." She preferred oily to heavy, she noted, "but if you wanted to work, you wanted the money, you worked."

On one occasion she stood up for herself. "We were facing some kind of wall, and I said, 'Why do we have to face this wall?' I mean working is bad enough. I spoke *up* that time." And it worked: "Finally, he moved us someplace else." It was difficult to take that risk, she explained, because "I keep things inside, I don't express. I don't like to fight." She was grateful for the support she received from the UAW: "You didn't have to be scared that you would be fired, because you had the union working for you." In addition, she learned to withhold judgment of coworkers: "This one woman that sat like two women away from me, she never talked to anybody, and then I heard that there was a fire and five of her children were burned. And I thought, 'Oh my God, how could she even *work*?' Some things stick in your mind, you know? I said, 'Oh my God, I don't think I could live with that.'"

Caring for two young children required help. The family lived on the second floor of a house owned by Dorothy's grandmother, who lived downstairs. "She would watch the two children when I went to work midnights," and when the tired mom needed sleep, "because I would go to bed when I come home from work." All this time, Dorothy's marriage was unraveling. At the beginning of the war, her husband still worked at the Plymouth plant and also served as a local air raid warden, making sure lights were out at night to prevent the possibility of enemy aircraft spotting targets. At home, there were constant arguments and fears for her safety. Once in the early '40s, she recounted, "I was pregnant. We went to a dance, maybe a wedding or something. My sister and her husband was there." To her husband, Dorothy said, "'I don't want you dancing with any gal that you see.' So then we went outside to argue or something, and he grabbed me by the throat. Then he let go, and I couldn't breathe anymore. And then my sister said, 'You're doing this to your wife, and my sister? How dare you! And especially, she's pregnant!' And he says, 'How do I know that's mine?'" Not expecting to recall such things, Dorothy declared, "Thank God. It's a wonder I'm living today!"

Her husband was eventually drafted into the Navy, and Dorothy wasn't sorry to see him go. Still, there was a financial drawback, because instead of his Plymouth paycheck she received only $15 a month from the military. To compensate, she picked up a second job. A woman who ran a corner grocery store "wanted me to clean her house. David was just a little baby when my husband was in the service, so I brought the baby with me to her house. She was really good to me because she used to give me bacon and butter and things like that, so I didn't mind working for her." The food gifts were special, Dorothy emphasized, "because everything was rationed." Dorothy remembered the end of the war: "It was wonderful. It was really, really a celebration." On the other hand, she knew her husband would be returning from his base in Bremerton, Washington. She hoped their relationship would improve after the service-imposed time apart.

Although Dorothy hoped to keep her job at Plymouth, the reconversion to civilian production was disruptive, especially for women. After a lengthy layoff immediately after the war—"It was quite a spell before they turned the factory over to the cars, you know"—she worked "off and on," always subject to layoffs. Her husband also experienced uneven employment.[1] The couple hoped to purchase a home and had some savings, which they tapped into to get by. At one point they placed a down payment on a house, but Dorothy's husband was convinced that many of the wartime workers who came to Detroit would leave, creating a buyer's market, so he withdrew their deposit and waited for bargains to appear. Sadly, housing prices only rose. So they continued to live above Dorothy's grandmother, and Dorothy resented their missed opportunity.

It was difficult to run a household with young children in an upstairs apartment. To provide heat in the winter, Dorothy explained, she "had to go out to the barn because that's where the coal was." She carried the coal up to the second floor and loaded it into a stove. There was no hot water, so to do laundry, including soiled diapers again after her third child, Linda, was born in 1947, Dorothy had to boil water and carry it to the washing machine. Her grandmother couldn't offer much help because she was looking after an adult daughter, Dorothy's aunt, who suffered from rheumatism and required constant attention.

Dorothy's husband was rarely around, either because of work or extramarital affairs. Dorothy learned that her husband "had women over there" while in the service. "That wasn't a happy thing." After the war, she recalled "washing clothes in those hard times, somebody called me, and they said, 'If you want to see your husband come down to' such-and-such a bar. I turned the gas burners off, and I took a streetcar to this bar. And sure enough, he was there with a woman. And I took the beer bottle and I threw the beer at him—not the bottle, just the beer. So then the bartender said, 'Oh, we can't have that.' He said, 'You got to leave." I said, 'I'm going.'" But to her husband, she said, "'You're not coming back to my house.' And he didn't. Then I threw his clothes out and God knows where he went. But he never did come back. I don't know where he went or what he did. He probably went to her, because she is the one he married."

It was 1949, and Dorothy's life was in turmoil. She knew she needed a divorce, but she had no income and wasn't sure how she and her kids would survive: "What did I have? Maybe just furniture. I didn't even have a car." As a Catholic, she was uneasy about divorce. She went through with it anyway and stopped receiving Holy Communion, which gnawed at her. A friend warned her, "Don't tell my husband that you're divorced, because he wouldn't want me hanging around you." Her grandmother became seriously ill as well, and "had to sell her house and she sold it to Black people," who moved into the first-floor unit. "Not that I have anything about Black people," Dorothy insisted, "but they used to have parties down there, and I thought since my grandmother wasn't there anymore, it was time that I moved." She also wanted to be farther away from her ex-husband.

She found an apartment, available on a short-term lease, on the west side of Detroit, which seemed worlds away from her family and friends on the east side. Although Dorothy had been close with her sister, now they hardly saw each other except on holidays, "because I lived here and she lived there." Forced to move again after six months, Dorothy found a spot in the Herman Gardens public housing project, on the far west side of the city. Lila Johnston, a friend from her days at the Plymouth plant, looked out for her. Lila's husband "was a union representative," Dorothy explained. "*He's* the one that got me the job at Dodge's." So with a ten-year-old, an eight-year-old, and a two-year-old, Dorothy settled into life as a single parent, juggling parenting with a job at the Dodge Main plant in Hamtramck, about ten miles away from her new home.

Decades later, the 1950s remained mostly a blur for Dorothy. Despite clear memories of her work at Plymouth in the 1930s and in wartime, Dorothy had difficulty recalling what she did at Dodge Main. She emphasized instead how she enjoyed carpooling with coworkers: "I bought an old clunker of a car, and I used to pick up two other women, and sometimes the car broke down halfway. So this gal would get out, and she'd take a bobby pin out of her hair and she did something and it got the car started." She also appreciated having an understanding foreman.

Dorothy's most powerful sense of her life at the time was of the relentless rhythm, "rushing to work and coming home" to care for her children. When she first moved into Herman Gardens, Dorothy had a cousin, Mary Ann, stay with her to look after the kids while she went to work: "She must've been about eighteen." Later, a next-door neighbor helped out while Dorothy worked the evening shift, from 4:00 to midnight: "Her name was Vi, and I was paying her fifteen dollars a week for watching the kids." Staying with their neighbor was OK with the children, although it sparked some envy in Dorothy when Vi "got a television set—because I was paying her fifteen dollars a week—before we did!"

Money was always tight: "I remember when things were really rough. I was working, and my boy said to me, 'How come these people have oranges and we don't?' I had to pay rent and pay telephone and pay everything else. So I don't know if I bought him some oranges or not. Whatever. But I remember that. Just little things, you know, you remember." At one desperate point, Dorothy sought assistance from the Detroit Welfare Department: "I had to cash in bottles to get twelve cents for the streetcars to take me downtown and tell them I needed help. That was a bad time." She received minimal assistance and some useless advice: "They gave me six dollars. All of six dollars. And they said, 'You have to get after your husband. You have to go to Friend of the Court.'" It was her ex-husband's responsibility, they said, to support his children. The problem, Dorothy emphasized, was that "he wasn't very good at paying child support—at that time it was twenty-one dollars a month, for three kids." She would gladly have accepted seven dollars a month per child, and child support arrived more regularly after her ex-husband remarried, but many times it wasn't enough to stave off a crisis.

Instead, Dorothy risked physical and emotional injury whenever her ex-husband visited the children. He'd stop by "maybe like once or twice a month," she recalled, "but then he used to drink beer and he'd get violent with me." Details about work life mattered little given the enormity of the challenges and abuse Dorothy experienced.

The pastor at St. Christopher Church added to Dorothy's distress when he refused to accept her children into the parish school unless she made a financial contribution: "And I thought, 'You S.O.B. How could I give donations?'" Although the pastor eventually relented, the episode bothered her. Her relationship with the church was tested again when her son, about twelve years old at the time, was invited by a priest "to a cottage for a week. I thought that would be good for him. So then when my ex-husband came over to visit the kids, he says, 'No way, he's not going with no priest.' Maybe being a man, he would realize why this priest would want these young boys to go to this cottage. They didn't get it from a woman. They'd get it from little boys. So I didn't send him, because my ex-husband said no."

In 1957, when her daughter Patricia turned eighteen and got a job, Dorothy was called into the Herman Gardens office: "They told me that I had to move" because the family "was making too much money." She had enjoyed living at Herman Gardens and didn't want to leave neighbors and friends, but rules were rules. Unfortunately, this change occurred on the eve of the 1958 recession, when employment at Dodge Main was sporadic at best. Yet somehow she made it through.

When her youngest child, Linda, graduated from high school and got married in the mid-1960s, Dorothy started taking business classes to fulfill her dream of becoming a secretary. Before that she quit auto work and found jobs at a winery and an animal feed store. She also remarried in 1967: "He was such a good man compared to the first one." But her second husband, Tony, died twelve years into their marriage. "Fibrillation of the heart, because he had high blood pressure," she explained. "How did I ever survive all this?" It helped that she completed her coursework and eventually was hired as a secretary with the State Highway Department: "I got back to what I went to school for, and I really enjoyed that." But she was quick to add, "I never minded working in a factory, and I wasn't ashamed of working in a factory." She also traveled to Las Vegas and to Poland. It was also significant, Dorothy emphasized, that "I talked to a real nice priest. And he said that I could go back to receiving Holy Communion. That was good. So, I believe in God and I think I lived a pretty good life."

9

L.J. Scott
(1931–)

"I come a long ways," L.J. Scott reflected. "I've learned a lot. It has been hard, though. It's been hard. A lot of times things get at you, but nobody told me life was going to be real easy all the time." Times were difficult for L.J. from the start. He was born in 1931, the last of fourteen children, in Linwood, Alabama, about fifty miles southeast of Montgomery. His parents were sharecroppers. "By the time I came along," he explained, some of his siblings had already "gotten married and moved out." His mother and father were originally from China Grove, about fifteen miles to the northwest, but they worked their way to Linwood: "Most of the time we was sharecroppers, and there was sometimes when we rented the land from the person who owned it. If you saw a better deal—maybe it had some pretty good land, pretty good soil, and you'd know that you could raise a good crop on there—if you could get it, you got it, even if it did mean moving. I lived in about four different places right around Linwood, wherever my dad moved us." No matter where they were, L.J. emphasized, "it was kind of rough. We were poor. We didn't have no money or anything, but we survived. We had plenty of food to eat. It might not be the food that you wanted, but I ain't never went to bed hungry."

To meet their obligations to landlords, the Scotts planted cash crops, mainly peanuts and cotton. But they were also able to grow food for themselves and their livestock: "Corn and millet, sorghum and cane—anything you can name we just about did it. We ate peas when they were green and when they got dry.

We picked them and put them in sacks and hung them up in the roof of the loft, to keep rats from getting to them." When his mother needed more peas, L.J. explained, "you'd go up there and you'd take down a sack and you'd get your stick and you'd beat the hell out of the sack—and that makes the peas break up. And then you'd bring them back in the house."

L.J. had a wide variety of duties from a young age: "The first chore I had was feeding a little calf. And every day, at a certain time I knew I must feed that calf. There was no backing out of it, no 'I don't want to.'" Everyone understood the rules: "You could be off having fun or what have you, but if it was time to feed the hogs or cut some wood to take in the house to have a fire, you come and do that and then you go back again." L.J. began milking cows when he was nine: "I was small when I first started to do that But I knew how to do it, and I did it." Although he and any siblings who were still home helped with the crops, L.J. admitted that he "never liked working in the fields. I didn't like the insects. I'm scared of spiders, and definitely afraid of a snake! I woke up one morning to find a snake in bed with me."

In addition to peas, the Scotts ate lots of pork: "We'd kill hogs during the wintertime and we'd have barrels of meat in the smokehouse. We had meat all year round." The trick was to layer salt and meat "until that barrel is full. And you didn't have to worry about no flies getting in there where that meat was because they couldn't stand that salt. We would have smoked hams. We'd make sausage. We did it all. We knew how to survive. You could put me back down there right now and give me a mule and a plow—no tractor—and I could survive."

L.J.'s mother was in charge inside the home: "She kept the house and she cooked. Canned everything she could get a hand on. She had a big old pressure cooker. I think that thing would hold twelve quarts. We had hundreds of quart jars of all kind of stuff in the storage room." Since the children worked hard outside, their mom handled the dishes, laundry, and cleaning: "You never found a bed unmade. You could go in there and eat off of the floor, because she used that old potash soap—we made our soap too." For laundry, she boiled clothes in a block "cut off a big old tree," with plenty of "old lye soap" and a stick to "beat the stew out" of the stains. Meals were "always on time, but there was a rule at our house—you didn't go and cook after my mom done cooked. You either ate what she done cooked, or there was always some syrup and bread that you could eat." In the winter, L.J.'s mother kept the fireplace going, and he recalled huddling around it to stay warm: "You'd burn up in the front and freeze in the back." None of the places the Scotts lived had electricity, so they used kerosene lamps after dark.

Farm responsibilities took priority over formal education: "You had to drop out of school as the fall went on, getting ready to plant your crops. By the time stuff in school started to get a little hard and get interesting, you had to come out of there and work the fields." School was only available through 9th grade, but L.J. dropped out before that year "to work at a sawmill. I wanted some khaki pants, and my parents didn't have no money to buy them. So I bought them myself. That was about all that was going out there in the country that you could make some money at."

During these years, L.J. developed a close relationship with a niece, Louise, who was about a year and a half old when her mother, one of L.J.'s sisters, died in childbirth. Louise's father was working in Florida when the delivery turned tragic in Alabama. The Scotts embraced Louise. "Matter of fact, I raised her," L.J. emphasized. "And I'm only nine years older than she." When he had any income, like from the sawmill, he'd "give her a little spending money, just as she's my kid."

There were diversions from hard work. Although farms in the area were spread out and "the houses wasn't close together, you knew everybody, and everybody knew you. And we boys, we always going to find each other, playing and all that kind of stuff." The Scott children also enjoyed any free time available between chores and dinner: "We'd go out in the yard and play ball until they called us in to eat. And if there's any time left in between eating and going back to the field, we went out there and played ball again." They'd play "grab ball, just throwing the ball to each other and just any kind of ball." Whatever game they were playing, L.J. reminisced, "that was our favorite."

Church divided the family: "Religion were taught by my mom. My daddy never mentioned nothing about it. We weren't strict religious people." L.J. looked forward to the annual, two-day camp meetings: "It started on the fourth Sunday in August. That was a big day. People come in wagons and trucks and cars, and I mean that place would be packed. They had their little stands, selling stuff. And all the women, they'd bring trucks of food, and then they would put some benches together" to set up a buffet. "If you didn't like what you seen there on one bench, just go to another. That would kick off the revival." Baptisms took place the following day, "and that was the last until the next year." L.J. was always amazed: "That was a foreign type of thing. You didn't have no lot of money to be buying a whole bunch of stuff, but you going to beg a penny or two out of somebody, and you're going to be able to buy something. And you'd get that homemade ice cream. It'd be so hot down there in August. And they'd put it in that cone, and it'd go right down to the bottom and start running out, you sucking on that bottom and try to keep from losing it." The barbecue was also excellent, although farmers were concerned about the health risks of butchering a hog in August: "In the summertime, the sap is in that hog. It could make you sick on your stomach, give you diarrhea. Everybody knew about it." Equally memorable was the "homemade hot sauce. That stuff'd be so hot it almost turn your mouth inside out. It'd be so hot, you'd take a bite and you'd just keep turning it around in your mouth. The first thing you know—whoom!—you done swallowed it. That was good! Those were the good times."

The Scotts rarely went to Troy, the nearest town—"Linwood wasn't nothing but a whistle stop, two or three little country grocery stores, two gas pumps, and a gristmill"—unless someone needed medical attention: "I used to have asthma when I was a little small, and I had it so bad they had to take me to the doctor. They felt they was going to lose me, I was breathing so fast, panting. We didn't have a car, but somebody else close around had one. The doctor gave me something to make me feel better, and right there is when I started wanting to be a doctor. The doctor had a big, old, high-back chair, and he gave me something to make me feel better. And oh, that's what I wanted to do. I could just imagine myself sitting there and somebody coming in there and I got the know-how to make them well. That was my dream." He held on to that dream for "ten or fifteen years," he said, before realizing "that I wouldn't ever be one."

When L.J. was fifteen, his father was diagnosed with prostate cancer. His older siblings had left the farm, so as his dad weakened, most responsibilities fell to L.J. A brother lived in Detroit and convinced their father to come north for medical care: "But he got homesick right away. I'm down there milking the cow, and I look back up to the house, and somebody's standing in the kitchen door, and it was him—my daddy. He done come back home. He ain't never been in no city. He was used to the country, where you walk out the door and walk through your yard and walk in the fields." Detroit "was like foreign to him. He wasn't used to being away from home. Home was in Linwood, Alabama." L.J.'s father lived three more years before the cancer "took him down."

L.J. was eighteen, and he felt pressure after his father's death "to move myself over into his spot, as far as looking out after my mother, and there was my niece, Louise." A brother in the area was supposed to help out with earnings from the sawmill. But things got tense. One time, L. J. asked him for a quarter: "He said, 'Boy, I ain't got no quarter.' I said, 'Well damn, give me a dime or something!' He didn't give me a dime. But we had a house that we all went to. It was like a good-time house. They sold whiskey there, and two or three girls there, and all that stuff. And my brother bought a pint of whiskey and left it sitting on the table. He went across the field to somebody's house to shoot dice. And that pissed me off. Ooh that got me. He couldn't give me a quarter and he done bought this pint of whiskey and left it there and he'd gone somewhere to gamble. That ain't sitting right with me."

As the family system broke down, L.J. wanted to leave Alabama. Racial indignities provided an additional motivation to get out. As a child, L.J. had carefully observed, and hated, the subservience that white people demanded of African Americans in the Jim Crow south. He occasionally challenged racial expectations, although doing so could have life-or-death consequences. Sometimes this involved what would otherwise be considered just a prank. For example, a landlord had a pond on his property and "didn't want nobody to fish in it." A bunch of boys in the area, "about maybe eight or ten of us," enjoyed "mudding" in the pond. They'd stir up the water, "mudding" it, "to make them fish sick and they'd come to the top." The boys wanted to catch those fish: "We met at our house, and we were making all kinds of little doodads—bow and arrows, driving nails through a piece of board, stick end of the board—you'd take it and hit the fish and he stuck right up on there." The boys knew that the landlord, Horace Williams, went to town every Saturday, so one of them sat on a bench at the train station until Williams left. The plan worked: "The sentry came back, said, 'All right boys, he's gone!' And away we went. Had buckets and tubs and everything—yes, we were going there to muddy that pond. We had a lot of fun, and got a lot of fish out of there too—catfish, perch, breams, also what they call blackfish. It had good fish in there." As for Horace Williams, "He never did know it."

Although the fish heist was conducted in secret, another time L.J. had a direct disagreement with Mr. Williams: "I'm sixteen at that point, and I'm an angry young man, and we rented this land, and this land had a peach tree on it." Williams claimed the peaches: "So I told him, 'No sir, Mr. Horace,' I said, 'we rented the land, and whatever's on that land belongs to us. The fruit of that tree belongs to us, not to you.' And he didn't like that. He told my dad, he said, 'You'd better talk to him. He's getting biggity'—that's one of the words that they used when you're sassy, you know. Well, I didn't think anything of it. But I just knew I was going to get those peaches." Williams still "had a knack of going to town every Saturday, just like clockwork. So I'm watching the peaches as they get ripe." When they were ready, "I goes down to Linwood there where the train stops at and I watch him when he leave, going to town. I go back home and I get this tub. I go down and I *strip* that tree. I took them peaches home and me and my mother peeled them and she canned them."

In the fall, L.J. crossed Williams in an even more dangerous way. L.J. bought a ledger to keep track of expenses, income, and debts, and recorded "everything that we got on credit" from Williams. "We borrowed money from Mr. Horace to get certain things, like fertilizer, seeds, stuff like that. There was times when we might have needed some for clothes or something. It was put in there—how much money we got, and what it was used for, the whole bit. Dated and everything." Over the years, L.J. recalled, "I'd seen my dad try to calculate in his head, and I know he was getting taken for a ride. But once you took some paper and write it down, that's going to stay there no matter where your mind go." At settling up time, Mr. Horace "was saying that we owed some amount. And so I told him, 'No Sir, Mr. Horace. We don't owe that much.' I said, 'Here's what we owe right here.' And when I did that, I opened that ledger and handed it to him. He ain't never seen nothing like that before. People didn't do that." There were consequences: "First thing I know, we're moving." His parents did that, he figured, "to save me."

If so, it wasn't the only time that L.J.'s father tried to protect his son from dangerous circumstances: "There was a man that had a store down there, and he had this young wife, and it just seemed like she took a liking to me. We had rented some land from her auntie that we farmed for a number of years. And I used to be singing in the fields, where I'd be plowing, at the top of my voice. And somewhere along the way she'd heard me sing, because she'd always be trying to get me to sing for her and I wouldn't ever do it. Anyway, she was real friendly. And one day, me and my dad was over there putting in some fence posts back on the pasture, and she and her family came by in her car, and she said, "Hey there! You going to town this Saturday?" L.J.'s father was livid: "I could feel them eyes on me. He didn't turn his head and look, but I could feel them eyes on me. He said, 'What did she mean by that?' I said, 'I don't know sir.' He said, 'Is she always friendly like that?' I said, 'Yes sir, she's friendly.' She'd talk to me when I'd go to the store. He said, 'Well, you going to have to stay away from her, because she can mean trouble for you.' He said, 'Don't go to that store no more.' He said, 'If you're someplace, and she comes, you leave.' Said, 'You go to a place, and she's there, you leave. Stay away from her.'" White men could maim or slaughter Black men with impunity for interactions with white women, whether friendly, unfriendly, or imagined. "I knew what he was saying to me," L.J. said. "I knew exactly what he was saying. And I acted accordingly."

It was frustrating that his father didn't fight back, even though L.J. understood why: "He had to raise me in a way where that I would be safe, where I could grow up and not get hurt. And even though it was not the right thing that was going on, you didn't have no win. The judge was white, the prosecutor's white, sheriffs is white, the jury's white. Where's your win? That's why I didn't have no good feelings for down there." He noticed, however, that a few Black neighbors took a different approach: "Some guys didn't take it, and carried guns and all that kind of stuff. They was deemed 'crazy.' You didn't mess with them."[1]

L.J. was happy to set off for Florida in 1949. Only responsibility for his dad kept him in Alabama, "so when he died, that was it." L.J.'s mother and Louise went to live with one of his sisters in Troy, and he left with his next oldest brother, L.C., for Orlando: "We had another brother, Jim, living in Orlando at that time, and he was picking fruit—oranges, grapefruit, and tangerines. Jim got us on with the guy that he was working for." L.J. was small, not a desirable attribute for picking fruit on trees. But his brothers "put me in the middle of them—Jim on one side and L.C. on the other one—and if I started to lag behind, they'd jump over on my row and pick some, trying to keep me up. We did that for a while, and then it got where I could keep up myself." Supervision was lax: "You was pretty much on your own, because you got paid by the amount of fruit that you picked. We were getting like 15 cent a box. The more boxes you picked, the more money you got. A few times I was able to pick a hundred in a day. And that was $15. That was good at that point." L.J. didn't keep all of his pay: "Every other week I'd send my mother some money. It wasn't much, but it was all I could afford."

When the fruit season ended, L. J. found "a job downtown at the San Juan Hotel, busing dishes." He also "picked a little vegetables." Then a niece convinced him that he could find work where she lived, in St. Petersburg: "I must have had about three or four different jobs over there. One time I was working at a nursing home, on the grounds, mowing the grass and keeping it clean and everything. I didn't like the people that was supervising me." Someone was always yelling out the window to "get hopping!" After a while, he "found a job at a bakery, where they made cookies. I helped the guy in all phases, mixing up the dough, putting the cookies on the pan, and putting them in the oven. I kind of liked working there." Then he moved on to construction, helping to renovate houses: "There was a white guy named Mr. Dick. He used to pick me up and take me to work. I used to carry his toolbox for him—he was kind of weak-like. I got to like him a lot. He was like a father figure. He started to teach me how to read a blueprint, and how to build cabinets and all that stuff. But then I left, and naturally there wasn't no follow-up. I done forgot all about that stuff. I left and came back to Orlando and picked fruit, because I could make more money picking fruit than I was making there."

L.J. certainly didn't think of construction or fruit-picking as long-term possibilities. He was twenty years old and didn't envision himself staying in Florida at all, although he had no hard feelings against the state: "It was a better deal than being in Alabama." All he knew was that he was "heading to Detroit. I just wanted to get a job. I wasn't skilled. But I wasn't scared of work. And I knew that if I worked hard, I could make it. I hit the city with $3.25 in my pocket." He had hoped to stay with his "favorite sister," Flora, but her apartment was full of boarders, including another sister, Rose. Flora and Rose worked as domestics. Instead, L.J.'s brother Charlie offered him a place to stay: "He was going to charge me $15 a week for room and board. He loaned me $5 in when I just got here looking for a job. And on my first paycheck, he asked me for that $5 back." L.J. was upset at Charlie's lack of generosity, especially because his brother wasn't contributing anything to their mother's support—L.J., L.C., and Jim had sent money to her from Florida—and Charlie had a decent job at Thompson Products, an auto supplier.

About a week after arriving in Detroit, L.J. was hired at Chevrolet Gear and Axle: "My brother was living on Holbrook and Chevrolet was on Holbrook, so I walked up there and I got a job and worked for a day and a half, and got laid off." L.J. was disciplined for inadvertently breaking plant rules, "smoking in a restricted zone." He had gone to the lunch wagon to buy a snack, "a roll and a little bottle of milk," which he took back to his job. As he returned to the wagon to claim the nickel deposit on the bottle, he pulled out a cigarette: "In between where I was and where the bottle had to be taken, there was a restricted area, and I walked through it with that cigarette in my mouth. I really didn't know I was in no zone like that. Tall machines and all that noise and stuff around—I'm busy looking at trying to keep myself safe." A supervisor caught him: "He told me to come along with him, and he took me to the office, and they told me they're going to lay me off for two weeks. I mean I made a mistake and I had to pay for it." That night he told his brother: "It was funny to him, you know, but it wasn't funny to me. Lost what I considered as a good job."

Determined to find work while on suspension, L.J. followed Charlie's advice and set off for a nearby Plymouth factory—but ended up at a Chrysler plant instead. He recognized it from his initial job search: "I went in there and put another application in. And do you know they hired me right there on the spot?" They even gave him his choice of shifts: "So I went to work that same afternoon." His Gear and Axle transgression, it turns out, didn't cost him much: "I missed a half of a day that week, from the time I got laid off at Chevrolet."

Chrysler put L.J. on a job drilling holes in rear axles. It was repetitive, but he "liked it. It wasn't too hard of a job." Still, you had to be attentive: "I almost got hurt. You had to put oil on those drills—the ones that tapped the holes out. And I've got this glove on my hand. Got my hand too close to the drill that was turning. It started pulling that glove right off of my hand. And I reared back and I gave it everything I had. I tore my hand out of that glove. It could have messed me up, you know." That job lasted eighty-four days, just short of the ninety needed to gain seniority and the job security that went with it: "They wasn't going to let me get that in. Chrysler was good at that, for not letting a person get their seniority in—lay them off. If you didn't let nobody get no seniority, that mean that benefits, and all that kind of stuff, they didn't have to pay." It seemed that the company didn't discriminate in these layoffs, as both Black and white workers were fired before they lasted ninety days. As L.J. saw the situation, "As long as there's people looking for jobs, they could get somebody to fill a vacancy."

In his short time at Chrysler, L.J. saved enough money to bring his mother to Detroit. He wasn't sure that she would accept, "because that was her life back there," and "at that time she was old." She was ultimately convinced to leave by the constant physical and sexual threats from white men: "The old sheriff down there, called Ben Reeves—he kind of run roughshod over people. My sister was living right there by the depot. And my mother always said that you'd be in that house, and all of a sudden the door would open, here's Ben Reeves walking in, looking for somebody. And she didn't like that. She didn't like that at all. That was an invasion of her privacy."[2] L.J. was thrilled to have his mother in Detroit, and Louise was already there, having moved north to stay with her father when L.J. and L.C. left for Florida. The three moved in together, and as L.J. declared, "We were a family again."

Any joy was tempered by unemployment, which was widespread in Detroit in the early 1950s. L.J. placed an ad in a local newspaper, announcing that he was looking for work, and received job offers, including one from a steel mill. He considered taking it, but decided instead that his brother Jim, who had recently arrived from Florida, needed it more: "He had four or five kids at that point. So I said, 'Jim, why don't you take this job, because you got a family.' And he did. And Jim worked that job until he died." L.J.'s ad also resulted in a job offer from an army surplus store: "I worked there about a year." He didn't like it at all, because his boss "was using people and cheating them a little bit, messing with their time. If they worked six hours, he might say you worked five, that kind of stuff." The boss hired a number of people who were down on their luck, "that were pretty much like homeless people," who probably wouldn't complain. But L.J. still had his ledger: "I carried it with me all the time. When I got there and started to work, I wrote it down. And when I quit, I wrote it down. And whatever the date was, I wrote it down." He did this, he said, because the owner "turned the clock when I walked in so I couldn't see the face of it. But I had other ways of knowing what time it was. We argued about my paycheck almost every week." Finally, the boss "said I need not come back. So I said, 'Fine with me!' We were arguing pretty heated. So anyway, then I was without a job for a few months. I'd get up every morning like I was going to work. Usually, I would hit three places every day. And then I'd pick me out three more." L.J. insisted that he was prepared to do "anything I could do to try to make a penny."

In the spring of 1952, a newspaper ad offered hope: "This one day there's a whole page: 'Pontiac Motor, General Motors Division, wants skilled and non-skilled.'" The ad contained a long list of positions available. "Wow! Then I asked myself, 'Where the heck is Pontiac at?' So I called a bus station and asked, 'How do I get to Pontiac?' And they told me how to get out there, told me to catch the suburban bus on Woodward. So in a few minutes, I'm standing down there on Woodward. There's jobs in Pontiac, and I'm going to get me one." But he hopped on the wrong bus and got lost, which wasted time and could have undermined his chances at the hiring gate: "A *long* line was there. I mean all the way out of the office, all the way and then crooking down the sidewalk." Fortunately for L.J., the line "was moving like crazy. They were hiring everybody and his brother that day."

L.J. could have gone to work "right then and there," but he was wearing his "Sunday clothes," to make a good impression, and he "didn't want to get them all oiled and all that stuff." He passed his physical, took a tour of his new department, and met another worker who lived in Detroit and offered a spot in his carpool: "Told me where to be at, at what time." The meeting spot was only a block or two from where L.J. lived: "Next day he picked me up. Had me a ride." L.J. began as a press operator, running a machine that drilled holes in rods that connected to pistons: "This machine would hold something like six rods, and it clamps down and the drill comes down and drills the hole right down in the middle of it, all the way down through there. And it would come back up. You'd take them out. Put some more in there."

Things were definitely looking up, but after only a few weeks on the job, L.J. received "this letter from Uncle Sam." It was hardly a surprise. The military required a continuous supply of new troops for the Korean War, he had passed his Army physical back in November, "and this was in April. I knew I was going. I was just waiting until the next drafting come up. And it came up right after I got this job at Pontiac Motors."

L.J. was never deployed to Korea. He did basic training at Camp Breckinridge, in Kentucky, and then was sent to Fort Gordon, near Augusta, Georgia: "I stayed in the States all the time. They made me a cook." He ended up liking the cooking part, although he "didn't in the beginning because I thought that was a woman's job. You know, that little macho thing that was in me. But after I got into it and everything, I liked it. I fell right into it. I already knew how to cook, even before I got in there, from watching my mother cook. It's different because you're cooking so much. But it's the same. It's just the way you go about doing it." He figured they made him a cook because he was Black and because he tried to get himself disqualified from the military altogether: "I was trying everything I knew to try to get out of the Army. I tried to pretend that I didn't have very good sense and all that stuff," including on aptitude assessments. "So it could have been on some of those tests where I didn't test high on or something. I didn't want to be in no service. That's not for me. I don't like nobody hollering at me and making me do stuff I don't want to do." Despite his efforts, L.J. wasn't discharged, so there "wasn't nothing to do but to grin and bear it. You got to take it just like anybody else. You can get mad all you want to, but you just don't let it show too much. Because you could get in trouble if you revealed too much. I told myself that I was going to make the best of it. I was supposed to be in there for two years. I wasn't going to rock no boat, or nothing like that. Make it as easy on me as I possibly could, and get out. But I ran into some rough people while I was in there."

L.J.'s frustrations with the military centered on his company commander, a white lieutenant from Plymouth, Michigan. Things started out well: "We used to talk about Detroit and what have you, all the time. I thought that we had a little thing going." Problems started when the officer bent the rules by hanging out in the kitchen and expecting to be fed whenever he was hungry. L.J. worried about violating regulations, "so I told him the food service didn't want us to have nobody back there anywhere unless they had a health certificate. So when I told him that, he would go out, but he didn't like it. I would know that he's boiling. And then he started his little vendetta."

L.J. began receiving nasty assignments: "One time we had to paint the mess hall, and we had this walk-in cooler" with maybe two feet of space between its top and the ceiling. "You know who had to paint back there? Paint dropping all down in my face and everything, but I got through it. I knew what he was doing, but I wasn't going to let him get to me. One time he had me out there on the side of the road cutting grass with the recruits." It was unfair, L.J. thought, but he didn't raise a fuss: "He's messing with me, you know." Still, the aggravations piled up: "One day he made an inspection and didn't nobody get a gig—that's like a write-up—but me. I think I had one shirt that didn't have stripes on it. I was a corporal at that time. And I got gigged for that." This time, L.J. defended himself: "There was a lot of guys walking around with no stripes on. I said, 'Sir, why am I the only one to get a gig for not having a stripe on their shirt,' when here's so and so and so and so—three shirts, no stripes—and just went on down that line. Everybody got quiet. There was some sergeants just sitting back there where I was with him. Nobody was saying nothing. I went through my litany of accusations, and then I turned around and started out. And then he hollered, 'Come back here soldier!' And then he chewed me out." L.J. knew that he "was out of line," but, "I just had took all I could take." The lieutenant threatened to demote him: "So I told him, I said, 'Sir, I don't even care about the rank. The only thing I want to do is be treated like everybody else. That's all I want.' Well shoot, he wasn't listening to that kind of thing, man. You know he did take a stripe. He took a stripe."

At that point, L.J. recalled being "messed up. I was completely messed up." The day he left the Army for Detroit, he bought "a .25 automatic, a little Beretta," hoping to shoot the lieutenant from Plymouth. In friendlier times, the two had talked "about how he'd come into Detroit and places he'd go. I bought the .25—I'm going to kill him. That's why I bought it. I carried that thing for a little over a month. Every day, it was in my pocket." Occasionally, L.J. would stop and look at men in their cars, or on the street, "to see if it was him. I don't think about getting in no trouble. My mind don't go to that point. My mind is still messed up to the point of where the only thing I want is revenge. I felt like if I saw him, the first thing I'm going to do is hit him with my fist. I wanted to just feel my fist hit his jaw—tear his nose up or something. And then I'm going to shoot him."

L.J.'s anger led to potentially dangerous confrontations. Several times he got into arguments with men in bars, once with "a big-ass guy—I mean *big*—and I stood right on up to him with my arms folded, and he knows darn well that I ain't standing there for nothing." L.J. wanted people to know that he was carrying a gun and that he was no one to cross: "I got the thing in my hand. I can shoot him before he can mess with me." Another time, while driving on a snowy day in Detroit with his gun under his seat, he had a confrontation with a taxi driver. Cars were parked on both sides of the road, with barely a lane between them: "The cab was coming up the street, and he passed a place that he could have pulled out and let me by. So I stopped, and he stopped. And then he stayed there for a little while. He's thinking I'm going to back up. Well he pulled up and he bumped his car into mine. And then he backed up. I was saying, 'This has got to be the world's biggest fool here.' So I bumped him, and then I backed up." The cab driver opened his door, and L.J. reached under his seat: "He saw me. He saw my head go down like that. He knew I was getting something. He backed up into that empty space and let me by. I would have stood there until all hell froze over. I wasn't going anywhere."

L.J. shook his head when thinking about those days: "That's craziness. I could have been in all kinds of trouble. My whole life could have been messed up." He was obsessed with the lieutenant and thought that "nothing could touch me. But I was wrong. You still got laws and things governing you. But that's just how I wasn't thinking. Hey, my mind was ready to snap. Done already got it to a point where it was drawn too tight." Eventually he cooled down: "Either somebody talked to me or I came to my senses and I stopped carrying the thing. Started leaving it at home. I still wanted to mess with him. That didn't go away. But I had sense enough to know that sooner or later I could get in trouble, because when I was carrying that thing, I didn't back down off of nobody."

L.J. gradually re-entered life in Detroit. He remembered that Pontiac Motor gave him "a month in which to get back on the job, and I was there maybe about three days before the month was up." He returned to his old drill operator job: "I was happy to be back, because I'm getting back into my normal routine, and I'm looking at the money that I was making, which wasn't much, but it was like steady work. I mean you got laid off sometimes, but it still was one of the more steadier jobs that you could get." Although he was fortunate that he accrued seniority while in the service, he was still relatively low on the list. Others around him "had more seniority than what I had, and they weren't getting laid off like I were."

He had some ideas about alternate employment opportunities: "When I was in the Army, I was dreaming about having me a TV repair shop when I got out. First I was going to have me a whiskey store, until somebody told me about the license and all that stuff, and how they had them all hooked where you couldn't get them. I gave up on that. And that's OK. I'm going to have me a TV repair shop. I always liked to tinker around with stuff." But then he found out he'd have to know trigonometry and chemistry to get licensed, "and I hadn't had it, because I hadn't finished high school." He took a series of career tests: "I made my best test on tool and die," a skilled trade. Yet everybody knew that African Americans were not accepted into apprenticeships to become skilled tradesmen. L.J. sat down with the man who administered the tests: "And I told him, 'I don't have no money, but if I sacrifice and go to school for something, I must be able to work at it after I finish.' I said, 'Tool and die, I can't work at that because they ain't got no Black tool and die out there. It's all white.' Then he said, 'I think you're making the right decision.' In other words, he wasn't going to tell me what to do. He let me make up my own mind, but he concurred with me after I told him that I think the best thing for me to do is go back to school and at least get a GED." It was one more example of the harsh racial realities in the north: "I thought that I was coming to a utopia, but it's nothing like that. That's fantasy, and I got to figure out how to cope with that."

L.J. worked at his old drill press job through most of 1955: "I know '55 was a *boom* year, because I bought me a '55 Star Chief Pontiac. My second car. My first new one, though. Oh, I was feeling good. Things were looking my way, because in '55 you could work all you wanted to. I worked a lot of overtime." Unfortunately, however, "it didn't last. Like, '56 is when it went down again," he recalled, making a swooshing sound, "and '57 wasn't worth nothing."[3] Fortunately, L.J. had enough seniority to remain in the cylinder head department during the worst of the cutbacks. Compared to the drill press job, he said, the new one "was harder, because the cylinder head, naturally, is bigger than a piston rod. I did some work there that was so hard I had to rub my back before I could get out of bed in the morning time. There was another guy that his job broke down one day and they brought him around there to give me a hand. He looked at the job and he said, 'Shit! This ain't no job for me.' And he went to first aid and got a pass and went home."

A lot of the job involved material handling, hard, physical labor moving heavy parts from one line to the next, something that required lots of workers and created production bottlenecks: "In '55 they was putting in a bunch of automation. But it only went so far, because they hadn't got it all hooked up. I was feeding the line with the cylinder heads. The line was coming up this way, and they got this opening, so I got to pick up the cylinder head and put it over in that line, like so, and set it up right. All that is pulling like crazy, my belly and my back." It might have been the worst job he ever had, but there were several contenders: "There was some hard jobs." Eventually, automation eliminated cylinder-head handling by workers: "They hooked it up right." With his seniority "there was other jobs there in the department," and he was happy that he no longer had to do such backbreaking labor. "I felt *good*!" L.J. declared, when asked about the impact of automation on his life. On the whole, L.J. "thought it was good to automate. Naturally, if they had been doing by hand there would have been more men there, but I wasn't exactly looking at it from that angle." It's uncertain how he would have responded if he hadn't remained employed, but his reaction did speak to the heavy toll on workers' bodies when performing the most physically demanding jobs in the plant.[4]

Family life for L.J. took twists and turns during the late '50s. When he was discharged from military service, he lived with his mother and Louise. He got married in 1956, but "that didn't last no time—a year, a month, and four days." While separated, he started a relationship with a woman from Alabama, someone he met through a nephew: "My divorce became final on Tuesday, and I got married that Saturday. That one lasted for twenty-eight and a half years." L.J. and his wife, Morene, had three children in the late '50s and early '60s, and Morene had a young child from a previous relationship. With a growing family, making money had to be a priority, so L.J. buckled down at Pontiac Motor and also became the carpool driver, "so that give me a few extra dollars." He preferred to commute from Detroit: "I didn't like Pontiac. I always liked the big city. Pontiac was a small city."

Employment became even more uncertain at the end of the decade, especially during the 1958 recession: "I got laid off in March, and I didn't know when I was going back or *if* I was going back. And that's as poor as I've ever been in my life." L.J. collected unemployment pay while it lasted, and received "a little bit of SUB," the Supplemental Unemployment Benefits the UAW won in its 1955 contracts. But he emphasized that "it was very hard. Every penny that I took in, I could account for. I had to have my car refinanced to keep from losing it." The bank allowed him to pay only the interest on his loan while he was out of work: "I didn't have nothing. I tried to get a job, car wash and everything. I couldn't find a job nowhere."

L.J. decided to become a barber: "We were having different layoffs, and it kind of did something to me when I'd be laid off like that. I'm trying to make it, and I'm thinking, if I learn how to be a barber, I can get a job in any city that I go to." But he needed $75 for classes to get his license through Michigan Barber School in Detroit. He cobbled together the tuition, with some help from Morene: "She scraped it up from somewhere. I guess she could see farther in the future than I could." In November 1958, around the time that he gained his barbering credentials. L.J. was recalled to Pontiac Motor. He hedged his bets, returning to the factory and opening a barber shop with a fellow laid-off autoworker, a business they ran together for nine years. As a barber, L.J. explained, "I worked part-time. I couldn't give up my job at Pontiac Motors." To fulfill the requirements for his barber's license, he "was supposed to be working full-time at the barber shop." But he "couldn't afford to do that." So he cut hair whenever he wasn't scheduled at Pontiac Motor. Throughout this rocky period, he never considered moving back south: "No. No. It's too many bad memories from there, from Alabama, this discrimination crap." Besides, he enjoyed barbering: "Before I start, I could look at your head and tell what your head's going to look like when I finish it. It's a lot of creativity in cutting hair, you know, shaping it and making it look a certain way. And this was what I liked about it."

L.J.'s new job at Pontiac Motor was stock handling, making sure a particular production line had what was necessary to run without interruption: "I was thinking that if I worked hard, somebody would notice and reward me, like give me a different job or make me a foreman or something, which at that time didn't hardly have no Black foremens out there." As usual, however, "they noticed the white guys' effort, but they didn't notice mine. I'd be working along with a white guy, and that Monday, maybe they'd bring him in there and make him a job setter. That's a higher-paying job, and you needed every penny that you could put your hands on. Because I've got a family." It was galling. A new white guy would be "in charge of running the stuff through the machines, running the line, and I'm still out there handling the stock. And it got to the point where I realized that I wasn't going anywhere like that. So then I started doing what I had to do to get by. No extra. No extra at all."

Things got worse when there was a cutback in his department and twelve white workers got promoted to inspector positions while the two Black employees, L.J. and Lawrence Coleman, were demoted to the assembly line: "That hit me real hard there." Decades later, the memory brought tears: "I try to bury stuff like that, but sometimes it comes out and hits you." He convinced Lawrence to join him in filing a grievance charging racial discrimination: "We got together, and we demanded that we also be put on inspection." The foreman responded quickly and negatively: "No discrimination. Request denied." But at a higher stage of the grievance procedure, L.J. and Lawrence won. Although company officials did not admit any wrongdoing, they agreed to put L.J. and Lawrence on inspection jobs. Yet it turned out to be a trick. L.J.'s foreman arranged to transfer him back to the cylinder head department, but not on inspection. When L.J. learned of the plan, "man, the anger started coming on. I said, 'I don't want this.' I said, 'I ain't put in for no transfer.'" That was the trap. Soon the General Foreman appeared, charged L.J. with insubordination, and fired him. L.J.'s union committeeman was of no use: "I found out sometime later that he was behind it." The foremen and the committeeman knew they were wrong and backed down after L.J. refused the actual offer. L.J. finally ended up on inspection and vowed to outlast his supervisor: "I ain't *never* going to leave. I'm staying in inspection always. And that's exactly what I did. When I retired, I retired off of inspection." It wasn't the first time he had experienced on-the-job discrimination, but the lesson "was driven home at that point." L.J. liked the inspection job. Much of his work involved determining which machine in a long line of automated equipment was causing a faulty hole or poor threading: "It's better to look at something than to have to attach something to something. Much better."

By the mid-1960s L.J. became a union committeeman, trying to do right by his fellow workers: "I loved it. I had read the national contract and the local agreement. I read them over about three or four times. I knew the things almost like my hand. Plus, I used to read the minutes from labor relations and shop committeemen meetings, so I had a good feel as to what was going on. Talk about giving somebody some hell. I gave them some hell!" Indeed, L.J. developed a reputation for being "hotheaded," doing his job with all his heart: "I'm a high-strung type of person. You know, I let things get to me. And I have shed tears about a guy, and I wouldn't have known him if he'd have walked in the room. But I just believed in his case." A friend once said to him, "'Scotty, you're letting the case get too close to you.' But that was me. That was my ability. I'd fight like a cat. There were cases that I didn't win. There were cases that I did win, too. But if I had one I believed in, I stuck right to it. You know, in a place like that, everybody ain't going to do right, and you got to put out them prayer mats, do a lot of begging for them. I did whatever I had to do." He was particularly adamant about safety issues and unfair punishments. But, he said, "anything that you can think of happened." He always considered what the aggrieved worker must be thinking: "When I want my committeeman, I'm mad at that point. And the sooner I can talk to somebody, vent that anger, the better it is. I knew how it was being on that other end." L.J. also served about twenty years as a UAW benefits representative, helping workers in his local resolve problems regarding health insurance, pensions, and such: "I got a lot of money for people. I loved being committeeman. I loved being benefit rep, because that was helping people. And you remember I told you that I wanted to be a doctor, right? All that kicks back in there, as to me being the type of person that I am. I like to help people. And it's part of who I am."

Because his committee work was steady and time consuming, L.J. eventually gave up his share of the barbershop: "We ran into a situation where we were working seven days a week, and we continued to work seven days a week, and it just got to be too much." He cut back his barbering hours, reduced them some more, then offered his half of the business to his partner. Working two jobs had exhausted him, but it was also the first time his family was able to make any financial headway.

L.J. reflected on the differences between Alabama and Detroit: "I thought that when I came here, that I was leaving all that stuff behind. But I found out all that stuff here just been swept up under the rug. That same stuff is right here too. And I made myself a promise, I ain't going nowhere. I'm staying right here and fighting it. I ain't going nowhere, trying to run away from the type of stuff that's out there in that world. Right here is where I take my stand. When something come up, I face it. I confront it." It was the right thing to do, for many reasons: "All that stuff would burn, and turn, and wiggle around, and one day, bust out, you know, come out in crazy ways. Maybe you shouldn't get that angry over something—all of a sudden, *bam!* Here come all that stuff out that you've been holding back. That kind of stuff can mess your mind up, your body up, because it's a form of hatred. It really is. You get to hate a person and you don't come out with it, you keep it pushed back in there, it will eat away at your butt. But all in all, you know, I look back, I come a long ways. I've learned a lot. I've become more wiser, with more wisdom that I can dispense out to my family, to my grandkids. You know, hey, it all hasn't been a waste. It has been hard, though. It's been hard. It's been hard. A lot of times when things get at you, you just have to hum a little tune or something, do a little walking or what have you. But nobody told me life was going to be real easy all the time. So I learned how to take the bitter with the sweet, mix a little bit of religion in there, and I get by. Do pretty good. Do pretty good."

10

Thomas Nowak
(1921–2009)

Thomas Nowak described himself as a "hustler," in a good way, for creating options during difficult circumstances. The fifth of six children, Thomas was born in 1921. His parents were Polish immigrants who lived on the west side of Detroit, just south of Livernois and Warren Avenue. When Thomas was three, his family moved a few miles west to Dearborn, where his father worked for a while at the Ford Rouge Plant before opening a bar near the massive complex. Thomas learned a lot hanging around his dad's business: "There would be five or six or seven guys that would come by, and they'd want a beer and a shot to go to work in the morning. Can you imagine that?!? And the same people would come back in the evening to do the same thing again. It was hard—I'm sure it was. You know, labor was terrible. You had to have a Ford, or you didn't drive into that parking lot. And the Service men," referring to the Ford Service Department run by Harry Bennett, "they watched everything. And you had to have that badge on, on your chest, or somewheres around there. They had to see that badge all the time. And they had all kinds of rules and regulations. And them were the good old days, when you couldn't go to the bathroom unless the boss told you to do so."

Thomas started out in Catholic school, then went to Charles Lindbergh Elementary. Students there were proud to attend a school named after "Lucky Lindy," who became a national celebrity after his solo trans-Atlantic flight in 1927. Definitely an American kid, Thomas never learned Polish and said that his parents spoke their native language only in private. When Thomas was a teenager, the family moved to Belleville, about twenty miles southwest of Dearborn. Before long, he found a job at the Peninsula Paper Company in Ypsilanti, another ten miles to the west. It was a printing business that eventually produced government documents, including draft notices. Thomas and a friend were moved by the many successful union campaigns of the mid-1930s—although not at factories owned by Ford—and tried to organize their coworkers. "Most everybody was *bettering* themselves," Thomas recalled, and in his view certain things needed improvement at his workplace: "You didn't get no breaks, hardly at all. You kept going all the time. We worked two shifts, twelve hours a day, seven days a week. The conditions were really not very good. We used to have a place to change your clothes and take a shower, and that was a filthy place in there. They never did take care of it very good. And we never did ever use the place—just to change clothes. Of course, the money was not very good there either, probably thirty cents an hour. And they didn't give you much of a promotion at all. There was no such thing like that. My friend and I, we got talking about it, and we complained and grumbled. We just didn't think it was fair. And before long they canned us both."

While unemployed, Thomas had a conversation with his priest. According to Thomas, the priest said, "Well you know, I have a friend in Milan," a small town a few miles southwest of Belleville that had a Ford plant. "I'll talk to my friend." The priest's connection gave Thomas a letter of recommendation: "That's the way we used to get employed—through somebody, a friend, or a letter, or something. And he give me this letter, and the superintendent, he called me, and said that I got a job. So that's how I got into Ford Motor Company." The reason for Thomas's firing at Peninsula Paper must have remained a secret, because Ford was notorious for ferreting out and firing anyone who offered even a hint of sympathy for unions.

It was 1941, and there was a lot for Thomas to consider. He was dating a woman named Rosella, and they hoped to get married. She was still in eleventh grade, and he was facing the likelihood of military service. After seeking advice, the couple decided to wait a year before setting a wedding date, allowing Thomas to fulfill some of his military obligation before they wed. He signed up for three years with the National Guard, figuring that the hardest part of his service would be over within a year, and headed north for training to Grayling, Michigan and then to Wisconsin: "First time I was ever in a train in my life." The plan seemed to work, because after a few weeks Thomas was back home and could complete his National Guard obligation by reporting once a month to the Armory in Detroit.

Thomas focused on his job at the Ford plant, helping to assemble ignition coils: "It was strips of metal. We used to bend them like a horseshoe, so that we could put them inside of the casing. I think it was fourteen strips on each side. And then they would seal it with tar and some wax." The utility men, who knew every job in the department, taught him what to do, a process that took about an hour. "We used to switch every thirty days from the afternoons to days," Thomas remembered. He was eventually promoted to "checker," ensuring that the ignition coils met specifications: "I would stamp it 'OK' if the tar wasn't leaking out of there or anything like that." He also had to confirm that "the terminals were on there right." It was important to catch the faulty coils before they headed off to an assembly plant: "You would see some leak in there once in a while. Sometimes the casing—I think it was Bake-o-lite—would crack because of the heat, and that's why the tar would leak out of there. They would tear them down and salvage what they needed to and then start it all over again." In Thomas's experience, checking coils was better than producing them. On production, "when you first started, you cut your fingers. After a while, you toughened up your fingers, and then it was a simple job." As a checker, however, "all I had to do is see that it wasn't leaking anyplace. I think got three cents or four cents more an hour, something like that. I was worth a little more, I guess."

Ford emphasized that the plant was a professional workplace and must be kept clean. Thomas recalled an incident when one of the Milan Ford workers, a friend of his who was also a dairy farmer, left the factory abruptly, "took off for about an hour, an hour and a half. Come to find out what it was—he had manure on his shoes, and they run him out of there and told him he had to get those shoes cleaned up." The bosses were strict like that, Thomas said, but on the whole conditions were a lot better than at Peninsula Paper. At the Milan plant, "whatever the foreman told you to do, that's what you did." It worked for Thomas. That's how he got the checker job. Although there was widespread discontent a few miles away in the Rouge plant, Thomas didn't see any signs of union activity in Milan, and he certainly wasn't going to stick his neck out again. "I think I got my message," he said, referring to Peninsula Paper. "There, it didn't work out so good."

Even though war seemed imminent, Thomas still hoped that his life would proceed according to plan. But he was called to active duty in early April, 1941: "The day I went in the military, my boss come along and he says that the Rouge is on strike. Everybody's got to clear out except me. He said I'm on military, so he would let me finish the day. He gave me fifteen minutes short—he wouldn't give me my eight hours." The Milan plant shut down during the Rouge strike, but Thomas didn't care because he was heading to Fort Knox, Kentucky before assignment to Fort Leonard Wood, in Missouri: "I didn't really think about it. We were kind of busy trying to learn how to be a soldier." Meanwhile, Rosella worked for a cleaning company in Ypsilanti before landing a job at the new Willow Run Bomber Plant after the U.S. officially entered the war. In early 1941, Thomas and Rosella had monitored the construction site outside Ypsilanti: "They were clearing out woods and stuff, cleaning it all out. They shut off a whole bunch of roads in through there. Something was telling me in my mind that there's something going on for some reason. We didn't know what it was, at that time, but that's what it was—Willow Run was being made right at that time."

After the Pearl Harbor attack, it became clear that Thomas would be in the military for the foreseeable future, so he and Rosella revised their plans and were married in December 1942. Rosella quit her Willow Run job: "She would follow me around. I went to California. I went to Louisiana. And we went to the Carolinas, and then we went up to New York. And then I shipped out overseas." In New York, Thomas was stationed briefly at Ft. Slocum, which occupied an eighty-acre island in Long Island Sound, near New Rochelle on the mainland. Rosella arrived shortly before Thomas departed. Fortunately, he was able to obtain overnight passes from the base so he could be with his wife at night: "At that time, I was very sad. I found an inn in New Rochelle, and we stayed about ten days." Then he learned that there would be no more passes to leave the island, and he had no way to contact Rosella. He knew that a woman who worked on the base lived in New Rochelle and he asked her to deliver a message to Rosella at the inn "that I'm going to ship out, and go on back to Michigan. Then come to find out that very fortunately, my wife got pregnant" during their time together. He received the news in a letter while in Europe. "I think you're going to be a father," Rosella wrote. She had returned to the bomber plant for a few months until the pregnancy slowed her down. Then she moved back to her family's farm in Willis, a bit south of Ypsilanti.

Across the Atlantic, Thomas spent time in Ireland before training in England for the D-Day invasion in June, 1944. His unit crossed the channel fifteen days after the initial assault, long after the worst of the carnage. But he was wounded in fierce combat during the Battle of the Bulge, which began in December that year. "This is where my good buddy died right alongside of me," Thomas recalled, with tears. "His name was Ken, from Chicago. We were from all over the United States. And he was a good friend at that time. So it was a sad day there. It was a terrible war. I think that many, many times, these young fellows, eighteen, nineteen years old, didn't have a chance. That was it. Life was gone. I was fortunate—I was wounded, but for some reason or another, I don't know, someone's watching over me—my wife, or somebody. A lot of times it come pretty close and all." After three weeks in a field hospital in France, "they moved me back into combat again. Same unit. So we went back and we finished the war over there."

Thomas was somewhere in Czechoslovakia when Germany surrendered, and his thoughts switched from survival to returning home as soon as possible. The military established a point system, based largely on length of service, for assigning spots on troop ships.[1] Thomas learned that he was three short of being eligible to leave in the first wave, but he was certain that the Army hadn't yet processed the points he was due for having been wounded: "I got a medal. I should have been the first ones shipping out of there." Instead, he waited a number of weeks, anxious to finally see his son, who was almost a year old.

Thomas took a train from Pennsylvania to Detroit, where Rosella and her sister picked him up and drove him to Belleville: "Oh, it was great. It was just so great. Especially that son, the little guy. It was a great feeling. You don't have to worry about the war." He did, however, have to find work. He could have returned to Ford's Milan plant, but in the military he had served as a telephone lineman, and he wanted to work outside, so he got a job with Michigan Bell. Thomas and his crew of five extended telephone access along country roads west of Detroit, creating infrastructure for new suburbs: "It was rural. It really was booming there. From time to time, it would be two crews getting together. But as a rule, it was just one crew. We'd run wires, and we'd put telephone poles up."

Most of Thomas's coworkers had served in the war: "Some were from the Pacific, and some from someplace else. And I was in Europe. And we'd talk this, that, and the other." Their foreman, however, had no military experience and would "get upset all of a sudden" when the veterans began telling war stories: "'Quit talking so much about the Army all the time!' He was an older man, and he got irked pretty many times about that. Sometimes he would take his lunch and he'd go someplace else."

Although for the most part Thomas enjoyed working outside, winter often meant cold, dangerous conditions. Once, he recalled, "they had a real storm, and there was probably an inch of ice on the poles. We were changing some wires from old poles to new poles, and some were rotten." One snapped and he fell twenty feet. "There was snow," he said, which softened the blow a bit, "but there was about an inch and a half of ice in there and I fell down on my back there." He escaped without serious injury, and said to himself: "'I'm going to get up and do it again.' And I did."

Thomas remembered that Bell Telephone operators, all women, launched a strike a few years after the war as members of the Communications Workers of America, and that the linemen supported them: "I had my turn on the picket line. Every three days, we'd go there. They'd give us sausage, or bologna, and sandwiches, and coffee." The strike was about "mostly wages. Because there was no money in it. And my wife, we'd talk many times about it. I says, 'Geez, we're just barely making it.' And I was trying to build a house at that time too. And I had another child," a girl, born in 1946. "We were out over a month. I know that. I think we did get a few dollars. I'm pretty sure we got a little better. And I think conditions got a little better." Nevertheless, it bothered him that line crew members still had to provide their own overalls, "because they were quite expensive at that time."[2]

Thomas wanted to build a house for his family. His father-in-law wanted it to be on his farm and was willing to give Thomas and Rosella an acre of land. Thomas wanted to accept this generosity, but hesitated: "My father-in-law, we didn't get along. We never had no big arguments or anything like that. It was something that didn't match." Thomas recalled Rosella saying to him, "'You know, Dad's never going to get along with you. Don't do this.' 'Oh no,' I says. 'We'll be OK. We'll build a house over there, on the farm.'" In the end, Rosella won out. The couple found another piece of property for their house, and Thomas came to understand that "she knew better than I did."

Then came the actual construction. Rosella had saved $3000 toward a house—"she was very thrifty"—and they figured they needed another $3000. Their bank, however, wouldn't offer a loan unless it covered the entire cost of the house: "So of course, me, I'm going to do it my way, you know. And I did. We went on our own. I had a friend—he was a carpenter—and he and I, and then my two brother-in-laws, helped each other. And 90 percent of it, I think, or 80 percent of it, I'd say, we done it ourselves. It's still mine. I never had a mortgage!"

While working on his house, Thomas looked for better economic opportunities: "They were recruiting linemen all over. And they wanted me to go to Florida, to the Everglades. They needed a lot of work over there, and it was giving us premium pay. But I had two children. I said, 'I just can't do that.' Instead, he took a position at Industrial Wire, an auto parts supplier in Wayne, Michigan, a small town a little over twenty miles from downtown Detroit: "It was mostly all stamping. Big sheets of metal. We made oil filters, big ones, for Ford." They also produced carburetor parts and radiator caps. Thomas was a press operator, helping to shape sheets of metal into finished products. The work "was fast, real fast," and potentially dangerous, despite safety systems built into the machines. “One fellow, a brand new guy was there maybe a week,” Thomas recalled, and was assigned to stamp out air intake screens. “He took his safety off one day, and oh, geez, it took his fingers right off. And there was four girls sitting right there. That was terrible to see that. He just ignored it, I guess, or something. I don’t know what it was.” Once Thomas was hit in the back with a box full of brass radiator caps: “Oh, it hurt for the longest time. And they took me to the doctor, and checked me out there. Anyhow, I had to write up a big accident report, but nothing ever happened. It was just a lot of paper.” There was no union to back him up at Industrial Wire. “No, no, no, no,” he laughed. “They were pretty much anti-union.”

Thomas thought he could earn more at Kaiser-Frazer, the upstart auto company that had taken over a part of the old Willow Run plant outside Ypsilanti after the war. In early 1953, he left Industrial Wire and was hired as a trim repairman: “The money was good, and the union was in there.” He joined Kaiser-Frazer’s UAW local right away: “As a matter of fact, I was really starting to get active with the union. I was on the Veterans Committee,” helping ex-GIs solve problems with their military benefits. Kaiser-Frazer was going broke, however, and the Willow Run plant began phasing out operations. “I was one of the last ones—about the last fifty or maybe a hundred people that was there. It was one holiday we had there,” he said sardonically. Finally, the last vehicle came down the line, “and they had that little joke—they put their old shoes on the last car” and a sign “saying, ‘We’re going to Kentucky,’” where so many of the workers had been born. Thomas was deeply concerned. He and Rosella already had a third child—they would eventually have ten—and job openings were scarce at the time, during the 1954 recession: “I went all over. There wasn’t anything. Everybody was looking for work, and there was nothing there. I had to get hustling.”

He found a job on a construction crew, building a “paint house” that was an addition to Ford’s new Mercury assembly plant in Wayne, Michigan: “I think I went there ten, fifteen times, waiting for a job. And the foreman come along, and he looked at me one time,” and asked, “‘Have you got fifteen bucks?’ That was for the union dues, I guess. I says, ‘No, but I can get it to you in about five minutes.’ He says, ‘You be back in five minutes.’” Thomas got the job after quickly borrowing the money from a friend who already worked on the crew: “I was pretty fortunate.” He passed his first challenge when he demonstrated to a boss how to tie knots to keep a chalk line straight: “Two half hitches, so it would be real taut. He was my friend from there on.” One of Thomas’s responsibilities was to watch overhead and warn the crane operator if the equipment came near power lines, “so that this guy wouldn’t get electrocuted. That was a good job. I’d just stand and watch.”

After the paint house project was completed, the construction company offered Thomas a job on a project in northern Michigan, near Traverse City, about 250 miles from Wayne, but he didn't want to uproot his family. Instead, he got a job at the Wayne Mercury plant where he had helped build the paint house. Given how unstable his jobs had been, he also took a position handling baggage for American Airlines at Willow Run Airport, near Ypsilanti, which at the time was a major commercial hub: "I had to hustle for my kids." He had "another kid coming along, my fourth," and he was still building his house. Thomas worked days at the airport and evenings at the Mercury plant, with about forty-five minutes between shifts to drive about nine miles from Willow Run to Wayne. There was usually no time for food on the way, so he ate during evening lunch break about four hours into his shift. He rarely saw his family: "After a while, it had got to a point where I couldn't see going back home. I run off the road a couple of times. I was getting too tired." He thought to himself, "'I'm going to kill myself one of these days.' I was burned out."

Thomas quit the airline job after three and a half months. Mercury paid more and he liked it better. In addition, after his eight hours on the assembly line, he could "put another three or four hours in as a repairman, whatever they needed." It could be moldings that weren't installed properly, or "maybe some paint damage," or "nuts and bolts were stripped, or something. It was a good job, and I made good money because of overtime. It was time and a half, all the time. That's where I was making a lot of my money for my house." The assembly work, considered unskilled, was more difficult for Thomas to master. He had to install several bolts, "and the line is moving along all the time. I tried to keep up, and I told the foreman, 'Geez, I'm putting you in the hole.' The foreman, he told me, 'Hang on. You'll get it sooner or later.' And I did, believe it or not. In about a week, I got a little more skilled with it. I could stay even with the line all the time." He couldn't remember needing union representation while on this job, and it was only later that he learned that he had already accrued Ford seniority from his time at the Milan plant. In a few months, he was selected for a job off the assembly line, servicing the machines that connected the bodies of cars to their frames. Everything had to be aligned properly before being welded together: "Those outriggers would get damaged sometimes, and get out of line. So what we had to do is loosen them up, then set them where they're supposed to be all the time so they'd be true."

Things went well for Thomas in the Mercury plant for "a little over a year," he remembered, "and then things got bad. Everything went down slow."[3] He was laid off, with no sense of when he might be recalled. Two months dragged by. Unemployment pay helped a bit, but was hardly enough to pay the bills. Then, at a family wedding, Thomas struck up a conversation with his mother-in-law's brother, Ike, who worked in security at the Ford plant in Ypsilanti. A few weeks later, Ike contacted Thomas to say, "They're hiring at Ypsi. Come down and see me." When Thomas arrived at the Ypsilanti plant, Ike greeted him and "talked to a fellow in the office there." The personnel guy, Thomas recalled, "liked my record. He said, 'I see you worked for Mercury.' He says, 'We got a heater job going down, and we're going to start it going here at Ypsi. You want to go to work?' I said, 'Why not?' And so I went to work there."

Once again, a key connection brought a new opportunity. But it was also true, as Thomas emphasized, that he "was hustling all the time. I had enough kids, I had to keep going." He was back on a production job, manufacturing heaters to be shipped to various Ford assembly plants. He also spent time making air ducts. After he helped solve some production snarls, his foreman moved him to a repair position, much like what he had done before at Wayne: "That's what I wanted in the first place. And then I would do other odd jobs, whatever had to be done. I know they had people ahead of me, but I got the job."

Thomas appreciated that nobody hovered over him on the repair job, telling him to hurry, and no moving line dictated his pace: "You had your own time. You did the job, and when it was completed, that was it. So you moved along to the next station." But after another big layoff, he had to start over, returning to assembly, this time on generators, before working his way back to checking and quality control. For all of his hustling, he hadn't accumulated enough seniority throughout the '50s and early '60s to withstand the volatility of the industry.

Thomas was aware, however, that there were problems in the plant regarding arbitrary transfers from job to job, including some directives that kept him from fulfilling his regularly assigned duties. It seemed to Thomas that local union representatives were colluding with management, allowing such abuses to continue: "I was reading the contract. I was watching it pretty good." One problem, from Thomas's perspective, was a lack of responsiveness from shop committee members about protecting job classifications. He agreed that there had to be some leeway for flexibility, but it seemed that lines had been crossed: "We would complain about it," but "they just ignored us. I felt that the committeemen were not doing the job." Sometime in the late '60s or early '70s, Thomas ran for a committee position, but came up just short, close enough to be named an alternate. "They were cheating on the votes," he claimed. The third time he ran, he won a full-time committee position.

Thomas enjoyed the responsibility, even though the job could be exasperating: "One particular time—and I feel bad about the guy even to this day—he was probably fifty-five years old, and he stole a starter. And the security people were watching him. And the guy had all kinds of seniority, you know. And I had to represent him, and I tried my darndest to give him thirty days, or a year off, so he wouldn't lose his job. And he lost it. It was one of the worst things I ever seen. It was his own fault. And it was *dumb* to do that. That's his whole life. It was gone." On the other hand, Thomas had some unambiguous triumphs. In one case, a worker with "long seniority" was "off three days in the hospital. He was sick." The worker "was a utility man," and as punishment for missing shifts the company was going to demote him to assembly, which would also mean a cut in pay: "He didn't call because he was in the hospital. And he tried to tell them what the problem was, and the foreman said no. And so we went to the hospital and found the doctor, said that he was in the hospital and couldn't communicate. We won the whole thing there."

Heightened racial tensions in the late '60s and '70s were difficult for Thomas to comprehend and navigate as a committeeman: "We were hiring quite a few more people there—minorities, you know." Younger Black workers, in Thomas's view, "were hot. They were angry. The older guys, they were much better. But the young bucks, they had a chip most of the time." Indeed, economic disparities, discrimination in hiring and promotions, and racism within the UAW provoked widespread activism.[4] From Thomas's vantage point, that manifested itself as Black workers making unreasonable demands of committeemen: "They felt they wouldn't get a fair shake. They felt we were discriminating all the time. And we weren't. I just bent over backwards to try to be honest with everybody. And they would call you all kinds of things. No matter what I said, I was wrong, and they were right. They was just mean about it. You know, they were trying to embarrass you, I guess, anyway they could. I'd tell them, 'This is a contract, we got. We can't change the contract. That's the way we have to do it.' I tried to be as honest as I possibly could. There were some times when maybe you weren't doing it right, but the intent was to be honest about the whole thing, as much as I could. But, you know, it's not a perfect world." As the roster of shop committee members diversified, Thomas was offended when Black workers demanded Black union representatives: "It wasn't right. And there was discrimination right there. If I had a case of Black and white there, the younger bucks, they'd say, 'No, I don't want him.' They'd want this one Black fellow. And that wasn't right either. We were all the same union."[5]

Given how hard he had hustled for so many years, it was difficult for Thomas to see how he had benefited in ways that his Black coworkers could not. For example, he had gotten leads on auto jobs through personal connections that were unavailable to African Americans and thereby accrued valuable seniority; he had been hired in on a construction crew when the building trades were highly segregated; and he had been allowed to advance to more challenging and higher-paying jobs, such as repair work, when Black workers were not allowed to hold those positions.[6] Union contracts might have appeared to be racially neutral, but they tended to lock in such advantages and disadvantages, especially regarding seniority, something that Black workers understood but which shop committeemen alone had little power to challenge, even if they recognized the unfairness.

Thomas's devotion to fairness and his union was genuine, but his primary focus throughout was supporting his family, even if work meant long hours away from home. His children grew up and scattered throughout the country, from Washington state, to Texas, to New York, with several remaining in southeastern Michigan. In the early 2000s, one of his sons worked for Ford Motor Company in Germany, which provided an added incentive for Thomas to revisit the Normandy beaches and Battle of the Bulge sites that had made such a profound impact on him. One of his daughters accompanied him, but unfortunately Rosella, his wife of fifty-six years, died a year earlier: "My son was there, and my daughter, and we went to Normandy. And we went down the same roads, just about, where I went, that I could remember. And I had a good buddy of mine, got killed right alongside of me. And I wanted to see him. So we wound up in Luxembourg, where my buddy's buried there. That was the main reason I wanted to go to Europe, to see him."

11

James McGuire

(1925–?)

James McGuire was four years old when his family moved to Prenter, West Virginia, in 1929. He had lots of siblings, and it was tough for his parents to find a place to live. The coal company that hired James's father offered what passed for affordable housing, three rooms in a house that had settled in the middle of a stream, "with the creek running around both sides of it, like it's a big pile of rock," after a flood swept it down a hill. His father had worked as a carpenter for various coal companies, including stints in five different mining towns since James was born. The McGuire family grew at nearly every stop, eleven children in all, plus taking in two young relatives after an aunt became incapacitated and a neighbor boy whose parents were killed in a car accident.

The extended McGuire family experienced some stability in Prenter, despite the Great Depression. Eventually, they moved to company housing on dry ground, which offered new opportunities: "We had eleven little gardens, up and down that little holler where we lived. And my dad got a horse, to help us plow—help us to hoe the corn." They also had a cow: "If you had two, you'd have too much milk. You'd be dumping it out because you can't sell it. Nobody had the money." And they raised pigs: "If you don't have a pig, you don't have pork in the winter. We had a pig every year." The routines were relentless: "Somebody has to feed the chickens, somebody has to feed the horse, somebody has to feed the cow, somebody has to do something."

The family always had "a shortage of money," James noted, even when his father worked side jobs, so everybody helped out. James earned some cash by "hoeing peoples' gardens." He also "took up three paper routes for the *Charleston Gazette*. I'd get out at 5:00 in the morning and deliver papers." And he delivered the Sunday *Pittsburgh Press* to seventy-five customers in Prenter, "but my mother got the money. That's OK with me. She made good use of it." The paper routes helped James develop his math skills, which were evident as early as age three, when he learned to add fractions, a necessary skill for ensuring equity when apples were sliced for so many children. The *Charleston Gazette* offered prizes to carriers with the highest percentage increases in subscriptions during special periods. Before those competitions, James was strategically lax about collecting money, subscriptions would lapse, then he had customers resubscribe when the contest started: "It's easier to get the biggest percentage on a forty-paper route than it is on a seventy-five or a sixty." While some carriers won roller skates, James won trips to Washington, D.C. and Cincinnati, Ohio. While delivering papers, James also became aware of the local class structure. "The *city* women," he observed, "got their groceries" with ease. "The doctor lived in one house and the secretary of the company, he lived in the next house." From a child's perspective, the inequity was obvious: "They'd buy a bicycle every year and we'd never had a bicycle."

At some point in the '30s, James's father brought electricity to Prenter. He chopped down dead chestnut trees, used their trunks for poles, strung electrical wire a half mile to the nearest power lines, and connected their house to the makeshift grid. That allowed him to reinstall the original electric motor on a washing machine that he had converted to gasoline power. As part of his job, James's father collected coal samples from hillsides for the company to assess, and he took enough for family use as well: "That coal was to heat the house." James's mother experimented with coal for cooking, but "she was picky," and it did not suit her that "coal will burn a biscuit before it makes it done." She preferred wood for her stove, so "we sawed wood every other day."

James's mother was "an American Indian," but his father "didn't allow us to go back—and I have never been back yet—to where my mother was born, where my mother was raised, or where there were Indian people." In 1932, his mother's family lost their farm for nonpayment of taxes, and his father wanted to help but "didn't have no money to pay that—probably would have been a hundred dollars for taxes." James remained interested in this part of his heritage, and when people hassled him too much, especially on the job, he used what he called his "Indian stuff" on them. "It's worked three times for me," he insisted.

Although the McGuires aspired to self-sufficiency, they still needed help. Once a month, James's mother rode along in their neighbor's pickup truck to shop at the nearest store—at "the top of the hill, maybe twelve miles away"—that wasn't owned by the coal company. There she'd buy sacks of beans and flour, baking powder, and canned goods that were all significantly cheaper than at the company store. People in the mining village tended to support each other that way: "If you got extra food, you helped your neighbors. I've eaten other people's food." At one point, so many Prenter residents who had converted to gas stoves were unable to pay their bills that the company "cut off the town." In response, those with functioning wood stoves let others use them. A lot of people "was using our cook stove," James recalled. Community extended to entertainment, as villagers would "go down to the schoolhouse" in the evening "and sing songs."

James enlisted in the Navy in December 1942, "but they throwed me out." He was color blind, so he was assigned to the Seabees, the naval construction division, to support the Pacific war effort: "I started out at Guadalcanal, Bougainville, and the Admiralty Islands, and then all the way up to Marshalls, Gilberts, Peleliu, up to Okinawa, next door to Japan." Although colorblindness made him ineligible for combat, James often landed in the second wave of attacks, amid chaos and mayhem, to establish the infrastructure necessary for battle. Nevertheless, his scariest moment came in training, when he practiced a shore landing off a landing ship—the "whole front end opens up and it'll drop a ramp right out on the sand." This time, however, the ramp ended in deep water: "Twenty feet to the bottom! And I got a pack on my back and I got a rifle. So I says, 'What am I going to do?' I says, 'I can climb that bank.' And I started digging right up that bank and come up. I carried my rifle and my pack and I walked out. And they'd already had a scuba diving man ready to go after me." He attributed his survival to hard work in Prenter: "My lungs was bigger than everybody else's at that time. I could stay down underwater four minutes. I guess it was because I was sawing wood. You know, when you saw wood, your lungs gets bigger."

After leaving the military in 1946, James was convinced that he had a future in refrigeration and air conditioning, so he headed to Pittsburgh and enrolled in training courses, including an eight-month class in appliance repair. On the side, he learned to operate a transit, a piece of surveying equipment, and helped lay out sections of the Pennsylvania Turnpike. He enjoyed surveying enough that he considered making it a career. But he lacked confidence: "I wasn't the man to run the whole outfit. I'll run this transit, I'll lay it out, and I'll fix you the curves—inside radius or outside radius." It was a mathematical challenge, something at which he had always excelled, including in school: "My math was way ahead of some of the others, but my English and literature and history was way down below everybody." With his various training classes, James absorbed higher-level math, including algebra, geometry, trigonometry, and calculus: "Every bit of education you get along the line, you take it." He recalled with pride that one of his teachers told him, "You're coming up as good as some college people." James left the turnpike job, however, to gain more experience with electrical work. He ended up in St. Petersburg, Florida, which also had demand for his air conditioning skills, and found a job working on heat pumps. On the side, he worked for Sears, Roebuck as a truck driver: "I had two jobs all the time."

Money became increasingly important because he had started a family. He and his wife, Mary, were married in 1947, and had a daughter, Joyce, in 1948 and a son, Danny, in 1952. He found few good job opportunities in Florida, despite his extensive experience. He could have joined a survey crew but didn't want to work in the heat and swamps. Instead, the family moved to West Virginia, where James worked for a coal company. He "pulled pillars," a dangerous job when closing down a section of a mine, and was a "shot foreman," inserting explosives into coal seams. After a year, he asked his foreman if he "could get on the electrical force," but the foreman didn't even know his name: "I walked off and left." Soon he also left West Virginia.

This time James and his family set out for Detroit: "You find out that Detroit is the only place that's capable of hiring people. And what happens is, I came up here during a steel strike." Indeed, a long national steel strike in 1952 shut down much of the auto industry.[1] Still, James was committed to Detroit and had to find a job. As usual, he found two, one in Ford's Highland Park plant, which had military contracts during the Korean War, and another at a GM Fisher Body factory. At Highland Park, James worked on bomb casings, making sure they were balanced, "because the center might be off." The job involved placing the casings "in a big pan of mercury. Light side will float up." At Fisher Body, he helped install fabric on a car's ceiling, called headliners, for Chevrolets and Cadillacs: "You stretch it up and tack it and put it on the little hooks. And you have to stretch that liner just perfect, otherwise start all over again." Although it violated UAW rules to hold two union positions simultaneously, nobody noticed. But with low seniority, James was vulnerable to layoffs and his Fisher Body job didn't last long. He still had his Ford job and soon hired in at Dodge Main as an electrical inspector. His postwar training in Pittsburgh and St. Petersburg paid off: "They thought I was smart enough with electrical background. I even caught cars with the wrong motors in them." But from his perspective, the key was that he "had two jobs again."

James's refrigeration training also proved valuable. In 1953, Dodge introduced air conditioning as an option but much remained to be figured out:

"They said I'm the only one they've got that knows anything about air conditioners or refrigeration. So they said, 'You are it. Put an air conditioner in this Dodge automobile.'" It was difficult to make the unit fit under the hood: "I had to bend the pipes. The engineer already had mounted it and put a fan belt on it. It's hooked up. So now, I have to bend the pipes and put it in front of the radiator, and put in the controls on it. And I made it fit." Management liked his solution and had pipes manufactured to the new specifications. "The next thing I know," James remembered with pride, "I got a great big box, and it's full of pipes all bent to order. And I had eleven men building up and putting air conditioners on these things."

The thrill didn't last long. James received a layoff notice after demand for cars plummeted late in the summer of 1953. He still remembered exactly how many air-conditioning units his crew had installed: 356. But no matter his contributions, he didn't have enough seniority to stay on the job. Adding to his frustration, James had to train his replacements: "A man brings in three older men and those three men has top seniority, fifteen-year men. I only had two years. He wants them to have my job when I get laid off." It still exasperated him nearly fifty years later. Chrysler thought that James's four years of refrigeration training and his heat pump experience could be transmitted to anyone in three weeks: "You can't do it in a short time." He would do what he could, he said, and the engineer would have to do the rest. But James saw obvious flaws in that plan: "He had an engineering degree from U. of M. [the University of Michigan], but he doesn't have no experience. I had to break the engineer in. He didn't even know which way to twist a screw in." The layoff also interfered with James's aspirations: "All I'm interested in is getting my refrigeration license. You got to have ten years' experience. All I want is the ten years' experience, and then I can get licensed. But I couldn't get that experience."

The immediate problem, however, was the loss of one of his jobs. In August 1953, James found a second position at a Ternstedt parts facility, which was located in a portion of the GM Transmission Plant in Livonia, just west of Detroit. Unfortunately, though, he began at Ternstedt just days before an explosion and fire destroyed the entire factory.[2] Several months later, he noticed a "Now Hiring" sign at the Square D electronic parts plant not far from his Ford Highland Park job. He was unaware that Square D workers were on strike and that the company wanted scabs: "I walked in the job, and they had guards to get you in. And also they had guards to get you out. I walked right out. I wasn't the only one walking out. When they go in there and find out that they're hired to take good men's jobs, the union men walk out."[3] He had learned this lesson back in Prenter, when fellow miners and their families shunned anyone who scabbed. Yet James knew little about the UAW at the time, and his position on strikebreaking didn't equate with general support for unions: "If you're a normal person, you'll never have any problems. The ones that have trouble with the boss, they're not normal."

James eventually hired in again with GM, this time at the portion of the Ypsilanti Willow Run plant the company acquired after the Livonia explosion. He also transferred from Ford's Highland Park facility to the Ford Ypsilanti plant, near Willow Run: "I had seniority at General Motors and I had seniority at Ford at the same time, for four years. I was working the day shift at one and the night shift at another." This still violated union rules, but James again escaped detection. To him, it was justified because when layoffs struck one of his jobs he still had another to rely on. As he remembered the pattern, "General Motors would lay off in the wintertime and Ford would lay off in the summertime." He also moved his family out of Detroit, where they had lived in "a little old apartment near Hamtramck." He purchased an outbuilding that was no longer needed at the Eloise Psychiatric Hospital complex in Westland, just west of Detroit—"They was selling those little old houses out there for three or four hundred dollars"—and moved his new house to Milan, Michigan, a rural community about fifteen miles south of Ypsilanti: "I put blocks under it and set it down. I put a toilet in it, and went out and drilled me a well on this side and put a septic tank on that side." By 1956 James and Mary had four children and appreciated the open space: "I had two acres of ground, and I had a garden there."

But James was laid off from both of his auto jobs that year when the industry contracted after a boom in 1955.[4] Always enterprising, he found work as a "maintenance man" for the Lawyer's Club, the University of Michigan Law School's residence hall in Ann Arbor: "It don't matter what the maintenance was, I'll do it. And they said I'm the only one they've ever had that would do that." There was plenty to do. Every year James refinished all the desks and tables, which were expected to look like they did when purchased in 1924. He was in charge of the heating and ventilation systems, electricity, plumbing, and everything in the kitchen: "I found three valves in the steamer put on backwards by the contractors." There were also over 400 locks to maintain. Before long, he was head of maintenance, supervising fourteen janitors. Despite his position, James encouraged his staff to unionize. The tipping point for him was when he discovered that white janitors received significantly more pay than their Black coworkers: "They all got the same number of rooms to clean up every day. One section is almost the same as the other section." James's skill set and multiple responsibilities helped him support the organizing campaign: "I'm a maintenance man, and I'll talk to anybody everywhere—I can talk to you out there in the middle of the yard, and nobody knows what I'm talking about. I can talk to you down in the basement, and nobody knows what I'm talking about." University officials did find out, however, and threatened to fire James and his staff. But James encouraged the janitors to hold firm, certain that the risk of unmet cleaning and maintenance needs gave them leverage. He was right, he said, and the janitors voted to unionize.

At one point both GM and Ford sent James recall notices, giving him the option to return to auto work. He turned them down. The varied responsibilities at the Lawyer's Club appealed to him more: "I was having fun. I was enjoying myself." Besides, maintenance was steady work. Still, he realized that auto jobs paid far more money if work was stable, which it appeared to be by 1963. That didn't mean he could just show up and get a job: "They're not hiring at Ford's every day." His chance came at the Ford Ypsilanti plant in 1964, first as an electrical inspector, and then as an electrician.

Despite his many efforts, James never obtained his electrician's license. Still, he was proud of his vast skill set, including expertise in hydraulics that he obtained at a community college. All of that eventually brought him a measure of stability, but only after years of insecurity in his quest to be an autoworker. James didn't get involved much with the UAW until retirement, perhaps because he flaunted union rules for so long by holding two auto jobs simultaneously. "I never even got the right to go to Walter Reuther's hideout," he remarked, referring to the UAW Conference Center on Black Lake, in northern Michigan. "I wasn't a big shot."[5]

12

Edith Arnold

(1916–2011)

Edith Arnold loved the outdoors. She grew up on a farm in Oswego, Illinois, about fifty miles west of Chicago, and since there were six girls and only two boys in the family, she had lots of outside responsibilities. Edith's family name was Schlapp, pronounced as if there were no "ch," which according to family lore was appropriate because on their first date, her mother slapped her father for kissing her on the cheek. Edith was born in 1916, the twelfth child in the family, eight of whom lived past infancy. Her oldest sibling was born in 1899: "I mean, Mama had to be pregnant a whole lot of the time. The story went that my mother wanted a baby girl with blonde curly hair and blue eyes. And it took twelve kids to get that combination. After me, she quit."

Farm life involved hard work for the entire family: "We all had our chores. No question. My sister and I had to bring in the cobs and the wood for the cook stove." They loaded each other's arms, enduring "pickers and slivers." Some eighty years later, Edith remained indignant that her mother called hauling wood "lazy man's work." Edith also spent many hours in the family garden: "We lived off of that. I knew the vegetables from the weeds." She and a sister would "go out and fight hens for the eggs that they laid. Some of them didn't want to give them up. And I didn't like being pecked on the hand. My sister would grab it, but I gingerly would get in there, and I'd get pecked on the hands." Once they were tasked with killing a chicken for Sunday dinner: "My sister and I was told to go chop the chicken's head off. We had a stump, and there was two nails—you'd stick his head in here." Her sister, Esther, refused to do the chopping: "She hangs onto the feet, and I come down with the ax, and all I did was cut the skin here and she lets go, and away the chicken goes, flopping around, blood flowing all over the place. Oh, horrible. And then we never had to do it again. You would think I'd have been smart enough to figure that out and do it on purpose!"

The family's orchard provided opportunities for work and leisure. When the fruit ripened, Edith's older sisters did the canning and she cleaned up after them, one of her rare indoor duties. She had a favorite spot in the orchard: "I'd get way up in that apple tree, and I could lean out on a branch and twist my ankles around the branch below me and read a magazine, laying in the branches. Nobody would know where I was at. I heard my mama call my name, and of course I 'didn't' hear it. Soon here comes my sister. 'Didn't you hear your mama calling you!' And that was the end of that favorite tree." That particular sister "was ornery sometimes," Edith said. But to be fair, "probably I did something to her and she was getting even with me."

Edith was a prankster. She recalled an example from when she was "probably ten years old. My cousin was there from Minnesota." Edith looked out a second-story window and saw her cousin talking with others directly below: "The window was open. I went and got a tub of water and dumped it on my cousin's head. And when I walked out the kitchen door to go outdoors, he was waiting for me and grabbed me, carried me all the way up to the horse tank and dumped me in that really yucky old tank. And everybody said my arms and legs was just going every which direction." Her dad just watched, "standing there just a'smiling. I had it coming!"

Most income generated by the farm came from cattle and hogs. The Schlapps raised steers for beef and had milk cows: "One sister worked outdoors with the guys, like she was a boy. She wore these bib overalls all of her life, practically. I don't know if it was because she wanted to or because dad asked her to. He didn't have enough sons!" Her father was generally "even-tempered," but nobody dared "mess with his animals." He once hired a man to help on the farm, and the hand used a pitchfork on a horse, "prodded him, you know, a little prick on the rump to make him move." Edith's dad grabbed the pitchfork "and went after *him*!" Her dad "loved his animals."

Some of the livestock also fed the family. Her dad and her brothers butchered hogs twice a year: "I could stand off at a distance and watch, if they didn't chase me away. They would scald these pigs in a great big cauldron of hot water. They'd stick them in there, and then scrape all the hair and stuff off them. Whew. The first thing that come out of the animal would be supper that night—the liver and the heart, stuff like that. Never did eat the brains." She recalled fondly the smell of their smokehouse: "The ham hocks would hang in there and get smoked by certain woods. There would be apple wood, and there would be hickory wood. There was a hedge that had good smoking woods."

Sometimes Edith watched her dad working in the fields, where corn grew to feed the livestock. Once he "was digging this quack grass stuff. He would take the fork and dig up the roots and pull it out. We went in this one little field that had been plowed, but these wads were coming up. And I laid my foot down in that cool, black dirt—oh, that was pretty soil, in the corn belt, and that soil was black. And he come down with the pitchfork and he hit my foot. And, aw, he felt so bad, he had tears in his eyes. And this skin right between the toes, that's the only place it hurt. He had tears in his eyes. I know my daddy loved me. That was worth the hurt."

Edith remembered tender moments involving her father, but nothing comparable from her mother. Perhaps the physical and emotional strain of twelve pregnancies and four lost children had taken a toll. The surviving kids suffered as well through the era's common childhood diseases: "I remember mumps and measles. And I had scarlet fever. They made me stay in bed for that, and boy, they don't do that now. It's a wonder I didn't get sick and die, making me lay in that bed." When she was a bit older, she had whooping cough. For whatever reasons, Edith's mother focused on getting chores done rather than on explanations or nurturing: "We did not ask questions. Never asked her why. We did what we were told to do." Edith loved her mother, but she felt belittled by constant reprimands. "I hate to admit it," she said, "but I was closer to my dad than I was to my mother," even though her father also demanded obedience without explanations. Her mother got a short respite each summer when a local midwife spent a week or two at the Schlapp house to help out: "I don't know if I really thought that she was my grandma. We called her 'grandma' all the time. And she would sit in that rocking chair and darn all our socks."

The Schlapps didn't travel much, since dairy cows don't take days off. Occasionally, however, when dinner was over and dishes were done, they'd take a Sunday afternoon drive in their Hupmobile, a Detroit-made car that competed with Ford's Model T.[1] Edith's siblings knew that their dad was more likely to say yes to her, so "they always put it up to me to go ask him. Was I a favored one, or a spoiled little brat, or what?!" The Schlapps rarely stopped to visit anybody. They'd just drive around the countryside "to see what the other farmers are doing, and what the fields look like. Never to town, hardly." They occasionally visited relatives, especially during the winter when there were fewer chores to be done and they could travel by horse and sled. Edith remembered that the sled "was loaded with hay, that we would keep warm, and all the kids in it. Hitch up the horses, and we would go." Sometimes the parties would last late into the evening, and "I'd fall asleep on the couch, trying to stay awake, and I'd hear all these noises. It would sound like a beehive. It would get me dizzy—I'd be gone. I couldn't stay awake." When it was time to go home, "My daddy would be carrying me out to the bobsled. I remember waking up, that cold air, and then I'd go back asleep once I got in the bobsled." When they got home, dad would "carry me in the house. Nice, nice memories to have."

School provided mixed memories. There was a country schoolhouse, a two-mile walk away, that went through eighth grade. At most, around thirty farm kids attended at any point in time, and there was only one teacher: "She would have—my goodness—reading and writing and arithmetic, geography and history. How could she do all of that?" But teachers at the time were also trained to believe that all students should use their right hands for schoolwork, which directly affected Edith: "She wouldn't allow me to write left-handed. She whacked me with a ruler." High school wasn't her favorite time, either: "I didn't feel like I belonged. I wasn't a loner, but I wasn't in a clique either." With each year, fewer of her grade school friends remained: "Boys dropped out more than girls, because they needed to work on the farm."

Edith enjoyed the Presbyterian Church her family attended. They all went together until her dad's rheumatism got so bad "he couldn't sit on the hard pews. It was just too hurtful, and he would stay home and the rest of us walked to church." He carried on with farm work, however. The minister's wife made an enormous impression on Edith, beginning one Christmas season: "We weren't going to have a Christmas tree that year. I thought, I don't care if we don't have presents. I don't care about anything else, but not to have a Christmas tree on Christmas, I just couldn't tolerate that." She thought of the tree that had been used in the church's Christmas service: "I'm thinking, the program in church was over, and I'm going to go see if the tree is there, if it's been thrown out. So I went trotting off—didn't tell anybody where I was going. And here it was, laying out there in back of the church." She asked permission to take it home: "This minister's wife had been a missionary, and she had me come in. She showed me her big old cabinet with all these things that she got from China. And I was just thrilled. I couldn't imagine all that. And I think that's why I thought I would want to be a missionary, because of her. She gave me a cup of cocoa and a cookie. And she told me I could have the tree. You don't forget something like that. That was my Christmas present for the family that year, and I had the privilege of decorating it all by myself." Still, Edith didn't want anyone to recognize her dragging a tree along the road.

On the whole, her family did reasonably well at this time: "I didn't know we were in the Depression. I had all the food I needed. I had clothes on my back. We weren't cold. I was eating well on the farm. We were in the same boat everybody else was. Holes in our shoes. Cardboard in our shoes. We weren't ashamed of it. It's what we did. Made things last. Got to do what you got to do." Edith's dad liked to stay up-to-date technologically: "He was one of the first farmers to have a windmill to pump water." He was also one of the first in the area to buy a car, that "big old Hupmobile." In addition, since there was no electricity in the countryside, he rigged up carbide gas lights: "You turned on the gas, and put a light to it, and here you are. It's a wonder you didn't burn the house down!" At the time, though, they thought, "Hey, we're coming up in the world!"

Edith often experienced conflict between her independent streak and her learned obedience. After she graduated from high school, she did what she was told: "I wanted to go on to college. But I didn't. I wanted to learn to be a secretary. They had a college in Naperville, close by, to learn to be a missionary, and I really wanted to do that. There just wasn't the money for it, I guess." Instead, somebody from Oswego "come out and asked my mother, 'Do you have any daughters yet that can come and work for me?' I didn't question it. I had nothing to say about it. Away I go, trotting along, and went to work for her." It was a miserable experience: "Just helping out with housework." There was one saving grace: "I never had to do the cooking. Hah! I could have learned something. I didn't do cooking at home. I was *outdoors*."

She lived with her employers Monday through Friday and went home on weekends: "It was five days of the week I didn't like at all. It was *housework*!" She also had to help care for the couple's baby, the younger of their two children, mostly in the afternoons. She would take the infant for walks "in this huge wicker baby buggy. I think I knew every street in that town, because I would walk all afternoon. The kid took its nap, and I just kept walking." As for the mom, "She's just reading her magazine, doing whatever she did." Things got worse, in Edith's view, when her employers moved to La Grange, Illinois, about thirty-five miles closer to Chicago: "I went with them. So every other week I'd get two days off, get on the train and go home."

In 1935, after about a year of live-in housekeeping, Edith abruptly left. Only her brother knew why. He had already moved to Pontiac, Michigan, on the advice of cousins who had jobs in auto factories, and he had an extra train ticket, which he mailed to Edith, who fled to Michigan with it: "That was a terrible thing I did. I just can't believe that I was that inconsiderate. I didn't tell them. I just left. Didn't say I'm not coming back." Eventually, she returned to La Grange "to get my stuff, and maybe apologized a little bit. I was really feeling guilty. I almost didn't even go back—what little I had there wasn't worth going for—to go through the humiliation." With that encounter behind her, Edith returned to Pontiac.

Her brother was determined to show her a good time: "He had a date for me with a different guy every night of the week." She had dated a bit in Illinois, and had even gone out with one boy "for about a year, but I didn't like him that much. I double-dated with my sister and her boyfriend because we'd always go to the movies or something." The men lined up by her brother didn't interest her much either, but her brother's girlfriend's brother did. Edith's brother had a room in a boarding house owned by Harold Arnold, who also operated a neon sign company in town. Arnold's daughter dated Edith's brother. Arnold's son, Don, had an apartment across the street and had noticed "this strange girl going in and out of his folks' house" and "decided to go find out about it. That's how we met." Edith ended up marrying Don, and her brother married Don's sister.

Edith's courtship was fairly short, but during that time she landed a job doing, of all things, housework—"which I hated!" It was for a couple who lived in a wealthy neighborhood near Birmingham, a Detroit suburb. Once again, she lived with her employers: "Had my own room. I did like that. But I didn't want to be somebody else's servant. But you roll with the punches." She mostly helped with "cleaning and stuff like that. She even let me work outdoors in the garden one time. Of course, I liked that. But they had a gardener who did that work. I would have an hour off every afternoon to go to my room and read a magazine, take a nap, whatever I wanted to do. So I liked to just go outdoors."

Marriage offered a way out. The deciding factor for her was that Don showed interest. She visited her family in Illinois whenever possible, and one time "Don came down to get me. He did the running. He did the chasing. And I finally let him catch me." She wasn't wild about the idea: "My sister and her husband kind of talked me into it, like I didn't have anything to say about the matter." The wedding wasn't meticulously planned: "At least it was in the church. It wasn't at the Justice of the Peace. But I didn't have any flowers. I didn't even think about it, you know. Went to buy a dress, and couldn't find a pretty dress—it was the ugliest dress I ever owned. I hated that thing. It was green. I did not look good in it. Glad I don't have any pictures."

Don was working at the Fisher Body plant in Pontiac, but he was laid off shortly after the wedding. The newlyweds had to live with Don's parents for a few months while Don worked at his family's sign company. During his layoff, Don landed positions at two other major auto plants in town, Pontiac Motor and GM Truck and Coach: "He was working two jobs for a couple of weeks until they caught up with him and had him quit one or the other." He opted for Pontiac Motor because it was closer to home. He also worked a second job on weekends, hauling new cars to dealerships on the west side of Michigan or on the east coast.

Edith gained her father-in-law's trust and took a job at the sign company: "I worked for almost a year doing his office work. He taught me everything I had to know and what to do—make out schedules and worksheets and made their checks, but he had to sign them." Although it was an indoor job, she found it fulfilling: "That was kind of a little dream, either be a missionary or be a secretary. I thought secretaries made a lot of money. And I was going to buy a car for my mother. She doesn't even drive. But I wanted to do something for my mom." She stopped working at the sign company during her pregnancy with their first child, Audrey, who was born in 1938. A son, named after his father, arrived in 1940.

Edith stayed home when the kids were young. Without much conviction, she said it was "OK. I kept busy doing stuff. I was always doing something of some kind. I was always making my own spending money. I did textile painting. Did ties and hankies and scarves. Whatever would sell. And I did pretty good." She used her earnings to buy birthday and Christmas gifts: "I was happy to be in the home. They were too little for me to be out." She still didn't like housework, but she was most resentful of her husband's insistence that it was *his* house: "I never said anything. But in my mind, I'd think, 'He could have said *our* house' when he's having conversation with somebody. It bugged me. But it wouldn't have done any good to say anything, because it would not have meant a *thing* to him." She acknowledged that "it was a hurtful thing," yet she questioned herself: "I probably shouldn't have felt that way."

Once again, Edith's independent streak clashed with her sense of obedience, or perhaps of duty. During World War II, her kids were too young for her to consider getting a job. Don didn't want her to work in an industrial plant anyway, she said, because he thought the "dirty jokes" and "nasty language" would be too offensive for her.[2] Ineligible for the military because of a ruptured eardrum, Don worked at Pontiac Motor during the war as an electrician, a skill he acquired at the family's sign business.

For nearly a decade, Edith and Don lived in an apartment: "That was wicked. Money down the drain." They "made do," Edith recalled, but "never got ahead." She did, however, enjoy the sociability with other neighborhood moms, "kaffeeklatsches and all that kind of stuff." Although Don had steady work as an electrician, they couldn't afford a house: "Every time we'd get enough money saved up for a down payment, the down payment would be higher. We never could quite get enough money together. So we borrowed some—I don't know where the money come from—and we borrowed the last of what we needed from his dad."

Social life once again provided her fondest memories of their new house and neighborhood, especially when the weather was warm: "In the evening, everybody would take their chair and go out—we had an extra lot on either side of us—and the guys would bring their chairs and would all congregate. Sit out there and yap." The women arrived a bit later: "We'd get our dishes done, and go out and join them until the mosquitoes chased us in. That was just kind of daily routine for a while there, and it was enjoyable."

As soon as her daughter approached junior-high age, Edith looked for a job outside the home. Auto plants were still off limits, at Don's insistence, but she found a position at an A&P grocery store, where her closest friend had a job. Edith inquired with the manager "and went to work the next day. Just like that. I didn't make too much, but it was a diversion. I'd get away from home a little bit, and the kids were old enough to be OK at home without me there." She worked Thursdays through Saturdays: "It was kind of bad in a way on the weekend, because the kids were home from school."

At A&P, Edith ground coffee to order for customers. The regulars would "come the same time every week, order the same kind of coffee every week, the same kind of ground, exactly. By the time they come to the counter, I'd have it ready for them. Oh, they'd then feel important. Made me feel good. And it saved time." She liked her coworker in their little department, where they also sold candy bars, gum, and cigarettes. Edith always looked for ways to have fun. The meat counter was next to them, so she'd "throw a package of gum for them and they'd throw back a hot dog or something. I had a good time there." But the pay was low: "We weren't getting ahead. We were just breaking even, payday to payday. Like everybody else. I guess I wanted more."

In early 1953, a hiring boom in the auto industry caught Edith's attention.[3] She insisted to Don that it would be a good idea for her to get a job at Pontiac Motor. "Paid better money," she pointed out. Without Don's approval, she applied and got hired: "He wasn't all gung-ho about it, but once he got used to it, it was fine." One thing he particularly liked was "having more money to spend for beer, and the good whiskey instead of belly-rot." She reminded him of those advantages whenever he complained about her working in a factory. Edith also treated herself. She was tired of arranging rides to work while Don drove the family car: "And I'm thinking, why don't I drive to work. I went out and bought me a car! Yes!"

Edith started out on day shift, in part because she was old enough that her foreman assumed she had worked during WWII and had accrued seniority since then: "So I just kept my mouth shut, and I'd get bumped onto the second shift once they'd find out." This happened several more times because she was transferred from plant to plant within the Pontiac Motor complex. It became a seasonal routine. She'd work first shift in the fall, get bumped to second shift sometime in the spring when car sales slackened, then get laid off in the summer: "I had it made. Kids would be out of school—I'm home for that. It worked out perfectly for me."

Edith almost didn't make it past her first morning at Pontiac Motor: "The day I hired in it was so noisy in there, I thought boy, one hour of this, I'm going home." A coworker yelled at her, "a great big old gorilla guy, and I couldn't hear what he was saying." She was miserable. "But three hours later I was getting better at it. I thought I guess I'll stay until noon." The hollering man, it turns out, "was breaking me in on the job, telling me how to do it. So about noontime, I thought, well, it ain't so bad. I guess I'll go to work the next day. And the next day I thought, well, I guess I'll do another day. By the third day, I'm all broke in."

Her first job was on a government war contract: "We were making rocket heads. Big old heavy things, and I worked on a drill press. I *liked* the job. These things were heavy, but I learned how to do it, and not hurt my body. Just do what they told me." A rocket head arrived on a conveyor line, "and we'd grab the handle, pull it out, and just flipped it over, one at a time onto the drill press." They'd fasten it in place, "and push a button. The machine comes down, and drills three little holes on the side of it. And then, automatically, turns off." The tricky part for Edith was grinding the metal burrs off the edges of the holes: "I'd take off more than needed to come off. I couldn't stop it quick enough. I was not good at that. But there would be two people that would change off, back and forth, and they'd just leave me on the drill press."

There was a mix of men and women in her department, although no Black employees. Edith fit right in: "I had a good time, throwing wet rags around until you get caught. One day, oh man—I had me a matchbox, and I had a live mouse. I took it to work, and turned the mouse loose. Those guys were up on the tables. They were afraid it would run up their pant legs. We were all laughing. Boy what a wicked thing I did to that poor little animal." Most of the women in her department, she said, adapted to the environment, becoming just "another worker, another one of the guys." Edith enjoyed being social: "You'd get to know them, and yak, yak, yak, telling jokes." Her foreman, she recalled, was "right there along with us! Yeah, he was a fun guy. One of the best foremen I had, for being a likeable person, and easygoing." In Plant 4, they had it down. They "didn't want to hurry up and work like madmen. You know. Slow and easy. Take my time doing it, and do it *right*. And use up the time."

Edith's Plant 4 experience lasted a little more than a year, then work life became less predictable. Her layoffs were longer, and she also had to take a year off on medical leave, during which she had two surgeries: "It was more than a bellyache! It's a wonder I even got back in." With low seniority, she was transferred frequently: "They shoved me around thinking that I would quit. I swear that that's the truth. I worked in every plant except the foundry. But I was glad *afterwards*. It was a lot more experience. I learned a lot more."

The entire auto industry, including Pontiac Motor, experienced lean times after the boom year of 1955, and Edith barely had enough seniority to cling to a position at all.[4] She followed Don's advice, this time supportive of her: "Don't ever refuse a job. Try it." If it was an impossible situation, "'Call a committeeman.' But there's only one time I called a committeeman, and that's because everybody bugged the heck out of me, because I would not do it. And the job was too hard for me." Fortunately for Edith, the union representative resolved the problem to her satisfaction. Nevertheless, Edith refused to call on a union representative again. She wondered what her coworkers would think of her if she relied on the union too often. Perhaps they'd see her as "somebody that's causing trouble." She said she preferred to handle things "my own way."

Edith had only one "cushy job" in this sequence, "light unitizing," which involved "putting small parts together" and "packaging them up to send off to suppliers." Yet it turned out to be one of her least favorite positions: "I had to work with two bitchy women that hated each other. I couldn't talk to this one, couldn't talk to that one, and I couldn't take sides. I didn't like it there. Women! They're not easy to work with. At least that bunch of women weren't." She once had the opportunity after a layoff to return to light unitizing, but she turned it down: "I'd rather work a little harder and work with the men!"

Although no jobs she had at Pontiac Motor measured up to her initial one in Plant 4, Edith made the most of every situation: "If I could make them laugh, it made my day." There were also a few unexpected surprises. For example, a coworker on a fender line had difficulty with part of the job. With fenders, Edith explained, "there's a right and a left, of course. On one side you have to use your left hand to hold the gun. And she couldn't do it. But I was born left-handed. They wouldn't let me stay that way in school, but I can use the left hand pretty good. So we traded sides. Did fine. She got along good and I got along good. There are weird little jobs in the shop that I could do and someone else couldn't."

Edith's home life, however, deteriorated. While on a job in Plant 8, "somebody in maintenance come over to me and said, 'Are you really Slug's wife?' People didn't know his name. He was called 'Slug' all the time. I said, 'Yeah.' And he says, 'How in the hell do you get along with him?' I says, 'Well, maybe he's different at home.'" But she knew better. He was, she said, a "gruff old bugger. Some people would consider him an alcoholic, but I never did, because he could hold it. You wouldn't know that he had that much to drink." Every morning, Don drank four ounces of whiskey before heading to work: "Lunchtime, a couple of beers to drown it down. He put away a lot of booze. But he was big. He absorbed it all. He didn't carry on. If he'd get a little bit drunk on whiskey, he could get a little bit ornery, but if he got drunk on beer, he was a happy guy." More often than not, though, "he'd just be grouchy. Give orders. He never got mean. He never hit me or anything, but it did get scary a time or two, when he was drunk on whiskey. Usually he'd just sleep it off. He'd get quiet. He didn't raise holy hog or anything like that, so I guess I didn't mind it too much." One Christmas Eve, Don "got home from work, three sheets to the wind. Sat at the kitchen table, fell off of the chair, laying on the floor. So I stepped over him and took off" to see her son and his girlfriend. When she returned home, Don hadn't moved, so she "stepped over him and went to bed." Alcohol affected Don's relationships with their children, especially their son: "He wanted his father to be a father to him. I don't think he ever really actually *felt* that. There wasn't the bond there."

Edith often felt like a stranger in her own home. She was also resentful that the family never took vacations. To be fair, Don's schedule and hers didn't mesh well. When she was laid off in the summer, Don's workload picked up "because he was on maintenance. That's when he did all of his overtime." They spent a week each summer in Illinois to see Edith's relatives. Still, she thought, "that's not a vacation. Vacation is where you get *away* from everybody." Nothing seemed to be working out the way she hoped. She tried a Baptist congregation for a while after falling away from the Presbyterian faith, but "they run down the Catholics, and I didn't believe in it. I quit going there. Started going to First Methodist," before eventually concluding, "I'm just not any of those—just be a *Christian*, not a denomination."

The 1958 recession hit the family hard, as both Edith and Don were laid off for a year. Edith immediately found a job in a junior high school cafeteria: "I worked out on the line during the lunchtime. I had my own little cart—apples and cookies, and frozen ice cream bars. They were all a dime apiece, no matter what. I had to take inventory of what I had, and how much I sold, and the money and all had to balance out." The job was very social: "I could yak with the kids, and you get to know them, and they get to know you. And I enjoyed that." But things were different when she worked the cash register on the regular lunch line: "Little pats of butter were supposed to be two cents. And they got these little pats of butter *hid*—oh those kids were slick—and then the manager comes along, she's yakking at my shoulder, 'Hurry it up. Hurry it up.' You can't hurry up everything like that. I didn't like that. When she'd leave me alone, I did fine." Edith found it ironic that Don preferred her to have this type of job to shield her from the rough culture in an auto plant. She insisted that she "heard more dirty jokes" in the cafeteria "than I ever did in the shop." It was worse than Pontiac Motor, "by far!"

Edith had just started her second year in the cafeteria when Pontiac Motor sent her a recall notice: "I thought, 'Now which one do I want to keep? I'm going all that many miles, working part-time, wearing the car out. I go in the shop, I'm making bigger money—a whole lot more. Full-time." It was that simple: "I'm going where it pays." She returned to Plant 8, on fender and hood assembly, which she liked well enough, although it didn't provide any challenges "because you just put the stuff on."

Edith left Pontiac Motor in 1972 when Don had to retire for health reasons. Things didn't go well: "He went home and he sat in a chair. He *retired*. *Nothing*. He just wanted to run me around. I was waiting on him all the time. I'd go to the store, and I come back and he'd be yelling at me before I even got in the back door: 'What took you so long?!' That didn't go over good with me at all. I wouldn't even answer him. Put me in a bad mood the rest of the day." This lasted nearly two decades, until Don died after spending his last couple of years in a nursing home.

Taking advantage of two UAW pensions, Edith finally got to travel: "I went to Alaska and I went to Hawaii within one year's time. Of course, now I'm out of money. I can't afford it. But then I've done it." She also got a tattoo to celebrate her 80th birthday, then went on a UAW Local 653 bus trip to Branson, Missouri: "The biggest highlight—oh Lord have mercy—I got picked to come up on the stage with The Platters. So here I am up there showing them this tattoo, and that whole theater came unglued!"

13

James Franklin

(1925–2020)

James Franklin's family was of African Canadian heritage. His mother was from Dover, Ontario, on the Lake Erie shore, about seventy-five miles west of Buffalo, New York, and his father was born in Maidstone, Ontario, about fifteen miles southeast of Detroit. Drawn by the prospect of work at the Ford Rouge Plant in Dearborn, his parents moved with their first child from Ontario to Michigan in 1924, a year before James was born. Some sixty-five years earlier, one of James's great-great-grandfathers on his mother's side had found refuge in Canada after escaping enslavement in the United States. James remembered his parents saying that the "Ford Motor Company was one of the best companies for a Black man to work for."[1] James's father quickly got a job in the core room in the Rouge foundry. "He built the water jackets for the head of the engine," which prevented overheating. The Franklins lived in Ypsilanti, Michigan, about thirty miles west of Dearborn, along with others who had followed a similar trajectory: "In the city of Ypsilanti, 99 percent of your Blacks at that time were all from Canada."

African Canadians stuck together: "I can almost name you every family in the city of Ypsilanti back in the early '30s. Everybody knew everybody. One of the oldest families in the city of Ypsilanti is the Kersey family. Their big nest of people was on First Avenue," just around the corner from the Franklin's home on Monroe St. "In fact, I think a whole city block was nothing but Kerseys." James remembered walking to school with his friends and returning home for lunch, even as a teenager. Reflecting back on those days, he said that everything "was safer. We never had a house key. Who needed it? If you wanted to sleep on your front porch in the summertime, sleep out there. Nobody's going to bother you. The police station was at one time, in the City of Ypsilanti, no bigger than a phone booth. You didn't have more than four or five policemen. So that's the way Ypsi was. It was a friendly city." The friendliness, James insisted, crossed racial lines. Some streets were integrated, as were the schools and the city's two theaters: "Everybody that had a dime went to the show on Saturday night. That was the relaxation that you had within the town. The children, as far as fighting and violence, you had very little of that, between even Black and white. I think the relationship was ideal, under the circumstances." James did recall some animosity, however, between Black citizens in Ypsilanti and African Americans in next-door Ann Arbor: "We didn't get along with the Ann Arbor people because they lived in a big college town and they thought 'ooh ooh,' you know. See, so we were the foundry workers, and they were the people that took care of the oopdy doopdy people."

In James's view, Ypsilanti's race relations changed in the early 1940s as local factories converted to war production and the mammoth Willow Run bomber plant was built just east of town. These developments brought a large influx of southerners, Black and white, to the city: "Everybody brought their tradition with them. If you lived in the south as a white man, your ideals of the Black man, you are over and he is down. And this brought a great problem to the City of Ypsilanti. At one time, in 1941, somewhere around through there, we had a little race riot at the Wuerth theater. That's where 99 percent of the people went, because they had a balcony and of course a downstairs. Now they started migrating the Black upstairs. We had no discrimination in where you wanted to sit up until this time. And here it come, upstairs, and people began to notice: 'How come all the Blacks go upstairs?' And that's what tradition did. Even our restaurants that we used to go in went to not serving Blacks. So, then we went to having trouble." He remembered this as a confusing and frustrating time: "Blacks who were living here, these old-timers from Ypsilanti, the young children coming up, we never run into segregation, or Blacks eat here and whites don't eat here, you can't do this, you can't do that. If it was there, it wasn't noticeable." James complained that newly arrived Black migrants seemed too comfortable with segregation: "They brought their traditions with them too. Their tradition was completely opposed to what the Blacks were living in the city of Ypsilanti, because we in Ypsi were not used to this discrimination, living all in a huddle by yourself." In James's experience, the established African Canadian families "did not partake" in the new segregation practices, "and they let the city know it, and things got back to normal again." The mini-riot at the theater, he said, had a lot to do with it. But there remained a division between longer-term Black residents and newcomers. Before the wartime migration, James recalled, "Blacks didn't have any problem with labor, because they were all intelligent, in the skilled trades—electricians, bricklayers, carpenters, and things like that." War production, however, prompted businesses, with the help of some local preachers, to "bring Blacks up here in boxcars, because of work."

Yet the Depression years had been far from rosy for the Franklins. James's father often had short weeks of work in the Rouge foundry: "My dad would work Monday and Tuesday, and another family would work Wednesday and Thursday. They split it up. That was a very, very rough time, because there was many a night that we didn't have food. We survived, but we didn't survive comfortably. Like a lot of people, we had decent clothes. Maybe they were raggedy, but they were clean. So we didn't have any problem with that, and we were all proud children." James's mother stayed home and stretched resources as far as possible: "She was always there for us, and she was a very good woman." There were strict house rules: "When I was a kid, being home in the house at 7:00, it meant 7:00. It didn't mean no 7:30. And that was it. And you'd be there." To supplement the family's income, James recalled, "My dad took an old car, an old Ford, cut it down and made a pickup truck. And as the boys grew older, he got another truck, and we had what we called The Franklin Hauling Company. We hauled trash." His dad could not sit still: "He would work seven days a week, even if around the house. He always found something to do. He was more contented working, and he was that type of guy."

In high school, James followed in those footsteps by getting a job at the Avon Restaurant: "I had to walk by it anyway to get home. After school I'd stop there and I'd work from, say, four o'clock up to eleven o'clock. Closed the place down. $2 a day." His pay went for a used car: "I bought a '31 Model A. Ten dollars down, and three dollars a week. That was living!" But life wasn't carefree: "I never will forget my dad told me—I had a date one time—he said, 'Well Jim, I'll tell you what you do.' He says, 'You leave as a man, and you come back as a man.' And he meant it. In other words, don't fool with this girl. He laid the law down. If you got somebody's daughter pregnant, you had a wife. That was it."

Like many of his classmates, James left high school in 1942 to work at the Willow Run bomber plant: "I never graduated. The war was on, and money was good. Your qualifications were just as equal to anybody else, because there was plenty of what you call 'common labor' work. You didn't have to be into the skilled trades to make a decent living." James started as a riveter: "They taught you how to drill, to carry your tools, how to buck a rivet, how to drive a rivet, how much pressure to put on it—everything that it needed." Many of his coworkers were recent southern migrants, sleeping in shifts in converted dormitory space. They crammed into trucks and buses to get to the plant. James worked with men and women, Blacks and whites, and even his high school science teacher: "He was making more money there than he was teaching."

The next year, James received his draft notice and joined three of his brothers serving in the military. He remembered the main question asked when he reported: "Do you want to go in the Army or the Navy? I took the Army because I always thought it was too much water to drink" out on the ocean. Sent to Louisiana for training, James experienced rigid segregation: "You'd go in the PX, they had a white line drawed right down the middle. White on one side, Black on the other side." Soon James was in Europe: "I spent a little better than eighteen months over there. Went to England, France, Holland, Luxembourg, Germany, all up through there." He was part of an engineering unit: "We built railroad bridges and different things that were bombed out, tore up. It was an all-Black outfit. Our work was very valuable, because we built a floating Bailey bridge across the Rhine River. And Patton and them drove their tanks across it. Now it took knowledgeable people to do that."[2] In the segregated military, African Americans were barred from combat, but that line became blurred late in the war: "I've got three battle stars. That don't mean I was in battle, but I was in the battle zone, right in the middle of it, doing work on different sections in there. We didn't shoot up nobody, but we did our work real good, and we got great honor out of what we did."

Before the Normandy invasion in June 1944, James spent eleven months constructing housing for the troops that would attack: "As far as the eyeball could see—tents. Then here come D-Day. Went over into France. Right behind them." After the beachheads were secured and Allied troops pushed inland, James drove supply trucks through the night as part of the Red Ball Express.[3] "We were in Belgium" and he had to "go back to France, pick up supplies, and bring them back up. My job was 6:00 in the evening to 6:00 in the morning." The next driver would be ready to go: "He'd gas it up, you'd check it over, and you'd give it to him. That evening when he comes in, I'm sitting there waiting, pick my truck, and away we go again." For security purposes, only limited use of headlights was allowed, making night driving especially treacherous. Red Ball Express drivers were predominantly Black. James felt the racism behind that fact, but he emphasized that the drivers "did very good work." He believed that all productive labor was dignified, and that all workers, military or civilian, deserved respect: "How could you survive in a restaurant if you didn't have a dishwasher? Look at the germs you would end up with. See, everything works together."

During the Battle of the Bulge, late in the war, military necessity broke down segregation barriers: "We had guys in our outfit went into the infantry. We had whites come into ours. It wasn't Black no more. It became a salt and pepper situation. So that was a good thing." James's integrationist vision extended through the postwar Civil Rights era. Black nationalism didn't interest him: "If you're talking about Black Power, I wouldn't want to never live in any place where it's all Black. Never. Because it doesn't make good sense. If you're going to pull yourself apart from people, it's no good."

James expected to join the fight against Japan: "We left Germany and we came back to Marseilles, France. That's a beautiful place. That's the port of embarkation to where they were shipping soldiers out, going to the Pacific, because the war was still going on there. So the next day we were shipped out. Then they dropped the atomic bomb." He heard the news while passing the Rock of Gibraltar. Needing thirty more days of service to become eligible for discharge, he ended up back in Louisiana: "The only thing I had to do was spend the time. So that was very good." Still, returning to harsh segregation was infuriating, "because we were never discriminated against overseas, even with the Germans. You take the Belgian people, or even the English people there, Glasgow [Scotland], Ireland—there wasn't no great discrimination, other than the white soldiers would tell the people that the Black soldiers had tails. But they found out what kind of tails we had, and we socialized with the people. We came out good, you know."[4] After a difficult month, James returned to Ypsilanti, got married, and "went back to Ford's" in January 1946.

By then, the Willow Run bomber plant was closed, so James worked instead in the foundry at the Rouge Plant: "I was like a utility man, a relief guy, relieving the guys, and took care of the stock." He appreciated that he was able to do "numerous different things. I was young, progressive, and I had the ability to move, to learn, catch on quick. So I got a job on the bull ladle, to where you would take your cup, catch some of the iron when you was pouring it, pour it into your mold. Then when it settled, crack it, and see how much difference between the temper of the steel, from the top to the bottom." All kinds of people worked in the foundry at that time: "Ford never did believe in all-Black" departments. "The Italian people, the Polish people, and Romanian people—Ford hired all of them, and the Blacks, right together." James said he had "no big problem" with whites in the foundry. "Good people to work with."

In September 1946, James and his fellow carpoolers, six in all, stopped at Kaiser-Frazer on their way to the Rouge. A new auto company, Kaiser-Frazer was hiring for production jobs in a section of the former Willow Run bomber plant. James's father already worked there. Offered jobs on the spot, James and his friends continued to the Rouge, but "instead of reporting for work, we went there and checked out." Kaiser-Frazer appeared to have a bright future. Henry Kaiser had gained a national reputation for his shipbuilding enterprise during the war and had now shifted his focus to passenger cars. Meanwhile, Ford was staggering in the early postwar era, with parts, material shortages, and strikes hampering production.[5] Some of James's coworkers at the Rouge gave up considerable seniority to move to Kaiser-Frazer. James welcomed the opportunity: "I've always been fortunate in getting decent jobs. If there was one there better, I could get it. I started out as a material handler, unloading them big eighteen-wheelers back on the dock. After a year or so material handling, I applied for a job called stock chaser. That's where you run stock all over where it's needed," to keep the lines running. "Then I became a production checker," a higher-paying position. "I was checking everything that comes off the truck, and make sure it was right. And from there I went to what you call an inventory checker, controlling all the stock on the assembly line, from where the body was dropped to where it come out a finished product. All that material was my responsibility to keep it in flow or banked." James prevented line shutdowns by recognizing when parts supplies were running low and getting more in place before anything ran out. "It was a high degree of responsibility," he emphasized.

Kaiser-Frazer's auto production floundered, however, although military contracts and airplane parts production temporarily kept the company afloat. At one point a General Foreman, who recognized James's ability, asked him to move from auto to plane production. Before long, James was in a supervisory, salaried position, with four stock chasers working under him. For this job, he had to wear nice shirts and ties, which "cost you more money, but it was a good job. I enjoyed it. The crazy thing about it was, I didn't graduate from high school. The qualifications was two years of college or equal experience. So even though I did not graduate, I still was able to qualify through experience." In the early 1950s, however, Kaiser-Frazer's military contracts expired and the company abandoned auto operations. Although everyone could see the end coming, James "worked right there until the last dribble," in 1953. When a GM transmission plant in Livonia exploded in August that year, Kaiser-Frazer was eager to rent out space in the old bomber plant so the top automaker could build transmissions there. Soon, Kaiser-Frazer left Michigan for good.[6]

As thousands of laid-off Kaiser-Frazer employees looked for work, James managed to land a job back at the Rouge plant, with a little help from a former Kaiser-Frazer foreman who knew him. But the nation was heading into recession, and soon he was laid off. His move to Kaiser-Frazer probably cost him, because he lost seven years of Ford seniority while working there. James looked for a job in Flint, Michigan, where a brother of his worked. Approaching thirty, James feared that he would be considered too old, even though he was younger than many successful white applicants. James was eventually hired at a Chevrolet plant, part of General Motors, and found it ironic that the city known for the famous 1937 Sit-Down Strike, the birthplace of the UAW, seemed far behind Ford, a latecomer to unionization, in both racial and basic workplace fairness: "General Motors had the greatest discrimination, as far as Black and white. A Black man at General Motors got the dirt. That was a fact. In order for me to get the job from the beginning, I had to take a test. Whites came up from the South, walk right in."

James learned that GM usually hired Black employees for the worst jobs, mainly in foundries. He also discovered that the company ignored basic contract provisions, negatively affecting all workers. Most critically, no shop steward could be found when workloads were too strenuous, and there weren't enough relief workers to spell people who needed to use the bathroom: "I went a lot of times without any relief, and I walked off the job and went to the rest room. And what happened, I got chewed out." James knew that this violated the contract, but he couldn't get any union help: "It didn't get better, so I quit. First job I ever quit in my life."

He was in Flint for about a year, living with his brother during the week and returning to Ypsilanti on weekends, an arrangement that proved stressful. He and his wife had started a family—they would eventually have three daughters—and believed strongly that "according to the Bible, man is head of the house." James emphasized that to be a good father, "you have to spend time with your children, and you have to show these children respect. But then you lay the law of the house down." Yet he was not home during long stretches each week.

After the Chevrolet job, James returned to Ypsilanti full-time. It was during the 1955 auto boom and he was quickly rehired at the Rouge plant. Soon, however, new layoffs loomed, and he had just enough seniority to claim a job in welding, but there was a problem: "I never welded a job in my life—never even put my hand on an arc welder." Yet he was desperate: "I go to the library and I got me a book on welding. I read that book that Sunday night. Monday, I went back to Ford's for my interview as a welder." Although he got the job, it didn't go well, because he had to weld on a production line: "It was moving, and you had to walk with it. Oh boy, if I didn't have a good foreman, I never would have made it. For three days, I was burnt—I'm telling you, I was in bad shape." James's foreman saw his potential and assigned him to weld at a stationary bench for a few weeks: "He could have kicked me right on out. But Ford don't operate that way." With some time to practice, he could weld, "no big problem." After a few months, "I could weld with either hand, smoke, and do anything I wanted to do." James liked this job, but it took a toll: "My eyes were so bad, that when I came home at night, I had to put an Irish potato on it to pull the heat out."

James remained a welder at the Rouge until he experienced a long layoff in early 1960. Since he could receive his unemployment checks at any Ford facility, he had his delivered to the Ypsilanti plant, closer to home. Eventually, someone in the Employment Office asked him if he'd rather just work at the Ypsilanti plant, which produced various auto parts. He started the next day, no longer a welder, but happy to be employed. In less than a month, however, he faced a layoff in Ypsilanti and a tough decision. He was still within the thirty-day period during which, according to the union contract, he could return to the Rouge. If he went back, he would retain his plant seniority there but still face possible layoffs. If he chose to stick with Ypsilanti, he would be starting almost from scratch with plant seniority, leaving him even more vulnerable during layoffs. Pride was also a consideration. James and several others who left the Rouge had been bragging to those still on layoff there: "We run our mouths about it." He and his friends chose Ypsilanti, "and luckily, two weeks, back to work."

James never regretted his decision. At Ypsilanti, "the relationship between he and she was good, between Black and white was good. I was drinking off and on during that time. We partied together. If someone got sick, or death in the family, the whole department would be there for them. The Ypsilanti plant's the best plant I ever worked in. Clean. Supervision is clean. And the people are good. Your discrimination there between Black and white was almost non-existent." He occasionally encountered white coworkers with racist attitudes: "But as you and him are working together and doing things together, his attitude leaves him, because you don't confront him to hurt him, or downtrod him. The union has the right attitude. You don't downtrod a person."

Over the years, James continued to find better jobs within the Ypsilanti plant, first on "starter buildup," then production checker, and finally on repair. He liked repair the best, and he stayed with it until he retired. When reflecting on his upward mobility he credited the union contract, which in his experience was enforced at Ford plants the way it was intended to work: "With Reuther and his system," it "got to where you could move up the ladder. If a job's available, whether you're Black, white, it didn't make any difference." Still, he had to excel: "I had to be the best because I'm Black. There's no disgrace of being Black, but for some odd reason, you've got to exceed over and above the white man. That's almost standard procedure. You got to be the best, so I was the best!"

The church remained very important in James's life. He was raised Baptist but joined the Church of Christ in 1960, in part because of the deep racial divisions among Baptists. He relied on his faith after the death of his first wife and during a second marriage that brought him seven stepchildren in addition to his three daughters. He insisted that he and his second wife buy a new home so they could establish their roles and responsibilities, including James as head of the household. They also moved to Alabama for a while, but the need to care for James's mother and father brought them back to Michigan. His mother suffered from Alzheimer's disease: "That's a bad one, because your children, you look at them, you don't even recognize them. And that's a hurting thing for anybody."

James's years at Kaiser-Frazer counted toward his pension, which allowed for an earlier retirement. He had no intention of just sitting around: "I had an '85 Town Car. I bought it on my 60th birthday. And I put 205,000 miles on that thing in no time. Because we went everywhere. Down through Florida, Mississippi, Alabama, Louisiana, over into Texas. You name it, we went there. I've been deep-sea fishing, and I enjoyed fishing. It's relaxing, looking at the water."

James was proud of his children. One of his daughters became a GM autoworker, along with her husband. When the company shut down its Ypsilanti plant and moved production to Arlington, Texas, James's daughter took the company's buyout while her husband accepted a transfer to Texas, where the couple bought a home. When layoffs and shutdowns loomed in Arlington, James's son-in-law was transferred to a GM facility in Flint, Michigan. Then he was shifted to a factory in Romulus, Michigan. It was especially tough on their four children: "Now they live in an apartment, because they say they're not going to buy a home, because they don't know what General Motors is going to do. You can't say, 'Well honey, let's go buy a house over here,' and six months later you've got to move." A second daughter was doing well in California, with a daughter of her own. And the third—"that's the only one that I had went to college—she's a chemist over in Maryland now. She's got a very good job. She's got one son. So they're all doing very good." The same was true of his stepchildren. In the early 2000s, one daughter was "a supervisor down at the assembly plant in Dearborn." Another daughter worked in engineering at GM. A son owned a small business. Another worked for GM—"been there a long time"—while others were involved in plumbing, managing a drug store, and working at a Ford transmission plant. There were tough times for some of the children, for example the multiple job transfers, but James could see the positive results of his hard work and faith.

14

Ernie Liles

(1932–2023)

Ernie Liles was born in northeast Arkansas in 1932 on a farm that was "eight miles from Monette, eight miles from Caraway, eight miles from Leachville, nine miles from Manila, twenty-two miles to Jonesboro—that's a bigger town—and twenty-three miles to Blytheville." The farm was in what locals once called "swamp country—swamp turkeys, swamp rats—but it was good country after we got it cleaned up." His maternal grandfather was the first in the family to plow drained land in that area. His grandparents grew "cotton, soybeans, and corn. They farmed it with mules, so of course they had to have corn for feed. But mostly it was cotton." They also raised livestock, "just for personal use, none for sale." Ernie's parents eventually farmed nearby.

Tragedy struck the Liles family in early 1937, when heavy rains raised water levels in the Mississippi River and many of its tributaries. Massive floods covered much of eastern Arkansas and affected many other states: "That part of Arkansas, the levees was breaking and they thought it was going to get worse. The water just got everywhere just about where the land was low, and the National Guard, they went around moving everybody out to higher country. You didn't have much to say about it. Now there wasn't no water at our house at all. I mean, it was fairly dry there, but they was going to take us out of there anyway. So they made us go."[1] "We was in a Red Cross camp, like prisoner camp. There was four of us, and they give us two bowls of soup a day. And it was February, so it was cold." The men, including Ernie's father, rescued survivors:

"They found them on trees, on top of houses." Almost everybody was "overexposed" and "underfed." In those harsh conditions, Ernie and his dad both caught pneumonia: "He died, and I didn't."

The family barely averted further disaster: "People got lost from their children, because the Red Cross doctors would take them to a hospital and not let the parents know where they're taking them. No records at all, so a lot of them got lost. My sister was taken to a hospital. She was playing on the floor, mom said, and they took her to the hospital. They said I was OK. I was burning up with fever and they probably thought I was going to die anyway. I got so bad they had to take me to the hospital, and when we went in there, my mother asked at the desk if they had a Stella Mae Liles registered there, and they said, 'No, no name like that.' So my sister was in a room there close to the receptionist. She heard my mother and she run out. If it hadn't been for that, she would probably have never been found." The family contemplated what might have been if they had disobeyed the National Guard, like Ernie's grandfather did, and stayed behind on the highest ground near Monette: "Mom said the water never did get even close to the house where we lived, so they should have left us alone."

Everything changed with the death of Ernie's father. Fortunately, Ernie said, "the families back then stayed fairly close. Especially farmers." Ernie, his mother, and his sister moved in with his maternal grandparents, where they remained for about seven years: "You just go *on*, that's all. I mean, you wasn't dirt poor. You could get by. You had plenty to eat. You had all kinds of clothes and stuff like that."

Ernie started chopping cotton when he was seven years old, and he had little patience at first for questions about what it was like: "I mean, you got a hoe in your hand, what can you do but cut weeds down? That's what you're there for." Offering more details, Ernie noted that "it was hard work. It was hot. And it depended on how the cotton growed up, how hard it was. Sometimes it got pretty hard, because if it rained, you can't clean it down, and the grass and the weeds, they get growed up in there, and then it's hard to dig out. So it was kind of frustrating sometimes."

Families in the area helped each other, but mostly in emergencies. Ernie remembered a Johnny Cash song about a child who thought his poor farm family was rich because neighbors "always come down there borrowing stuff. If you needed a cup of sugar, you went to your neighbor and got a cup of sugar. But we hardly ever borrowed anything. If we run out, we just run out," partly because it was so far to the nearest farm or town. "We couldn't just pull out of the field and go get a cup of sugar." As for communal work on each other's farms: "Naw, they didn't do that." If people helped neighbors with farm chores, "it usually wasn't free." Things were different with relatives. The extended Liles family "would work together, and they'd learn a whole lot about cooperation with other people."

Ernie enjoyed hunting with his grandfather: "We never went deer hunting, or boar hunting. We always got small game, rabbits, squirrels, maybe coon hunting once in a while." Ernie had a successful first outing when he was about nine: "I remember the rabbit sitting there, and you know it was a little bit of snow on, and he was sitting there in the grass. Well, my grandfather walked right by him. I see that rabbit sitting there. I says, 'Well I'll just shoot that thing.' So I stuck my gun right down to him, you know—had a 16 gauge shotgun—and before I pulled the trigger, he jumped up and run. But I held the gun right on him, and he got out there, maybe as far as here to the road, and I pulled the trigger, and whoo—that was the first rabbit I ever killed." He also learned that he should have paid more attention to his grandfather's location, but only the rabbit was hit.

When asked about school, Ernie responded as if he had fended off too many assumptions about white southerners. "We often read and write," he said sarcastically. But a lot of his classmates drifted away from the schoolhouse: "You know how kids are. They grow up, and they thin out." Although he admired his mom's level of education, he also had enormous respect for those who were self-taught, or who learned from experience. For example, he recalled that his grandfather was "never taught music, but I never seen an instrument that he couldn't play. I seen him one time with a steel guitar, and I said, 'Grandpa, can you play it?' And he said, 'I don't know. I never played it before.' And he laid it across his lap, and hit it a couple of times, then he played the 'Steel Guitar Rag,' just as good as I ever heard played. He wasn't real good on piano, but if it had a string on it, he could play it real good."

Ernie looked forward to family celebrations, especially during "lay by" time, before the harvest but after the hard summer's work was done: "We'd set lines across the yard and we'd hang up torches, you know, kerosene, and that would make some light. And they would start making music, and the neighbors would come over. Wasn't any dancing. They just sat around and talked, and they'd play. My uncle played the mandolin. The other one played the guitar. One played the fiddle, and grandpa, he'd play anything else. They would just pick and pick. After a while, they'd make me go to bed—I was just seven years old—and I'd lay in the bedroom and listen to them in there."

Ernie's mother remarried in 1944. Her new husband handled the mules on a neighboring plantation that was transitioning to tractors: "I really didn't see him until one day they said they was going to get married. She had been going with him, I don't know, maybe three or four months, so they decided to get married. And I was happy." It did, however, mean moving away from his grandparents: "Me and my stepdad farmed 210 acres. And it's hard work. We wasn't rich," but "we always had something to eat, and we always had good houses to live in, and we always had something to do. It was pretty good. Except the heat. I didn't like the heat."

Arkansas summers were certainly hot, and to add to Ernie's misery, the fields he farmed housed plenty of snakes: "A lot of water moccasins down there, and bull racers, and king snakes. All kinds of snakes down there." For her part, Ernie's mom would "sometimes get out there and chop cotton," but she mostly took care of the house and tended the garden: "She canned a lot, and it takes a lot of work in the garden." In the winter, Ernie hunted and fished with his stepdad, who "decided he'd be a commercial fisherman for a while, but it didn't pan out." Still, the area had many good fishing spots, including the rivers and ditches that flooded in 1937, and eventually in the backwaters of dams built to limit flooding and supply hydroelectric power.

Ernie recalled that his life as a teenager mainly involved "working. I was plowing, driving a tractor, chopping cotton, picking cotton." He also hired himself out during cotton-picking season: "I picked a lot of cotton for a lot of people. You'd get three dollars a hundred [pounds]. And I could get three hundred and fifty pounds, so that wasn't too bad. That was a little better than ten dollars a day." With a twinkle in his eye, he recalled his strategy: "I liked to get an early start, when the dew was kind of heavy, and the cotton was heavy." Working conditions mattered: "One time me and my uncle, we hired out to chop cotton. And we worked maybe three hours, and we run over and got us a drink of water. And the head honcho there, he come over and told us that we was hired to work, to chop cotton, not sit around and drink water. I sat around and drank water, and he told us to get back to work. So I just handed him my hoe, and said, 'You chop it.'" Ernie and his uncle went home.

Although Ernie didn't realize it at the time, if he had been Black a stand like that might have ended in his death.[2] But he hadn't seen many African Americans where he grew up and he was uncertain about southern racial etiquette: "I remember one time, Bryant Plantation, they had a lot of Black people working, chopping cotton. I'm sitting on a bridge—I'm pretty small there, and I'm sitting on a bridge—and was fishing, but then I got tired of fishing." A group of Black workers approached the bridge, but "they stopped. They wouldn't cross that bridge when I'm on it. Well I went over there and started talking to them. And I told them to go ahead, and they said, 'No, we won't go across when you're on it.' It's like meeting you on the sidewalk, you know. They was taught not to do that, and it didn't make me no difference."

Ernie and his stepdad gave up farming in 1950 and headed west into the Ozark Mountains to work on the Bull Shoals Dam. His stepdad went first: "All of his folks lived up there, and they worked on the dam. They just got through finished with Norfork Dam, so everybody went over to Bull Shoals."[3] Ernie followed a bit later: "I was real young, seventeen years old. They called me 'Peanut.' I was probably about a hundred and twenty pounds. Had to get a minor's release to go to work." To get to his job, "on cleanup crew," he had to climb a two-hundred-foot ladder to the top of the dam. A supervisor once asked him to carry a ridiculously large load of hammers, chisels, buckets, and hoses up the ladder, as quickly as possible. Eager to please, Ernie hauled everything in one especially hazardous trip: "After a while, my foreman come up, he says, 'Say did you get that stuff?' I said, 'Yeah, there it is.' He said, 'You mean you brought it up all at once?' He was just joking with me. They never used it either." When the dam was finished, Ernie "went to work on the clear-up" around the reservoir it created: "They cut all the timber down, moved all the graveyards. I was mostly hooking cables to trees and hauling brush." As that job neared completion and "the lake got up, I went to guiding fishermen on the lake. You'd make pretty good money. Fifteen dollars a trip." But there were obligations back home: "Grandpa was still farming. Every cotton-picking time, I'd go down there and pick cotton."

Although leading fishing trips was enjoyable, it was seasonal employment and Ernie wanted something more permanent. By the early 1950s, a number of his relatives had already moved to Detroit: "They didn't want to be farmers no more. I had three uncles work in forge for Chevrolet at Gear and Axle. I had a cousin who worked at the same place. Then my grandfather, he come up here and went to work for Hudson," an independent car company. "Everybody else come up here except my mom and stepdad." So, Ernie concluded, "I might as well do it too. Come up here on September the 5th [1952], hired in at Chevrolet Gear and Axle—to be a *press* operator." His uncles had alerted him that there were openings. He applied in the morning, had his physical the same day, and worked that night.

Ernie was eager to make a good impression. He learned his job in about two weeks, "running a great big old press for making spring houses. I was fast, and I was very accurate." Nevertheless, he preferred to "pick cotton. The worst thing on a stamping machine, or big presses, it's so boring. It's very boring. And all that noise." Yet he was committed to Detroit and his new job. One night his coworkers disappeared, leaving him to operate all four presses instead of only the one assigned to him: "I was always a fast worker, and I always believed in giving a person a fair day's work for a fair day's pay, and probably a little extra." Maybe, he thought, he was expected to take over the whole line. After a while, though, they came back. "'Hey, Ernie. What's going on?'" they asked. "'We're on break.' Break? I never was used to a break. That's what we had—a twelve-minute break. Hey, that's all right. And we had thirty minutes off for lunch, and that's not bad. And if you had to use the john, they'd have somebody to come over and relieve you, and then you could go take care of your body."

Ernie had been on the job for only five months, however, when he "got a little letter from my government, and they had a job opening for me" in the Army. In February 1953, as the Korean War was winding down, he was sent for training to Fort Hood, in Texas: "Oh it was hot. The hottest I seen it down there was 116." Ernie was amused that the Army didn't consider him to be an Arkansas native: "When I went in, I had a Michigan address, so that's what I was, a Michigander." He spent much of his two years at Fort Hood doing administrative work. "I trained to kill people," he deadpanned. "I learned how to kill a person with a clipboard." He also learned judo: "It would have helped me if I had went in battle. I would take on three people my size." Eventually Ernie was selected for the Non-Commissioned Officer Academy at Fort Hood: "I liked that pretty good. I graduated about the middle of the class." Nevertheless, he left the Army as soon as possible and returned to Detroit in February 1955, during an auto production boom.[4]

Ernie hired back in at Chevrolet Gear and Axle, this time installing brake shoes on an assembly line: "I didn't like it much. I didn't know the *job*. All jobs are hard when you're working on the line and don't know it. But you get the hang of it after a while." Working on the assembly line was significantly different from his old stamping press job: "I mean, it's *fast*. That thing never stops." He found solace, however, in his union. He was pleased that he accrued seniority while in the military. That left him a bit more secure against layoffs, especially since most of the employees around him were "young people." Also, "a union man" who was "a good friend" saw that Ernie was struggling on brake shoes and offered some advice: "He come out and taught me, said, 'Just take your time. You'll get the hang of it.'" Another coworker, "this old man, about fifty-five years old," taught him lessons about union history, especially the significance of being able to speak up without fear of being fired. His mentor said, "Back in the Depression days, we had a union, but it wasn't as strong as it is now. There's a guy down the line there, he had to go to the bathroom. And the foreman said, 'I can't get nobody to relieve you.' That guy just went in his pants." Ernie responded, "Well I wouldn't have done it. I would have walked off." The older man replied, "It would have been your job. And that guy had a family, and there's no jobs in town. That's during the Depression."

Union membership helped in other ways: "They had these people coming in, we called them 'bird dogs.' One of them would stand on the other side of the line and watch me, just staring. I never did like nobody to do that. I asked him to leave, and he just done a big, mad look on his face. Well I got tired of it, and I went and found my committeeman, and my foreman found me, told me to come back on the job. So I wrote a grievance up on that guy for bird-dogging. And I'm still standing there, and my foreman said, 'Go back to work, Ernie.' I said, 'Well I tell you what. You get him out of here, and I'll go to work.' So he did. He went over there and got him out. Well, I wrote a lot of grievances, you know, for pay, and overtime grievances. Because I was right. And when you're right, you're right. And when you ain't, you ain't." All of his grievances, he insisted, were settled quickly, because he was right.

After six months installing brake shoes, Ernie learned from a friend about an opening for an inspector job. Ernie had enough seniority and got the position. His new task was to inspect brake drums, and later, wheels and rims. Each brake drum weighed about fifteen pounds, which wasn't so bad, but he had to flip each of them over to inspect both sides, and they arrived at a rate of about 300 an hour. All in all, it was more strenuous than most inspecting jobs, and Ernie developed "shoulders like a weightlifter." He used a gauge to tell if the drums were out of round and if those that were faulty could be repaired. This set up some intriguing power dynamics in the plant: "Production always questioned your judgment, especially when you'd get a stack of rejects." Foremen in charge of making the drums would "just rant and rave." Ernie, however, deferred to his own foreman, who had frequent shouting matches with his production counterpart. Ernie remembered times when his boss, the inspection foreman, played hardball: "He said, 'Don't pass nothing.' We stopped the whole line. Wasn't nothing they could do about it. We'd get nitpicky and we'd stop the whole line. After a while, the foreman—the production foreman—come over and apologized to us."

While re-establishing himself in Detroit, Liles met and married a young woman named Mary Ann, also from Arkansas, whose parents had moved to Detroit in 1948. Mary Ann's dad hired in at Chevrolet Gear and Axle on a tip from his brother. Later, her parents bought an apartment building that housed mostly people from Arkansas, including Ernie's grandparents. "So when Ernie'd come up, he stayed with them," Mary Ann explained. "We met there. His grandfather and his grandmother with my grandparents took the whole neighborhood in. They were just that kind of people." "She was very young when we got married," Ernie remarked. "She was fifteen years old." Mary Ann dropped out of school after the wedding. "She wasn't pregnant," Ernie emphasized. Their first daughter was born the following year.

"We always made a living, and we always had plenty, and we always managed somehow to have the money," Ernie reflected, emphasizing that everything was relative to conditions in Arkansas. "I was raised where there wasn't that much extra." In the late '50s, Ernie and Mary Ann were able to buy a new car and a house in Madison Heights, a suburb two miles north of Detroit: "Paid $11,250 for it." They moved in part because Ernie's job relocated to a factory in Warren Township, also north of Detroit, not far from their new home. There were layoffs and strikes throughout the late '50s, to be sure, but Ernie said they had little impact on his family. Even the recession of 1958, he said, "didn't affect me." During some work disruptions, the Liles family would travel to Michigan's west side to pick fruit, but found they "couldn't ever make no money berry picking." During extended layoffs, they'd frequently "go back to Arkansas, see everybody. Sometimes we'd even go down there and pick a little bit of cotton." Although Ernie's mother and stepdad never made the move to Detroit, many others did: "We used to go to the park on a holiday or a weekend or something. There would be enough people out there for two softball teams. There would be about fifty or sixty people, family and friends. Everybody from Arkansas."

Just as life seemed settled, Ernie felt pulled by a lifelong desire. He quit his brake drum inspector job in 1962, returned with his family to Arkansas, and "went into full-time ministry." He had always been deeply involved in the church: "Oh yeah. Pentecostal Church. Assembly of God, or Church of God. But later, I was a non-denominational." No significant event prompted the change, he said, although their second daughter was born seven months before the move: "You had to choose sometime." Ironically, Mary Ann was apprehensive because she would be leaving her Arkansas relatives behind in Detroit. "I was very close to my parents," she explained. Congregations in Arkansas were small, not big enough to support a full-time pastor, so Ernie got a side job working in a plant that manufactured refrigerators and freezers. The family stayed in Arkansas for several years before they returned to the Detroit area, where Ernie landed a job with Ford.

Ernie remained grateful to the UAW for its help in providing him with a decent living: "The union is what got our wage up, and it got our insurance paid, life insurance and everything else, dental, eyes, and we're still making money. Instead of working ten hours a day, eight hours a day. Hey, it wasn't Ford's idea. That was the union's idea. Instead of having a fifteen-minute lunch, have a thirty-minute lunch. That wasn't Ford's idea. That was the union's idea. You know down South, they even got the old saying, to unionize is to be Communist." Ernie wondered why white southerners who moved north had a reputation for being anti-union. The people who came to the auto industry, he insisted, knew about the strong union presence in Detroit. The ones that clung to their anti-unionism tended to stay home: "They don't understand it. And I don't know what they don't understand about it, but if it was left up to Ford Motor Company, they'd still be working for five dollars a day." Ernie also appreciated almost all that the UAW did to encourage members to vote: "One time I remember they backed a Republican, and I don't know why. In fact, I would vote for a guy just off of skid row before I would a Republican. So you know where I stand now."

15

Paul Ish

(1930–2015)

"I was kind of wild, I guess," Paul Ish said. "But I got it out of my system and I settled down." Paul and his friends didn't care much for school. They'd often skip and "go swimming" or "go to Detroit to the ball game or burlesque show or just party someplace." Sometimes they'd head out on road trips, once ending up in jail in Ft. Wayne, Indiana. Paul's dad eventually issued an ultimatum: either finish school or join the military: "My mother was dead set on me going to college," but "college just didn't appeal to me at all. I'd rather do something with my hands."

As a child, Paul did plenty of manual labor. He was born in Pontiac, Michigan in 1930, but spent many summers with his maternal grandparents, first on their farm in western Michigan, and then in a nearby town called Fremont. This was a fruit belt, and Paul picked cherries, peaches, and apples that became baby food in a nearby Gerber plant. There was time for play as well: "I'd go down to the creek and go swimming and fishing. I'd catch little fish and my grandmother would fry them for me." Paul's younger brother stayed in Pontiac during those summers, and Paul never met his older brother, who died before he was born: "He got into a paint cup with paint brushes in it and he drank the turpentine and that was it." The tragedy affected his parents, and the family, for the rest of their lives.

Paul's parents scrambled to make a living. His father held many jobs, including with the federal Works Progress Administration and running the warehouse at Lewis Furniture. Paul's mother worked as a bookkeeper at Lewis Furniture. A young woman lived with the family during the week: "She'd do the laundry and clean the house and keep track of my brother and I." In the mid-1930s, money was so tight that the Ishes returned to the family farm near Fremont for a year. Back in Pontiac, Paul's father worked at a window treatment company before becoming a fireman in Waterford Township, where the family moved in the late '30s, while also managing a restaurant at the Pontiac Airport, which Paul appreciated: "I used to go down there and I'd get rides with different pilots." He was about ten at the time, and a few years later he took flying lessons. Then Paul's father took a job in plant protection at Pontiac Motor, where he stayed until retirement.

When both of his parents worked at Lewis Furniture, Paul got a job there too: "I started out running the old freight elevator." He also worked at Waite's Gift Shop, which sold "knickknacks and all that sort of stuff." During high school, Paul stopped spending summers with his grandparents, but he once ran away with a friend to work on a Nebraska cattle ranch, about 200 miles west of Omaha. The following year, his parents gave their blessing to another Nebraska adventure: "I worked all summer mowing hay, driving a tractor for about fourteen hours a day." When he and his friend began hitchhiking back to Michigan, "we got sidetracked and went to Lincoln, to the State Fair." They tried to make up for the time, riding "in dump trucks, in tankers, in all sorts of vehicles. But we got back and my mother—oh she was mad because I missed the first three days of school. My teacher ended up telling her I probably learned more in those three days out there than I did in school, so she kind of quieted down."

In the spring of 1948, a few months before he was scheduled to graduate, Paul ran away to Nebraska again, this time with two friends. On the ranch, he "rode for twelve, fourteen hours a day, horseback—because it was in the calving season—seeing if a cow was having a calf, if they were doing all right." Paul stayed in Nebraska, didn't graduate, and his parents "didn't like it at all!" That's when his dad issued the graduate-or-enlist ultimatum. Paul chose to finish high school, which he did a year and a half late in January 1950.

The next month Paul got a job at Pontiac Motor, where his dad worked. This was during a production boom, so the family connection might not have been a factor.[1] Paul started out in Plant 9 on the day shift, helping to make six-cylinder engines out of solid blocks of steel. He had that job "for probably a week, and then I got bumped to nights." There was pressure to transfer to Plant 8, on assembly: "They were always short of help, so I went over there and I worked putting brackets on horns before they went on the car." His foreman then stationed him "in a pit," from which he fastened molding to the underside of each car: "I worked down there for probably a month or so, and then I ended up above, putting hoods on the cars as they come down the line. Well that about killed me." The weight of the hoods and the pace of the line over an eight-hour shift—"they were running fifty-two an hour at that time"—wore him down the first few weeks, "but after that you got your muscles developed so that it was more automatic." Still, "everybody was waiting for the line to shut down" because of some mechanical problem or parts shortage, and when that happened, they'd all "hoot and holler."

After a few months, Paul moved from the hood job to become "an extra man in my department." He learned every job and filled in wherever needed: "They'd send me upstairs to what they called the merry-go-round, where they built the front end. The radiator, and the front fenders and the inner panels of the front fenders were all put on." Sometimes he checked that hoods fit correctly: "They'd slam the hood down and if it didn't fit right, they'd open it up and hit it with a hammer." He also helped solve the problem of leaks either by hunkering down in a faulty trunk or spraying water at the car's rear.

In October 1950, Paul got married and almost lost his job after he and his wife, Gerry, took a three-day honeymoon. Gerry's connections probably saved him. Her dad was a General Foreman, although not in Paul's department. It never occurred to Paul to seek help from the UAW. He wondered if he had even been a member at that time. Most likely, he had joined the union but had little idea what that could mean for him.

Although Paul enjoyed his job at Pontiac Motor, he thought about applying to trade school. Production work "wasn't something that I would want to do all my life. It wasn't challenging enough, I guess. It's like you could do it in your sleep after a while." He was effectively barred from an apprenticeship, however, until he had completed his military obligations. Companies, he noted, "didn't want to get you started in trade school and then have you get drafted," which was highly likely during the Korean War.

Paul's wild streak had come back to haunt him, because he would have been exempt from the draft if he had fulfilled his commitment to the Navy Reserve, which he joined when he was seventeen: "Just a whim. Liked the uniform at the time." He often skipped the mandatory monthly meetings. Once when he participated in a Navy Reserve activity, he and a few others took an amphibious vehicle, a DUKW (pronounced Duck), out for a publicity photo shoot: "Went in the lake and got stuck, high-centered on a sandbar. Couldn't go either way on it. They finally had to get a boat and a wrecker and pull the DUKW off." With such a spotty record, he ended up on inactive reserve and became eligible for the draft.

Rather than wait for the inevitable, Paul and a friend enlisted in early January: "I wanted to go in the Navy and he wanted to go in the Air Force. We flipped and I lost, so we went in the Air Force" and headed to San Antonio. Paul and Gerry had been married only two months, and she "went back to live with her folks." Thousands of new military personnel passed through San Antonio: "They didn't have barracks for them. The first night we slept on the floor of a gymnasium. We didn't have any blankets or anything. Then we got tarpaper shacks and they heated them with wood stoves." He stayed in Texas for about three weeks: "I had KP duty and one Friday I spent the whole day prying frozen fish apart. That was back when fish was mandatory, especially for Catholics. And that's about all I remember of Texas."

From San Antonio, Paul went to Fort George Wright, near Spokane, Washington: "They didn't give you time to think. They kept you busy." He learned of his grandfather's death from a phone call, but wasn't allowed to attend the funeral. He had already lost track of the friend who won the coin flip: "Out of the three weeks that I was in San Antonio, I only saw him once or twice." After a short stay at Fairchild Air Force Base, a few miles west of Spokane, Paul was sent to Forbes Air Force Base, a reactivated World War II facility near Topeka, Kansas. He ended up in the maintenance squadron, making parts for and repairing B-29s: "There was a machine shop. It had lathes, mills, saws, drill presses and that sort of thing. Then another section was a sheet metal shop. Then they had a paint shop and a wood shop. And off in another building they had a welding shop." It turned out to be excellent "on-the-job training as a machinist."

Once Paul was settled in Kansas, Gerry joined him: "I think I got a three-day pass and we got an apartment. It was actually a kitchen and a porch with a pullout daybed, and we shared the bath. This older couple in Topeka had a house. It must've been ten or twelve rooms, and they had every room rented." Gerry quickly found a job at a military supply depot near the air base, "working in the procurement section for a lieutenant colonel, as his secretary. She worked there until I left in November of '53."

Life was mostly good in Kansas. "We bought a new '51 Chevy, and I had that until June of '53." Then the couple decided they wanted a convertible, so during a leave they bought one, a Ford. "The payments on that convertible were $136 a month," which they covered with Gerry's military allotment check. Paul earned "something like ninety-five dollars a month. That went for the apartment." Everything else came from Gerry's paycheck: "We'd go to the drive-ins and play miniature golf and go to a show downtown once in a while." During that first year in Kansas, however, the Mississippi and Missouri Rivers experienced massive flooding, and Paul spent many days on sandbag duty: "We couldn't take the train from Topeka to Kansas City. You couldn't even get out at Topeka because of the flood. Kansas City was underwater, most of it."[2]

In November 1953, the Korean War was over and Paul had to make a decision. He could fulfill his four-year enlistment term or he could leave immediately in return for a six-year commitment to the Air Force Reserves: "I wanted to stay in the service, but my father-in-law said, 'Come on, I'll get you a job.' My wife had never been away from home. I'd been away, so it didn't bother me. But she was homesick." The couple moved back to Pontiac and Paul began work as an outside diameter (O.D.) and inside diameter (I.D.) grinder in Plant 15: "The O.D. grinds the outside of a part and the I.D. grinder grinds the inside."

Paul had that job until he entered the skilled trades in August 1954: "I wanted to get into trade school as either a toolmaker or die maker or machine repairman. I just liked working with my hands." Still, trade school involved academic coursework as well as practical training, and Paul's high school record was mediocre. He said that his father-in-law "hounded" the head of the trade school, "trying to get me in. It's who you know, not what you know a lot of the times. But after you got in, then it was up to you to cut the mustard." In the meantime, Gerry worked as a secretary for Consumers Power while they tried to start a family. She quit while pregnant with their first child, a daughter, who was born in August 1956.

Paul enjoyed trade school: "I just liked the work, tearing something apart, putting it back together, not having any parts left over." To fulfill the program's requirement for community service, Paul helped a disabled Pontiac resident: "He'd had some connection with Pontiac Motor, and he used to be a great golfer, but he had got arthritis and he was confined to a bed. We made a bed for him." Paul helped design a motor to raise and lower the bed so the man's wife "could give him a bath and change the linen and stuff. We made all that in trade school and then got everything chrome-plated." Paul liked machine repair the best and hoped to work in that field in the future.

As it turned out, by attending trade school from 1954 to 1958 Paul was protected from violent swings in the auto industry during those years.[3] The pay during his apprenticeship was not great, but it was consistent and unrelated to the market for new cars. He experienced a total of one week on layoff during the heart of the decade. Before the Ishes' first child was born in 1956, they purchased a house for $13,750: "We used to drive out there every day and watch them build it. It was just strictly a ranch house, a little over 1,000 square foot. We didn't have a garage. My house payment was $104 a month." They sold their convertible and bought a more practical car: "We were doing all right. We didn't have a lot of money to spend, but I was working every day."

Upon graduation from trade school, Paul "was all set to go to the foundry as machine repair." Instead, he joined the machine shop in the product engineering department, where parts were developed for cars scheduled to hit the market in the future. The engineers designed parts, and the skilled tradesmen produced them. The engineers and tradesmen often worked together to fine-tune angles and positioning to make parts fit together in tight spaces. Paul worked on flywheels, castings, ring gears and pinions, transmission parts, banjo housings, and more: "I enjoyed it. We used to cut thread, O.D. and I.D. threads, for days on end. I just like running a lathe. I was on everything—the mills and the blacksmith, making brackets. But most of the time I was there I ran a lathe. For thirty years."

The product engineering department had hired Paul on the condition that he work nights for the first year: "Well hell, nights was fine. In fact I liked it, because you didn't start till 5:00. And then you worked till 1:30. I could wake up at 7:00 in the morning and I'd have enough sleep. So I had all day to monkey around with." He liked night shift so much that he didn't tell Gerry when he became eligible to switch to days. This became an issue when their second child, a son, was born in May 1959: "She found out about it somehow, and either I went on days or I could leave. That was the ultimatum. So I went days. She just wanted me home at night, because she had my daughter and was pregnant with my son." Paul's shift switch caused a minor ruckus over seniority in his department. Some coworkers who wanted to work days had been on the evening shift longer than him and thought they should be allowed to transfer first. But Paul's time in trade school counted as seniority for transfers within his department: "Consequently, I could bump on days. And they were all up in arms."

Paul recalled another time that the UAW contract benefited him: "I didn't start out at the top wages. And usually after thirty days or sixty days, you automatically got a raise. At that time the foreman said I wasn't qualified for top wages. He said that he put me in for it but they turned it down upstairs. Well, the union rep said that that's not true. If your boss puts you in for a raise, it's automatic. I eventually got it. It just took me a little longer." On the whole, however, he said that he had more to do with the union after retirement "than I did all the time I was working."

Carefully managing their money worked well for the Ishes, who never seemed to be living from payday to payday. It certainly helped that product engineering did not experience layoffs, even when times were tough. New models had to be developed and built, whether or not they sold well. There was more of a cushion when Gerry began working part-time at Sears after both children were in school: "We'd take the kids on vacation. We went to Maine. We went to Washington, D.C. and Gettysburg and we'd go up to the U.P.," the Upper Peninsula of Michigan, "and we went out west to Denver and back to Topeka to see the people where we stayed. We used to pile the kids in the station wagon and go to the drive-in. They'd get their pajamas on and we'd pop popcorn and take some pop, and they'd be asleep in the back by the time the movie started, usually." There were plenty of social opportunities: "Our subdivision was real active. We had Fourth of July and Christmas parties and Easter egg hunts and Fourth of July they'd have a big tent and kid games for the kids." Product engineering also offered entertainment: "They had a picnic every year. They had a bowling league, a shotgun skeet trap shoot out at the sportsman's club every year. It was like a family, actually." The Ishes drifted away, however, from longtime membership in Central Methodist Church in Pontiac: "My folks were charter members. I was married in the parsonage, and I was on the board of Central Methodist for a while," but "it got to the point where they were always after money."

Paul had come a long way. He was "kind of wild," but then he "settled down." After military service disrupted his early career as an autoworker, he settled into an apprenticeship and a position as a skilled tradesman—with the help of family connections—and enjoyed a relatively stable, financially secure career: "I could of got out eleven years before I did, but I enjoyed it. If I'd retired and gone out and got another job, I'd a been at the bottom of the totem pole. And this way, where I was at, I had it made."

Paul's daughter, Terri, worked for many years in a salaried position in the Accounts Payable Department for General Motors in Flint. She worked with various vendors on contracts with the company. Paul's son, Mark, went to Northern Michigan University, in Marquette, Michigan, and worked a while for General Dynamics before layoffs hit. He ended up doing the same kind of job, producing tech manuals for tanks, but for a smaller firm. Most of all, he was a big hockey fan, rooting for the Detroit Red Wings.

16

Katie Neumann

(1922–?)

Katie Lapanowski was raised on farms outside Detroit. Her parents had migrated to the United States from Poland and lived for a while in Hamtramck, Michigan, a small city with a sizable Polish population, surrounded by Detroit, before renting their first farm near Stoney Creek, about twenty miles to the north. Born in 1922, Katie was the fifth of eight children. The Lapanowskis focused on dairy and vegetable production. One of Katie's earliest chores was to help prepare vegetables for sale on Wednesdays and Saturdays at either the Eastern Market in Detroit or the Chene-Ferry Market in Hamtramck: "Truck gardening is what they called it. We had to pick everything for the market. We used to have a lot of cucumbers, and we used to put them in a pile, and then we used to sort them out by sizes. And we used to have to clean the onions, and the beets, and the carrots." Her older brothers kept their siblings on task, and when they left home Katie's older sister Mary assumed that role: "She really kept us going." In addition, Katie recalled, "I used to have to take and watch the cows, with my brother." The cows had to be moved from pasture to pasture and then back to the barns for milking. Her mother was the best milker in the family: "When she filled a pail up, she could fill it up real quick. It would be my job to take and pour it in the can. We used to have to cool the milk, and the milkman would come with a great big truck there and we'd have milk cans, and he would take them." Katie also had "to help clean the horse barn, and the cows, too," including "the cow stuff, with a shovel. I'll tell you what, it made me what I am today." But when asked if she liked life on the farm, she answered emphatically: "No I didn't, because it was hard."

When Katie was about twelve, she began quitting outdoor work a couple of hours early to help her mother prepare supper. "And this is why I hate cooking now, I guess," she laughed. For many years, Katie was also responsible for doing the laundry, by hand. She used the family's big pot, the same one used twice a year for hog scalding to "get the hair off" before butchering. The scalding pot ended the day filthy: "I used to have to scrub it real good and clean it up." In the 1930s, the family's farmhouse was connected to the electrical grid, "and the first thing we got was a washing machine and a radio. And I washed clothes for days." It wasn't the most modern washing machine of that era because "it didn't have a wringer on it. But it was so good not to have to go scrubbing." And she was thrilled to enjoy radio programming while doing indoor chores.

Katie found jobs off the farm as well: "When I was about nine or ten years old, we used to have a neighbor. We called them *rich*." The father worked nights, and the mother was afraid to stay home alone with their son: "So I'd go over there and stay with her until he came home in the morning. That's the first time I ever had canned stuff to eat. And the only thing I remember about is she'd give me canned peas, because she knew that we never had anything." When Katie was a bit older, she looked after some neighbor children in the morning and made them breakfast and lunches while their parents, both teachers, got ready for work. As a teenager, Katie worked at a golf course: "I was everything from cooking and serving buffet to being a barmaid." During the summer, she "got a dollar a day," and in the fall, when she was in charge of hay rides, she earned "a dollar and a quarter." She was grateful for the pay: "I was able to save it for when I got married."

After a few years, the Lapanowskis had to move because their landlord sold the property. Katie's parents bought farmland on Leach Road, a few miles southwest of Rochester, where they rebuilt their dairy and vegetable operations. Conditions on both farms were rustic: "We never had a bathroom. We used to dig a hole, and when it got full we'd just move it further down and move the toilet over." Katie's mother and a neighbor woman "were midwives for each other, because they didn't go to the hospital to have babies." A younger sister entered the world feet first, a "breech birth," so her dad went to Rochester to bring a doctor to the farm. Although everything turned out well, Katie remembered being frightened when her mother asked her to go get some scissors: "She was going to cut the cord, but I was scared she was going to harm the baby." Equally memorable for Katie was that her mother worked the next day: "She was rough. She had all the kids at home. She never would go to the hospital.

She was sick, she cured herself." The kids learned to be tough and self-reliant as well. In addition to chores, they walked over four miles to school each morning and back home every afternoon.

Despite the relentlessness of running a farm, there were some breaks in the routines. In the winter, Katie recalled, the family "couldn't afford anything, but we'd make skis out of barrels, and we'd take some inner tubes and cut them in half and pound the nails in there to keep our feet in there." On Saturday nights, her brother John used the family's "stake truck," the one that usually carried vegetables to market, to drive to the movie theater in Rochester: "He'd take all the neighbor kids. We'd jump on that stake truck and go to a show for ten cents apiece." When she was fourteen, Katie got her first driving lesson in that same truck, from the farm to Hamtramck: "I mean, through Hamtramck—and they had street cars there at that time. And oh my goodness, the street cars would go in the middle of the road and those stake trucks are big!" With a hint of resentment, Katie recalled end-of-summer thrashing parties, when neighbors helped each other harvest wheat: "When the thrashers come, that's the only time we ever had real butter. And we had better meat because we had to have pork chops for the farmers that helped." Much more enjoyable were the frequent gatherings at a recreation area built by Polish immigrants: "We all got together, the younger people, and we used to go to Warsaw Park. They used to give Polish dances."[1]

Unfortunately, the Lapanowski family system disintegrated during the 1930s. Her older siblings struck out on their own: "Two brothers got a job in Detroit at Chevrolet Gear and Axle, and the other one went to Briggs." Her sister Mary left for a job at Fisher Body. During these transitions, Katie's parents faced bankruptcy and the loss of the Leach Road property. This was not uncommon during the Depression. Still, Katie knew that questionable decisions contributed to their predicament: "Dad was kind of careless. I can remember that he bought a piano. We lost that. He bought a car. We lost that. But he managed to keep our horses." Katie, her parents, and her younger siblings moved to a different farm near Stoney Creek. There were no buses to take her to high school, however, and her family no longer had a car, so she dropped out during her junior year. Katie's father took a job at a Briggs plant in Detroit. Her mother gave the city a try. "She lived there for a week," but her dad "played numbers a lot," hoping for a lucky break. Katie's mom did not approve and returned to the farm. Her parents "were never divorced," Katie said, "but they were separated."

In the late summer of 1941, just before she turned nineteen, Katie married Anthony Kardys. She had met him at a dance at Warsaw Park. Anthony commuted from his family's farm to a job at the Dodge Main plant in Hamtramck.

Although two of Katie's brothers entered the military during WWII, Anthony was exempt because of a broken eardrum. The couple had dreams of owning a home and having children, so to help earn a down payment Katie got a job at the Mount Clemens Pottery Company. She made plates, appreciated the income, and stayed there until her daughter, Nancy, was born in 1943.[2] Katie was a stay-at-home mother for a couple of years. Still hoping to buy a house, she and Anthony rented an apartment, but since they didn't own much to furnish a home, in January 1945 Katie looked for another job. Her top priority was to buy a washing machine. After leaving the family farm, she no longer had the modern appliance that transformed her childhood: "I needed a washer. Oh, I needed a washer."

Katie was hired at the Fisher Body plant in Pontiac, where her sister Mary worked. It helped that her mother lived nearby and was willing to look after two-year-old Nancy. At Fisher Body, Katie's job was burring. Many car parts would come down the line with metal protrusions, imperfections called burrs, that remained after the stamping process. Her task was "to make it smooth" with a tool that was like a whirring stone: "You'd used to just go *bzzzz,* and take the burr off."

Just two months into the job, however, she was laid off: "I never did go back." But she had to earn money, because she and her husband had purchased a house: "Our payments were forty dollars a month, and my husband was working at Dodge Main, but he was laid off, off and on. It was even hard to make that forty dollars a month payment."[3] She knew that auto work paid better than anything else, so she "stopped in to Pontiac Motors. I used to go past there to go to Fisher Body's. Pontiac Motors hired me that same day, and I went to work the next day."

Katie's job was in the core room of the foundry, where sand was used to make molds for car parts. It was hot, dangerous work, unlike her job at Fisher Body. When the sand molds were ready, "they'd pour that iron in. Many times, the iron would spill over. Like I always said, I did kind of a Polish jig." But her dancing wasn't always successful: "I got burns, you know, on my legs and that." Core room workers used powerful air hoses for cleaning, and occasionally lost control of them: "That hose would fly around all over. It snapped just like a snake. People got hurt, too. I mean you'd run like heck. I got hit a couple times. It stung, yeah it stung." Other times workers were spared because the hose got tangled in nearby machinery. There were serious injuries in the core room, and worse. Katie recalled when a coworker "had his fingers cut off. They wanted me to get that glove with the fingers in there, and I wouldn't do it." One day, when a repairman was working on a large machine, "somebody pushed a button, and the guy got smashed in it. And that was it. That was one of the worst ones that I can remember. It's terrible that I remember all that stuff. I got a lot of memories from there."

Most of the core room workers were either white women or Black men, with a few Black women. White men appeared on occasion, but "they'd only work a couple days and they'd quit because in the foundry it was terrible—the smoke and the smell. You could tell a person that worked in the foundry just by the smell." The white guys "was able to get jobs someplace else. They didn't want the foundry at all." Katie had worked in an all-white department at Fisher Body, so the core room was a huge change: "There was a lot of colored people, and I was scared. I don't know why, but some would talk rough and I was scared. I never was around colored people. I was just like on a farm there, and then when I took and got married, I worked in a pottery. And there was no Black people there in the pottery. But they were all right. You just had to show them that you weren't scared, that's all. I learned a lot, and they got to be some of the best friends that I ever had. I mean, they stuck up for you." Baseball teams and bowling leagues helped break down those barriers, and Katie enjoyed playing those sports.[4] Still, she remembered that it bothered her when a Black coworker said, "'Katie, you're going to go further than I will, just by the color of your skin.' I'll never forget that. And I told him, 'Alex, you know, that's the poorest excuse. You're just damn lazy. Where did I get ahead here? I'm working right here with you.'" Despite this disagreement, Katie and Alex produced a newsletter together reporting on issues in the foundry.

Katie took some time off in 1947 after the birth of her second child, a son they called J.R. She returned to work as soon as possible, though, because of the pressure to make house payments, and her mother moved in to take care of the kids. Many of her women coworkers didn't have such reliable child care: "They'd have to have somebody come over and watch them. If they didn't show up, they'd be late for work and they'd get heck from the foreman. Of course, if you had a good foreman, he'd kind of let it go."

Upon returning to the core room, Katie worked on the slingers, which delivered sand to the molds. The sand was stored "way up in the air" and would "pour down" through a tube that they called a slinger. "We used to have to move it back and forth. You had to be careful. When they didn't hit it just right, we'd get sand all over." To be able to cover for absences, most core room workers gained experience on different jobs: "I worked in every department in there except the wire room. So we weren't doing the same thing over and over again." She liked the variety, especially when she was able to avoid jobs that involved intense heat.

Occasionally, Katie was time-studied to determine workload expectations. Workers had an understanding that those being timed should do their jobs at a reasonable pace to keep workloads manageable. Katie recalled that when she was studied, she "was very nervous. I'd try to slow down, and yet I'm not a slow person. You're so used to working, because we had to get so many done." If she worked too fast, she said, her coworkers "would get mad—you're supposed to take your time." When not being monitored, failure to meet production goals would result in "a bawling out." Yet production shortages weren't necessarily the workers' fault. Sometimes "the machine broke down. They used to have a lot of problems." Indeed, there were times when workers took it upon themselves to break their machines "so they wouldn't have to do it, because they couldn't do it. And that bothered me." To be fair, though, she insisted that "a lot of people worked just like I did."

Katie stayed in the core room for eleven years, until 1956. During that time, she rarely had need for her union shop committeeman: "I maybe called him two or three times. And it was nothing really major. If I had a problem, I was able to talk it out with the boss." She said that when her foreman accused her of being responsible for problems, she "always proved that I wasn't." She was subdued but proud about her work in the core room: "It made me what I am. It made me strong." She never missed a chance to tell coworkers that "everybody should take and work in the foundry. They'd appreciate their job now."

Katie had no particular desire to leave the core room, especially after she landed a much easier position there, documenting the amount of scrap metal in the various departments. But the memory of her dead coworker bothered her—"that really got me, that guy that got smashed"—and some men tried to rid the department of women. There were also layoffs, which meant a wholesale shuffling of positions throughout Pontiac Motor. "They needed some people in the gun plant," Katie explained, and she had enough seniority, so she took the opportunity to transfer and worked on a milling machine, completely different from anything she had done before. After a year on that job, however, Pontiac Motor retrenched again, and Katie was transferred to Plant 9, where she helped make connecting rods for a while before switching to camshaft production. Her responsibilities included filing and burring, much like she had done years ago at Fisher Body. The difference was that instead of working on small parts with hand-held tools, she and her coworkers inserted connecting rods into "a great big round machine" that did the burring: "Two of us was working. One put them in, one took them out." In terms of technical know-how, "It was an easy job. You could do it with your eyes closed after a while." But the rods "were heavy."

The connecting rod job was on second shift, but to care for her children and for getting rides she preferred days, so Katie bid on a first-shift job and got one, inspecting camshafts. It was a lot of responsibility, and she could end up taking flak from both workers and foremen. Once a worker lashed out at her when she "red-tagged" his camshafts as unacceptable: "He was mad that I caught it, see? But I was an inspector. If I didn't get it, I'd catch heck." She brought the issue up with the union: "And he says, 'Well that was shop talk.' And I said, 'Well, as far as I'm concerned, that is not shop talk. My husband don't even use that.'" Another time a foreman tried to convince her that she had rejected parts by mistake, but she outsmarted him: "Whenever I used to check stuff, I would take a piece of chalk and on the bottom of that big basket, I would initial what was wrong with it. Well, one morning my boss called me over there and he says, 'Katie, these are red-tagged and there's nothing wrong.' So I walked around the basket, and I looked down to see what it was that I had initialed. And I went and got the gauge, and I didn't go to the first layer. I went to the second layer." As she suspected, the foreman had covered the faulty parts with acceptable ones: "They'd try to pull that because that's a bad mark against him. But hey, if I didn't catch it, I'd be at fault, too."

Throughout her working career, Katie observed the sexual dynamics when male foremen made advances on women employees: "Oh yeah, you could see it. Being-old fashioned, I was against that. Some of them got away with it, too. But as long as it didn't involve me, I didn't care what they did." Some women, she said, went out with their foremen "to get the good jobs. Yeah, they did. I've seen that happen." Another way to detect such relationships was if a woman failed to meet production goals but "never got a bawling out. A lot of women there were probably having problems at home then, too. I don't know. What they did, that was their business. I didn't care, as long as it didn't interfere with my thing."

Once when working with the local union during a strike, Katie grappled with her racial assumptions: "I used to think it was terrible that whites and Blacks would go out with each other. And I had to go way downtown with this colored guy. He took me downtown to the union hall for something. And I'm sitting in the car and I'm looking, and I see people are looking at me. 'Hey, she's with a Black guy,' you know. And ever since then, that cured me right then and there. That goes to show you what I was thinking before was evil."

Throughout the 1950s, Katie and Anthony never took a vacation. They "just couldn't," because they were "working all the time to make those *forty-dollar payments*. And paying for a car." Anthony's job at Dodge Main was an "off and on" proposition, in part because of layoffs, and occasionally because his parents needed help. Either way, he got to use the car and Katie had to find transportation to Pontiac Motor, about twenty miles away: "I had to hitch a ride with people that lived out that way." Her mother helped out in many ways: "She was Polish, you know, and she made pierogies and she made golabkis. And she took care of the yard. She still had the farmer in her." They always had a large garden, and they relied on it: "I froze a lot of stuff." For entertainment, "Warsaw Park was our main thing," but they also enjoyed socializing with their neighbors, several of whom had grown up on farms near hers when she was young. "They all moved someplace around here," Katie explained, while sitting in the home she lived in fifty years earlier, "and we'd go from one house to another house, and we'd have picnics at our houses." To all the neighbor kids, she was "Aunt Katie." Her place was the center of activity in the neighborhood, she said, "because I had the big yard, the big house."

Katie's marriage, however, did not survive the '50s. She and her husband were divorced in 1959, after a bit more than seventeen years together. "It was a sad thing," Katie said softly, "but we got along better after we got divorced." Still, she emphasized, "it was something that hurt." After the divorce, one of the first things she did was buy a blue 1959 Chevy: "I got strong enough that I went in and got that. I had to, because I couldn't find a ride to work, so I got enough nerve to get one." The house still wasn't paid off, though, and now she lived there on one income with her mother and kids: "It made it rough. I was kind of scared—I was worrying about this and that."

Although Katie grew up fairly isolated on a farm, she developed multiple skills, had a level head, and had a sharp eye for what was going on around her. She mastered difficult jobs in the core room, moved easily to connecting rods, and stared down foremen as a camshaft inspector. Around 1970 she began work in quality control, overseeing the inspectors and ensuring that their gauges were accurate. She credited the UAW with helping her become a better person. She also gave back, working hard on local union issues, including in-plant fund drives for retirement presents and the United Way, and organizing picket duty when necessary. She also continued to enjoy bowling leagues and baseball. She admired Walter Reuther and all the gains she attributed to the efforts of top-level UAW officials, but she was turned off by local union politics. "Boy they did fight one against the other," she said, referring to people vying for shop committee positions at Pontiac Motor. "And that I could never understand. Pass this literature around so you wouldn't vote for so and so. Nine times out of ten it was all wrong." Yet she held top local officers in high regard: "All the presidents at the union that we've had, they were all great." She and her second husband, Bill Neumann, continued to live with Katie's mother in the house whose payments had caused such worry. Katie could measure how far she had come when she considered where her mother had been: "She only went to the third grade. My mother could only spell her first name. And when she used to get her social security check, she used to make an 'X' and I would sign."

Conclusion

This sample of life history narratives demonstrates that when we settle for simple generalizations about postwar autoworkers, we're likely to misunderstand them as human beings. These stories place auto work in the larger contexts of people's lives, which were far more complicated than the label "autoworker" can capture. This conclusion will offer nuanced generalizations based on several recurrent themes in these life histories, but others might see different themes or emphasize other points in response to what they've read. If nothing else, these narratives suggest how complicated a more complete history of autoworkers would be, for example, if we were able to consider hundreds, thousands, or even hundreds of thousands of workers' lives.

Family Traumas

Autoworkers' lives did not begin when they took their first factory jobs. Early experiences might not have determined their life trajectories, but childhoods were formative. Margaret Beaudry had a loving mother, but rarely saw her father, who worked away from home for long stretches. Margaret's positive energy was infectious and her sense of self and self-worth could not be shaken. Paul Ross never met his father and his mother seemed burdened by his presence, which bothered him throughout his life. We don't know what Paul's mother thought about her situation, but it could not have been easy to be a single mom in the

1920s and 1930s. Again, no particular family dynamics determined ones' life, but personalities and outlooks had been influenced well before auto work.

Elwin Brown's parents separated when he was a child and he lived with an aunt and uncle for several years. Emerald Neal's parents divorced when he was young and he lived with an aunt through high school. Neal's older brother had died of pneumonia at age six. Lucky Coleman was raised mainly by older siblings and kind townspeople after his dad died. Joe Woods's mother was chronically ill. Ernie Liles's father died in a flood. Paul Ish's older brother died from drinking turpentine and his parents never recovered from the loss. Four of Edith Arnold's eleven siblings died either in childbirth or infancy, and her mother seemed distant and short-tempered, perhaps from these ordeals. Gene Johnson's older brother Calvin died when Gene was six, a family trauma that must have triggered terrible feelings when one of his daughters nearly died of illness. When he was a child himself, L.J. Scott cared for his niece, Louise, after her mother, L.J.'s sister, died in childbirth. L.J.'s father was diagnosed with prostate cancer, leaving L.J. in charge of the family farm at age fifteen. Katie Neumann's parents separated when she was a teenager, and Dorothy Sackle lost two younger siblings, her mother, and her father during her late adolescence and early adulthood. The resiliency demonstrated by this sampling of 1950s autoworkers is remarkable, but it also suggests that family disruptions and traumas were ordinary. These people persevered, often with unsettled quests for love and acceptance, while developing keen survival strategies, which ultimately but far from inevitably included auto work.

Education

Working in an auto plant during and after World War II did not require a high school degree, and relatively few of these people obtained one. Margaret Beaudry, Emerald Neal, Elwin Brown, Paul Ish, and Dorothy Sackle completed high school, although Paul's graduation came a year and a half late because of his escapades in Nebraska. Dorothy hoped that her high school degree would allow her to become a secretary, but she ended up as an autoworker instead before a career switch to her preferred field after she turned fifty. Tight family budgets prevented some from completing their schooling. Edith Arnold's parents couldn't afford to keep her in school and arranged for her to become a nanny. Katie Neumann dropped out of school because her family couldn't afford to keep their car during the Depression and there were no school buses. Paul Ross remembered "acting out" a lot in school, which makes sense given the chaos in his family life. James McGuire excelled at math, and in his estimation "was way down below everybody" at everything else. Later, in vocational training programs such as refrigeration, air conditioning, appliance repair, and surveying, he developed high-level math skills, but he was insecure about his lack of formal academic credentials. James Franklin dropped out of high school to take a job at the Willow Run Bomber Plant during World War II.

Those who grew up working in cotton fields generally missed several months of school each year. That was true for African Americans such as L.J. Scott, who regretted having to work all day just as classes got more difficult and interesting. But even white kids like Gene Johnson, whose family worked as farm laborers, missed lots of school each year. Ernie Liles drifted away from school, focusing instead on his family's farm and hiring himself out to chop and pick cotton. Joe Woods was limited less by the need to work in the fields than the reality that the local segregated school for Black children only went through sixth grade.

For most of the people profiled here, finishing high school was a luxury that families could not afford, whether or not graduation was a goal. It would have been interesting to see what would have happened if Margaret Beaudry had been able to develop her singing and theater skills, or if James McGuire had been able to pursue higher education in math or engineering, or if L.J. Scott could have had a fair shot at medical school. There was no shortage of talent, intelligence, grit, and resourcefulness in this group. But white-collar employment was never seriously on their radar screens, and we should be wary about assuming that achieving such status would have been an unqualified mark of progress.[1] Nevertheless, upward mobility in terms of seeking better, higher-paying jobs motivated most of these workers until they either found a position they liked well enough or couldn't see a clear path to anything better. The gold standard for blue-collar work was the skilled trades, and the fact that only white men, even those with marginal scholastic records, could reach that level during these years meant that the largest barrier was race and sex discrimination, not interrupted or unavailable educational opportunities.

Early Jobs

As children, all of these people contributed to the welfare of their families, either by earning cash, doing necessary chores, or eventually, by striking out on their own. Many of these autoworkers grew up or worked on farms, whether in Michigan (Paul Ish, Elwin Brown, Katie Neumann), Illinois (Edith Arnold), Missouri (Gene Johnson), Arkansas (Ernie Liles), or Alabama (L.J. Scott, Joe Woods). Others, for example James McGuire, worked in large family gardens. It's telling that so many 1950s autoworkers grew up on farms. Most of them weren't raised near auto plants and didn't observe immediate family members going to work in auto factories. Elwin Brown was the only one in this sample who followed his father into auto work, and Elwin preferred to be in the printing business. Whenever Detroit automakers ramped up production, they recruited workers in a wide radius, mostly from rural areas.[2] It makes sense, then, that farm chores were central childhood experiences for so many future autoworkers.

Margaret Beaudry babysat for neighbors in Michigan's Upper Peninsula. Dorothy Sackle, James McGuire, and Lucky Coleman sold newspapers. Dorothy later got a job at Kresge's, a dime store, while dreaming of becoming a secretary. Edith Arnold had enough sisters that she was assigned outdoor farm chores, which she loved, before her parents forced her to become a nanny, which she hated. Joe Woods helped his dad catch catfish to sell in a nearby town in Alabama. James Franklin got a job at an Ypsilanti restaurant. Gene Johnson sold illegal "home brew" and sawed firewood for cookstoves in Missouri. L.J. Scott left cotton fields in Alabama to pick fruit in Florida. Katie Neumann was a mother's helper before getting a job at a golf course as a teenager. Paul Ross lied about his age and latched on with the Civilian Conservation Corps in northern Michigan. Ernie Liles was still a teenager when he found work on dam projects in Arkansas.

Many of these jobs became frames of reference for auto work. Gene Johnson and Ernie Liles, for example, considered labor in a cotton field to be far more difficult than anything they did in an auto factory. The low pay in most non-auto jobs increased the allure of auto work when it was available. Jobs such as caddying, restaurant work, and even agricultural labor also became lifelines during layoffs in the auto industry. In any event, these autoworkers from the 1950s had a wide variety of work experiences before entering auto plants. Most were used to long, hard days on the job, if not the machines and noise they encountered in factories.

Religion and Church

Religion and church played complicated roles in the lives of these autoworkers. Most, but not all, attended church services as children. Paul Ish grew up as part of the Central Methodist Church in Pontiac and as an adult served on the board for that congregation before eventually leaving. Church was "drilled in" to Elwin Brown, first as a Presbyterian and later in a non-denominational congregation. He and his wife loved to sing church music together. Ernie Liles grew up in the Church of God, but eventually joined a non-denominational congregation. He felt called to the ministry as an adult and left auto work for several years to lead a church in Arkansas. James Franklin was raised Baptist, but was uncomfortable with the denomination's racial divisions and joined the Church of Christ in 1960. Strong religious beliefs about the man as head of the household influenced his decisions regarding where to work, especially during layoffs. Joe Woods was a devout Christian, with some acknowledged lapses. The mourners' bench at his childhood church in Alabama made a profound impression on him as a step toward atonement. Edith Arnold enjoyed her Presbyterian congregation as a child and dreamed of becoming a missionary. As an adult, she searched mostly in vain for a sense of community in a church.

As a divorced, single mother, Dorothy Sackle had a strained relationship with the Catholic Church. Katie Neumann grew up in a Polish family, presumably with Catholic roots, but she mentioned little about religion. She did, however, divorce her first husband in the late 1950s. Divorce had troubled Dorothy Sackle on religious grounds, but Katie, at least in retrospect, had no misgivings. There was no indication that church played much of a role in Paul Ross's life. L.J. Scott's family was divided by religion. His mother emphasized religious instruction while his father wanted nothing to do with church. L.J. had fond memories of the annual, two-day camp meetings held in the area and wore his "Sunday clothes" to apply for a job at Pontiac Motor. He spoke of the need to "mix a little bit of religion in there" to maintain his bearings during difficult times. Gene Johnson remembered his brother Calvin carrying him piggy-back to Sunday School before Calvin's death. Yet Gene's parents did not attend church, even before Calvin died. Gene and his wife, Agnes, ultimately devoted their lives to the church as part of a promise they made when a daughter defied the odds and recovered from viral meningitis and a son regained the use of his legs after several years of disability.

Although the interviews hardly covered this topic exhaustively, religion and church were clearly foundational for many of these workers and remained a touchstone if not always a dominant force through adulthood. In labor history, religion is often analyzed in terms of its role, positive or negative, in union organizing campaigns. Concerning the auto industry, with its largely immigrant workforce in the early decades of the twentieth century, the role of Catholicism in the organizing campaigns of the 1930s and into the Cold War era has received significant attention.[3] For the workers profiled in this book, however, religion did not seem to play much of a role in forming attitudes about unionization. The UAW was well-entrenched when most of them became autoworkers, and most Communists in the UAW had been ousted before the major upsurges in hiring at auto plants in the 1950s. But to varying degrees, religion and churches provided ethical guidance, community, frustration, and the possibility for redemption. Through the 1950s, religion appeared to play a more prominent role in most of these workers' lives than did concerns about the UAW's bargaining agenda or politics, local or national, topics that have justifiably been of great concern to historians. There does not appear to be any formula to predict what kind of religious upbringing might have produced activism or acceptance in response to injustice, any more than one can trace clear, secular explanations for personal behavior. But a congregation could be a significant part of one's life and identity, and a tip from a minister or parishioner often resulted in temporary or long-term employment.

Hobbies and Outside Interests

Paying attention to hobbies and outside interests also helps us better understand these autoworkers. Some of their passions were evident as children and extended into adulthood, while others were discovered later in life, sometimes flourishing in retirement. Among his many interests, Elwin Brown loved aviation, the Boy Scouts, model trains, and the American Legion. Polish heritage brought large numbers of people, including Dorothy Kudrycki (Sackle) to Warsaw Park to eat, dance, socialize, and seek romance. Ernie Liles enjoyed picnics with dozens of fellow Arkansas transplants, enough to field two softball teams for afternoons of competition. Before devoting his life to Christianity, Gene Johnson played music at "hillbilly" clubs, popular with white southern migrants. He continued to play music with his church orchestra, and he also played competitive softball well into his fifties. Margaret Beaudry was passionate about singing and dancing and bought a karaoke machine to be her backup band. Joe Woods was an avid gardener. Edith Arnold turned an interest in arts and crafts into a side business by doing textile painting and making ties, handkerchiefs, and scarves. She also enjoyed informal socializing with neighbors. She had to wait until widowhood to pursue her interest in travel, visiting Alaska, Hawaii, and Branson, Missouri before her money ran out. Paul Ross liked to sail, something he definitely did not do as a child. He also spent many years leading the Elks Club drill team. James Franklin enjoyed deep-sea fishing during his travels to Gulf Coast states. Lucky Coleman liked bowling and golf, while Emerald Neal developed an interest in antiques, a hobby that eventually became a business.

If we imagine hundreds of thousands of autoworkers in the 1950s, each with various interests, we can sense why UAW leaders were frustrated with the membership's lack of focus on union issues.[4] Unsteady work and the constant scramble to make ends meet mattered as well, as did broader family responsibilities, but these were human beings with likes and dislikes regarding activities that brought them pleasure. If we assess these autoworkers on the basis of what they liked to do, as opposed to what they apparently did not do, our analysis gets complicated, to be sure, but helps us understand more clearly how they approached their lives.

Marriage and Family

Marriage was a significant focus for each of the autoworkers profiled here, with widely different experiences. Edith Arnold married the first man who paid serious attention to her and was miserable until widowhood. Out of love and a sense of duty, she stayed home when her children were young, but she yearned to be part of the outside world, working and traveling. She overcame her husband's resistance with passive aggressiveness to work outside the home after her children were established in school. Margaret Beaudry dearly loved her husband, Marvin, but also felt compelled to tell him "white lies" to get his permission to seek a paid job after staying home with their kids while they were young. Paul Ish didn't tell his wife, Gerry, that he could transfer to day shift, and she was angry, but they overcame his mistake and were married for sixty-four years, raising two children. Les Coleman's first marriage ended after nine years with two kids and questions about where his wife went when she disappeared. Les gained custody of the children and was married a second time, for sixty years, to Marilyn, with whom he had a loving relationship and two more children. L.J. Scott and Joe Woods had very brief first marriages, followed by lengthy second marriages. They had children and stepchildren to support and care for, and L.J. also remained close with his niece, Louise.

Some of these autoworkers were wed when very young, for example Ernie Liles, who was in his early twenties when he married fifteen-year-old Mary Ann. They raised two children and remained together in 2023. Emerald Neal was still in high school when he married Cara Bent, who had recently graduated, and they kept their marriage secret for a year. Emerald became a responsible husband and parent to their children, and the couple remained lovingly together until Cara died in 2000. Dorothy Sackle's first marriage was abusive and violent, ending in divorce and single parenthood, and her much better second marriage ended with the untimely death of her husband. Paul Ross had two marriages end in divorce, with five children in all, and felt adrift late in life without a wife. James Franklin remarried after his first wife died, and he thought deeply about how to make his blended family—three daughters and seven stepchildren—function best for all. Thomas Nowak worked two jobs as much as possible—"hustling," he said—to support his wife, Rosella, and their ten children. He was away from home much of the time, but the couple was married for fifty-six years until Rosella's death. James McGuire also worked long hours and multiple jobs to support his family, and his wife, Mary, worked for pay as well, helping to run a University of Michigan dormitory. Mary sat with James during the interview for this project to help his memory, which had been affected by medical treatments. After leaving the military, Gene Johnson was completely devoted to his wife and children. Elwin Brown emphasized the importance of family in his marriage and in his role as a father to his daughter, Sherry. When Sherry had to move home with her two children, Elwin relished the time he could spend with his grandsons, even helping one with his Eagle Scout project.

It's impossible, of course, to measure the quality of a marriage in terms of years, number of children, and "on-balance" conclusions reached after decades. Even the best marriages include difficult times, thorny problem-solving, resentments, and crises, along with intimacy, support, and caring. But when these autoworkers reflected on their lives, the importance of marriage and family was evident, for better and for worse, with satisfaction and regret. In the 1940s and 1950s, especially as these workers were starting to have children, decision-making for married couples included serious family considerations, for example what shift would be best for child care arrangements, whether working outside the home or finding a second job was necessary, or in the case of Elwin Brown, whether they could find an apartment from which they wouldn't be evicted if their infant cried. A child with serious health issues made a possible military career impractical for Gene Johnson. Margaret Beaudry's husband, Marvin, learned how to curl their daughter's hair, slowly but perfectly, which gave Margaret some peace of mind while at work. Autoworkers cared about their jobs, for sure, but they also cared about their family relationships and desired to feel loved and appreciated, even if in some cases they discovered this through the loss of those connections. If we think of autoworkers as multidimensional human beings, again, the results are complicated beyond our ability to fully know and understand, but we'll be closer to achieving a meaningful sense of how they experienced these years.

Military Service

Military service directly affected most male autoworkers and indirectly affected the women profiled here. Some auto careers began after military service, while the draft interrupted auto work for many others. Thomas Nowak served in Europe during World War II and was profoundly affected by the death of an army friend during battle. James McGuire fought in the Pacific, in an engineering unit because of his color blindness, and almost drowned in a training incident before reaching combat zones. Paul Ross learned valuable technical skills as well as how to profit from graft while serving on a ship in the Pacific during and after WWII. Gene Johnson helped build a WWII military base near his home in Missouri before heading to Michigan for war work. Then he was drafted, and despite mediocre academic credentials, he was assigned to a high-security job at the War Department Personnel Center. Les Coleman was exempt from military service during WWII because he was a skilled worker, considered essential for the war effort. James Franklin's service confirmed in his mind the value of all types of work. Barred from combat because of his race, he drove trucks as part of the Red Ball Express, which involved harrowing, no-headlight drives at night to deliver critical supplies after the D-day invasion. Margaret Beaudry married her husband before he was shipped out for duty during WWII, and the wartime crisis allowed her to find work in a factory. Dorothy Sackle's marriage was in trouble before her husband was drafted, but his affairs while in the service hastened the end of their relationship when she learned about them after his return.

Paul Ish enlisted in the military to fulfill his service requirement, which would make him eligible for a skilled trades apprenticeship. Elwin Brown was drafted away from an inspecting job and served in Korea, training soldiers on the Browning Automatic Rifle and entering Non-Commissioned Officer school. Ernie Liles quipped that he fought "with a clipboard" during the Korean War. He was drafted too close to war's end to see combat and got out of the military as quickly as he could. Also drafted during the Korean War, L.J. Scott experienced maddening discrimination while serving as a cook. Joe Woods fought in Korea, and his service became a frame of reference for the racial discrimination he faced in civilian life before and after the war.

There is no way to consider the lives of autoworkers in this period without taking into account military service. Some experienced trauma that affected them the rest of their lives. Others turned military experience into membership in the skilled trades. Some felt part of a larger cause, while others questioned American values to their core. It was important that seniority in auto jobs continued to accrue while in the military. Those gains proved advantageous for job security during layoffs and for pension eligibility. But getting a draft notice while trying to be an autoworker or starting a family had a profound impact on one's life trajectory.

Secondary Support Systems

Because layoffs were so frequent, autoworkers had to develop secondary support systems. That often meant having a fallback job, or even holding down two jobs simultaneously. The people profiled here clearly identified as autoworkers. But in the early post-WWII era, it was hardly obvious to them that auto work would pan out. During layoffs, Emerald Neal occasionally went back to his home state, West Virginia, to look for work. When he stayed in Michigan during slack times, he got a job as a cyclone fence installer, which involved hard labor for uncertain pay. Les Coleman found a job at Argus Camera Shop in Ann Arbor, Michigan during unstable times at the Ypsilanti Ford Plant. Margaret Beaudry always had a backup job waiting for her at Neisner's, a local department store. L.J. Scott tried anything to make money when laid off and eventually operated a barber shop in addition to keeping his job at Pontiac Motor. Ernie Liles occasionally traveled to fruit orchards in western Michigan or back to Arkansas to pick cotton. Edith Arnold and her husband were each other's secondary financial support system, as they were rarely laid off from their auto jobs at the same time. Edith also found work at a junior high cafeteria during a layoff. Elwin Brown was a golf caddy during the 1958 recession. James Franklin's support system involved shifting between the Ford Rouge plant, Kaiser-Frazer, a GM plant in Flint, and the Ypsilanti Ford Plant. When laid off at one place, he usually got hired at another. Dorothy Sackle held a second job as a house cleaner. Gene Johnson drove a cab whenever he was laid off. James McGuire often held two auto jobs, a violation of UAW rules, but didn't get caught. Thomas Nowak held two full-time jobs for a while, in an auto plant and for American Airlines at Willow Run Airport. Paul Ross ran a gambling ring in the Pontiac Motor complex, making enough extra money when the plant operated to get through tough times.

It's fair to ask whether or not these people were autoworkers when they were doing jobs outside that industry. Business and civic leaders in Detroit hoped those who were laid off would leave auto work and the region when not needed in the factories and return when demand for cars picked up.[5] Often a version of that happened, because secondary jobs did not pay as much as auto work and most people were eager to return to auto plants when production resumed. For several years, however, James McGuire was an exception when he was in charge of maintenance at the University of Michigan Lawyers' Club and refused opportunities to return to auto work. If nothing else, the existence of secondary support networks demonstrates that it took plenty of ingenuity, often born of desperation, to make ends meet as an autoworker during these years. What Thomas Nowak called "hustling" was a consistent and at times a dominating force in these people's lives.

Danger at Work

Many people here emphasized the danger they faced on their auto jobs or the trauma they experienced from coworkers' accidents. Dorothy Sackle remembered dipping auto parts into vats of hot acid, a job one could only hold for six months at a time because of acknowledged but not clearly conveyed health risks. Katie Neumann worked in a department where a man was smashed to death on the job and she avoided that building for the rest of her career. At other times, Katie dodged molten iron, lucky to escape with only minor burns, and out-of-control air hoses. She also refused to retrieve a glove that contained a coworker's fingers, severed by a machine. James McGuire worked with mercury, apparently with minimal safety precautions. Gene Johnson lost hearing in one ear and much of it in the other before earplugs were mandated on stamping press jobs. It was common in his department for workers to lose arms or hands. Gene also couldn't count the number of times he ended up in First Aid for pieces of metal in his eyes, from grinding excess material off parts. Margaret Beaudry remembered several coworkers losing hands or fingers, and inexperienced workers always got the most dangerous assignments. Thomas Nowak saw a coworker lose his fingers in a machine accident. Once, Nowak was hit in the back with a heavy box of radiator caps and said "it hurt for the longest time." James Franklin's eyes were damaged by his welding job. Paul Ross remembered having to replace heavy pipes, often on forty-foot ladders: "We lost a lot of people in that pipe gang. You fall and you're dead." L.J. Scott barely saved one of his hands when a glove he was wearing got snagged in a drill.

When we focus on wages and benefits, we can overlook the courage and perhaps denial it took to go to work each day in an auto plant.[6] Company-paid health insurance couldn't replace an arm or fingers or bring one back to life. Nor could it erase emotional traumas. As Katie Neumann reflected on the accidents and deaths she had witnessed: "I can picture all that, a lot of stuff there. I got a lot of memories from there."

Relationships with the UAW

Although the people interviewed for this project identified as UAW members, their relationships with the auto union were varied and complicated during this period. Paul Ish never thought to seek help from the union when he nearly lost his job after his honeymoon. He maintained that he had more involvement with the UAW after retirement than in all the years he worked in auto plants. Ernie Liles, on the other hand, attributed everything good about his job to the UAW and never hesitated to file a grievance. Edith Arnold feared that she would look like a troublemaker if she used the union to solve workplace problems. Yet Paul Ross insisted that he would have been "dog beans" if not for the union, and he later became a benefits representative to help fellow workers. Dorothy Sackle resented the deduction of union dues from her paychecks in the '30s and '40s, because she and her husband were trying to save money for a house. Margaret Beaudry had her auto career saved more than once because of union protections and she eventually served a term as a shop committee member. Elwin Brown's father had participated in the organizing campaign at Pontiac Motor and instilled in his son a sense of loyalty to the UAW. L.J. Scott was painfully aware that corrupt white local committee members discriminated against Black workers, which inspired him to become a union representative. Joe Woods had his job saved by a white union shop committee member, but he also observed many incidents of racial discrimination within his local. Woods and James Franklin credited Walter Reuther and high-level UAW policies with opening all auto jobs on a colorblind basis by the mid-1950s, attributing racist union behavior to local union officials. Joe became a staunchly committed union representative. Les Coleman also became a local committee member, and worked hard at it, although he was eventually voted out of that position. Katie Neumann rarely called a union representative for help, but she volunteered during a strike to disburse relief payments. She credited Walter Reuther and top UAW officials for everything positive about the union and was appalled by the mudslinging and name-calling at the local level.

Most of these workers assessed the UAW by what they experienced in their workplaces. Southern migrants were as likely to be staunch union supporters as anyone from the north.[7] Some autoworkers were only vaguely aware of the union when they started in auto plants, yet several of them eventually became local union representatives, helping to resolve workplace disputes. Contract protections helped save jobs for many people, whether or not they fully understood how such processes came to be. Everybody was grateful for pensions and health benefits that, at the time of these interviews, still extended to retirees. Top UAW officials complained during the 1950s that autoworkers expected increased wages and benefits as a matter of course without any significant commitment to the union that negotiated for them.[8] But chronic layoffs and many other factors revealed in these interviews suggest that the relationships of ordinary workers to the UAW were much more complicated. In any event, there seemed to be more time to enjoy being part of a union after retirement, with opportunities to socialize at luncheons and go on bus trips to baseball games or Branson, Missouri.

Race

Superb scholarship on the UAW and Detroit has demonstrated that race played an enormous role in determining access to auto work, the makeup of neighborhoods, and union priorities.[9] These structural forms of racism were obvious to African Americans at the time, and race was in the forefront of interviews with Black autoworkers, whether focusing on the Jim Crow South or the north. These boundaries and limitations, however, were far less apparent to white people. It is difficult to gauge ordinary white people's personal attitudes and behavior with respect to race through interviews, let alone archival evidence. So much has happened since the 1940s and 1950s—civil rights activism, backlashes against civil rights gains, conflicts over language, culture, and history, etc.—that it's hard to get a clear sense of people's views in the past. When evaluating the life history narratives with awareness of structural racism, however, it becomes clear that race was a significant factor in how all autoworkers experienced the postwar years.

Joe Woods grew up in Jim Crow Alabama, so segregation came as no surprise to him, but he recalled the education in racial exclusion that white soldiers from the north received when on leave during basic training. Joe was struck by limited opportunities for Black employees at Pontiac Motor and housing discrimination in the area. He also encountered resistance when seeking a Veterans Administration loan to build a brick house. James Franklin also encountered segregation while in the military, but he thought that his hometown, Ypsilanti, Michigan, had been largely free of racial discrimination until southerners, both white and Black, brought expectations of separation north.

Elwin Brown recalled that his wife, Mary, from southern Indiana, was upset at what she saw as a lack of adequate segregation in the city of Pontiac. In contrast, Emerald Neal's wife, Cara, received threats for being a white woman willing to teach dance at a school for Black children in West Virginia. Katie Neumann was uncomfortable working with Black men at Pontiac Motor before she had a revelation when driving in a car with a Black man through Detroit and noticing stares and glares from white people. That seemed wrong to her. Katie hadn't encountered African Americans in the rural areas where she grew up, and one of her first jobs off the family farm was at a pottery factory that had no Black employees in a town about twenty miles from Detroit that had virtually no Black residents. Before recognizing that conversation and empathy could break down barriers, Katie's approach was "You just had to show them that you weren't scared, that's all."

When Dorothy Sackle's grandmother became ill and had to move, an African American family bought the house and lived on the first floor while Dorothy remained as a tenant upstairs. Dorothy felt uncomfortable. When she was nearly fifty and in school to become a secretary, she had difficulty understanding Black women's reluctance to wash their braided hair.[10] Margaret Beaudry struggled to reconcile her belief in fairness with racial assumptions: "They're not all alike. Just like the white people aren't all alike." Seeing race and racism in personal terms, Margaret noted, "I was never prejudiced. It's odd that some of my best friends are, and I don't like it." Thomas Nowak thought that the union contract should transcend race, and he was perplexed by Black criticism of the UAW and union officials' enforcement of the contract in the 1960s. Race was personal and structural for L.J. Scott, who tested the boundaries of safety in the segregated South before moving to the segregated north: "I thought that I was coming to a utopia, but it's nothing like that."

Many of the advantages of their race were invisible to white workers at the time.[11] Life was difficult enough that characterizing most white workers as beneficiaries of "privilege" might sound extreme, but in a relative sense, the term is accurate. For example, Paul Ish's father-in-law, a foreman at General Motors, saved Paul's job after a honeymoon mix-up, then got Paul into a skilled trades apprenticeship. Before that, Paul had learned machinist skills in the military. In contrast, there were no African American foremen at the time, there was no opportunity for Black workers to enter the skilled trades, and there was little chance that Black soldiers would be assigned to learn machining. Paul Ross could not have entered an apprenticeship without the experience he gained in the Navy, something unobtainable for Black men. Elwin Brown struggled throughout the 1950s before entering the skilled trades with help from a foreman who attended his church. It did not occur to him to reflect on how he had gained experience in several jobs that were off limits to Black workers, or that there were no Black foremen to make recommendations for Black workers from Black churches.[12] Les Coleman entered the skilled trades out of high school, while African Americans such as L.J. Scott, who were equally capable, had no chance to enter an apprenticeship. Katie Neumann observed that white men didn't last long in the foundry because they could transfer to other departments, something that Black employees could rarely do. Dorothy Sackle hardly led a life of comfort, but a friend's husband used a connection to get her a job at the Dodge Main plant. Thomas Nowak got an auto job because of a recommendation from a priest, then he landed a job on an all-white construction crew because a friend of his was already part of it.[13] Thomas also got a tip on a job opening at the Ford Ypsilanti plant. When African American workers like James Franklin got leads on jobs, with the exception of Kaiser-Frazer, it was for foundry employment either in Flint or at the Ford Rouge plant. Emerald Neal's in-laws offered $800 toward a Federal Housing Administration-backed loan, while Joe Woods couldn't get a VA-backed loan despite his military service. Margaret Beaudry's main backup job was at Neisner's, a store that was identified by the NAACP as engaging in discriminatory hiring practices in the 1950s.[14] That job, and many others, like cyclone fence installing, insurance repair work, and cab driving, were generally not available to African Americans. Through her sister, Margaret also got a much-needed job at Community National Bank, another position off limits to African Americans. Margaret had to look out for her family, which is what everybody was doing at the time, and it's difficult to fault her or others for not recognizing the ways in which the economy worked for white people far more so than for everyone else. But there were many more opportunities available for white workers, whether in auto plants or in the larger economy, with both short-term and long-term consequences for Black autoworkers.[15]

Working Women

These interviews provide glimpses into the working lives of women over many decades, beginning with earlier generations. Margaret Beaudry's mother had twelve children, James McGuire's mother had eleven of her own and cared for several others, while Edith Arnold's mother had twelve children, eight of whom survived infancy. L.J. Scott's mother had fourteen children, and Paul Ross's grandmother, who raised him for many years, had eleven children of her own beginning at age eleven. Katie Neumann had seven brothers and sisters, a number that now seems high for maintaining one's sanity, but which was in the mid-range at the time if this sampling is any indication. Unsurprisingly, a number of these women with large families were not in great health or spirits. They faced enormous challenges in raising children and running households while enduring the repeated physical and emotional tolls of childbirth.

In some families, children were assigned household chores when they were old enough, but for mothers there was still an endless grind of food preservation and preparation, dishes to wash, household cleaning, and laundry. L.J. Scott's mother put this burden on herself, allowing her children to work in the fields. Edith Arnold's mother had a midwife come help with chores for a couple of weeks each summer. Katie Neumann's mother was the best cow milker in the family, but she needed help with food preparation and laundry. Katie's mother and a neighbor were midwives for each other, and her mother took no recovery days after giving birth. Ernie Liles's mother was in charge of the garden and canning food. Although Joe Woods's mother was chronically ill, she prepared dinner every day, tended the garden, and canned much of the family's food. Some of these mothers of 1950s autoworkers had paying jobs of their own before taking on full-time homemaking. Dorothy Sackle's mother worked in a Detroit cigar factory, along with many other Polish immigrant women. Paul Ish's mother kept her bookkeeping job at Lewis Furniture after having children and Paul's parents hired a woman to look after the kids. Gene Johnson's mother had to marry at a young age because her father was disabled from an industrial accident and her mother couldn't support the family.

The women profiled here didn't necessarily start out as autoworkers or remain consistently in the auto workforce. Katie Neumann's first job was in a pottery factory before she took a position in a foundry. She faced no resistance from her husband about returning to work after giving birth to their second child. The couple needed the money to make their house payments and Katie's mother provided child care. Dorothy Sackle started auto work in her teens, but only because she couldn't find a job as a secretary, her preferred field. Dorothy dropped out of the auto workforce to raise her children, but returned when she needed to support them after a divorce. She relied on a neighbor for child care so she could keep her job at Dodge Main on the 4:00 p.m. to midnight shift. Margaret Beaudry worked at a department store and a drive-in restaurant before hiring in at a defense plant during World War II, while keeping her other jobs. She gave up auto work after the war to stay home with a young child and support her husband, who hoped to settle in Michigan's Upper Peninsula. Several years later, she had to tell "white lies" about helping the couple afford a new car to convince her husband that she should work outside the house for money, let alone in an auto plant. The same was true for Edith Arnold, who stayed home for a number of years to raise children—and run her own arts-and-crafts business—but was eager to work outside the home, especially in an auto plant because the pay was so much better than with traditional women's jobs.

Margaret Beaudry and Edith Arnold tended to be more assertive in the workplace than with their husbands. Margaret tolerated some teasing and flirting, but when a male coworker "patted" her when she was bending over, she pushed him. Later, when he said something nasty to her, she poured gasoline on his shoes. Margaret demanded respect, and she got it, even from plant superintendents and FBI investigators. Edith Arnold gained the upper hand with a group of her male coworkers by letting a mouse loose on the shop floor, then watching the men shriek and jump on tables. It might have required that level of dishing it out as well as taking it to survive the masculine culture in auto plants.[16] It often helped to work in a supportive, majority-women department, such as the one at Plymouth Motor that organized a baby shower for Dorothy Sackle. On the other hand, Margaret Beaudry didn't feel comfortable in a department with mostly women when she was their union representative, and Edith Arnold preferred working alongside men. Unlike Margaret and Edith, Dorothy had a difficult time being assertive, although one time she demanded to have jobs relocated so she and her coworkers didn't have to stare at a wall. Some women autoworkers dated or otherwise gained the favor of male supervisors to improve their situations at work, while others, like Dorothy's coworker who lost five children in a fire, endured stoically day after day.

The wives of the male autoworkers interviewed for this project tended to play supportive roles, providing what their families needed at any particular time, whether full-time homemaking or income from jobs in fields largely reserved for women. Paul Ish's wife, Gerry, worked at Consumers Power until pregnant with their first child. She got a job at Sears after their children were in school, which helped offset the loss of income from Paul's auto layoffs. Cara Neal found work at a jewelry store and as a dance instructor, and her income often supported the family during her husband's layoffs. Emerald hoped that Cara could get a job at the Ypsilanti Ford Plant, but company policy at the time prohibited husbands and wives from working in the same factory. Years later the policy changed, and Cara became an autoworker. Les Coleman's second wife, Marilyn, was a college-trained librarian who returned to work in her profession after their children were in school. James Franklin held strong religious beliefs that the husband should be head of the household and support the family financially while the wife should manage the home and raise the children. Although this stance caused stress during layoffs, James stuck with it during his first marriage, which produced three daughters, and, after his wife died, in a second marriage that brought seven stepchildren into his household. Religious beliefs contributed to Gene Johnson's wife, Agnes, staying home with their kids, but it was especially important for her to care for a son who had a serious physical disability. When pregnant with their first child, Thomas Nowak's wife, Rosella, left her WWII job at the Willow Run Bomber Plant to run their household. She remained in that role as the family grew to include ten children. Elwin Brown's wife, Hilda, worked at a department store. James McGuire's wife, Mary, worked in a University of Michigan dormitory.

There are limits to the conclusions that can be drawn from this evidence. But the trend, again, is toward a recognition of how complex the world of postwar autoworkers would be if we were to have more comprehensive data. Whether as autoworkers, or the mothers or wives of postwar autoworkers, women worked hard and were flexible in their roles, depending on what their families needed and what they could force or cajole their husbands to allow. Some women had to contend with their husbands' disapproval of wives working for wages at all or specific opposition to auto work. That resistance arose in part from a sense that men should be the family breadwinner, but also from awareness of the rude, masculine culture women would face in an auto factory. For the most part, these women were not dedicated, working-class activists. They were not frustrated by their inability to use college degrees, nor were they bound to their homes in some sort of Cold War domestic containment.[17] Although they were devoted to their children, Margaret Beaudry and Edith Arnold preferred working for wages to being full-time moms. They sought auto work because it paid so much better than service-sector jobs reserved for women. Katie Neumann thought she had no choice but to work outside the home so she and her husband could afford their house payments. Because auto work was so precarious, a number of these women moved in and out of auto employment during the early postwar years, and whatever jobs they held often compensated for family income lost when their spouses were laid off. For the most part, these are not stories of two-income families entering the middle class, but rather examples of resourceful couples, or in the case of Dorothy Sackle, a single mom, doing what was necessary to pay the bills. Both in absolute numbers and as a percentage of the workforce, more women worked outside the home during the 1950s than in 1940 or during WWII.[18] The examples here support that statistical analysis, although few of the women's paths or work histories were linear.

These are some of the thematic takeaways one can glean from the narratives. The intent is not to provide a comprehensive overview of the lives of autoworkers. That would be impossible. But unless the people profiled here are wild outliers, we can learn from them that autoworkers in the early postwar years were indeed multidimensional people, with aspirations and concerns of all sorts going way beyond their jobs in the auto industry and their relationship with the UAW. The story would only increase in complexity, and interest, if more ordinary workers became part of it.

Notes

Introduction

1. See *Labor History* (Spring 1996): 186; *The CIO, 1935–1955* (Chapel Hill: University of North Carolina Press, 1995).

2. See James Barrett's comments at http://www.lawcha.org/2018/12/16/40-years-of-working-class-history-the-series-and-the-field/. See Julie Greene's comments at http://www.lawcha.org/2018/12/20/newberry-working-class-in-american-history-40th-anniversary-comments/.

3. The Walter P. Reuther Library at Wayne State University, in Detroit, contains the records of the United Auto Workers. Longtime UAW president Walter Reuther's own collection within the union's holdings amounts to over 900 boxes of documents. There is relatively little material, however, on ordinary UAW members.

4. Jack Metzgar, *Striking Steel: Solidarity Remembered* (Philadelphia: Temple University Press, 2000); Cheri Register, *Packinghouse Daughter: A Memoir* (St. Paul: Minnesota Historical Society Press, 2000).

5. See for example Kevin Boyle, *The UAW and the Heyday of American Liberalism, 1945–1968* (Ithaca, NY: Cornell University Press, 1995), 107–31; David Lewis-Colman, *Race Against Liberalism: Black Workers and the UAW in Detroit* (Urbana: University of Illinois Press, 2008); and Nancy Gabin, *Feminism in the Labor Movement: Women and The United Auto Workers, 1935–1975* (Ithaca, NY: Cornell University Press, 1990).

6. *Journal of American History* 84, no. 2 (September 1997): 496–523.

7. See for example Steve Jefferys, *Management and Managed: Fifty Years of Crisis at Chrysler* (New York: Cambridge University Press, 1986); Nelson Lichtenstein, *The Most Dangerous Man in Detroit: Walter Reuther and the Fate of American Labor* (New York:

Basic Books, 1995); John Barnard, *American Vanguard: The United Auto Workers during the Reuther Years, 1935–1970* (Detroit: Wayne State University Press, 2004); Thomas Sugrue, *The Origins of the Urban Crisis: Race and Inequality in Postwar Detroit* (Princeton: Princeton University Press, 1996); Gabin, *Feminism in the Labor Movement*; Steven Meyer, *Manhood on the Line: Working Class Masculinities in the American Heartland* (Urbana: University of Illinois Press, 2016); and Jonathan Cutler, *Labor's Time: Shorter Hours, the UAW, and the Struggle for American Unionism* (Philadelphia: Temple University Press, 2004). For further discussion of the literature on autoworkers, see Daniel Clark, *Disruption in Detroit: Autoworkers and the Elusive Postwar Boom* (Urbana: University of Illinois Press, 2018), 1–2.

8. See Walter Reuther's comments in Barnard, *American Vanguard*, 263–64.

9. Daniel J. Clark, *Disruption in Detroit: Autoworkers and the Elusive Postwar Boom* (Urbana: University of Illinois Press, 2018).

10. Some oral history–based books offer more extensive profiles of workers. See for example Richard Feldman and Michael Betzold, *End of the Line: Autoworkers and the American Dream* (London: Weidenfeld and Nicolson, 1988); Michael Honey, *Black Workers Remember: An Oral History of Segregation, Unionization, and the Freedom Struggle* (Berkeley: University of California Press, 1999); Horace Huntley and David Montgomery, eds., *Black Workers' Struggle for Equality in Birmingham* (Urbana: University of Illinois Press, 2007).

11. This is not an argument against thematic chapters. One of my favorite oral history–based books, Jacquelyn Dowd Hall et al., *Like a Family: The Making of a Southern Cotton Mill World* (Chapel Hill: University of North Carolina Press, 1987), does that wonderfully, as do many others.

12. Consider the long print life of Hamilton Holt's 1906 book, *The Life Stories of Undistinguished Americans As Told by Themselves* (1906; repr., New York: Routledge, 1999).

13. Many of the recollections about the Depression in this book would fit well with the accounts in Robert S. McElvaine, ed., *Down and Out in the Great Depression: Letters from the Forgotten Man* (Chapel Hill: University of North Carolina Press, 1983).

14. See Steve Babson et al., *Working Detroit: The Making of a Union Town* (Detroit: Wayne State University Press, 1986), 52–110; Barnard, *American Vanguard*, 36–110; and Zieger, *The CIO*, 22–65.

15. See Babson et al., *Working Detroit*, 112–26; David Kennedy, *Freedom from Fear: The American People in Depression and War, 1929–1945* (New York: Oxford University Press, 1999); and Charles K. Hyde, *The Arsenal of Democracy: The American Automobile Industry in World War II* (Detroit: Wayne State University Press, 2013).

16. See Clark, *Disruption in Detroit*, 54–109.

17. U.S. Census data, 1950 and 1960. Sugrue, *Origins of the Urban Crisis*, 125–152. These 1950 and 1960 censuses classified residents as either white or nonwhite.

18. For basic information about Pontiac's industrial history, see the website of the National Park Service's Motor Cities National Heritage Area, for example https://www.motorcities.org/story-of-the-week/2015/the-early-days-of-pontiac-labor-assembly-lines; and https://www.motorcities.org/locations/building-bodies-at-pontiac-s-o-j

-beaudette-company. Also see Clark, *Disruption in Detroit,* 12–14. In the 1970s, Johnetta Brazzell conducted an oral history project with elderly Black residents of Pontiac. The recordings reveal much about segregation in many aspects of life in that city and are located in Oakland University's Kresge Library: https://library.oakland.edu/.

19. See James Thomas Mann, *Ypsilanti in the 20th Century* (Charleston, SC: Arcadia Publishing, 2003); Sarah Jo Peterson, *Planning the Home Front: Building Bombers and Community at Willow Run* (Chicago: University of Chicago Press, 2013); and Clark, *Disruption in Detroit,* 25, 28, 42, 80–83. Expansion of the Ford Ypsilanti plant can be tracked in the University of Michigan Library Digital Collections: https://quod.lib.umich.edu/y/yhsic1/x-yhs00329/yhs00329. Population figures are from U.S. Census data.

20. Chafe had recently published *Civilities and Civil Rights: Greensboro, North Carolina and the Black Struggle for Freedom* (New York: Oxford University Press, 1981), which relied extensively on the author's oral history interviews.

21. Daniel Clark, *Like Night and Day: Unionization in a Southern Mill Town* (Chapel Hill: University of North Carolina Press, 1997).

22. See Alessandro Portelli, "The Death of Luigi Trastulli: Memory and the Event," in Alessandro Portelli, *The Death of Luigi Trastulli and Other Stories: Form and Meaning in Oral History* (Albany: State University of New York Press, 1990), 1–28; and Portelli, "What Makes Oral History Different," in Portelli, *Death of Luigi Trastulli,* 45–58.

23. Recordings and transcripts for all interviews are located in the Metropolitan Detroit Autoworkers Oral History Collection, Walter Reuther Library, Archives of Labor and Urban Affairs, Wayne State University.

24. See for example *Hard Times: An Oral History of the Great Depression* (New York: Pantheon Books, 1970); *The Good War* (New York: Pantheon Books, 1984); and *American Dreams: Lost and Found* (New York: Pantheon Books, 1980).

Emerald Neal

1. See the Hinton Railroad Museum website: https://www.nps.gov/places/hinton-railroad-museum.htm.

2. For a description of Lincoln School, see https://www.nps.gov/places/lincoln-school-hinton-wv.htm.

3. See Clark, *Disruption in Detroit,* 80–83.

Elwin Brown

1. See https://kimon.hosting.nyu.edu/physical-electrical-digital/exhibits/show/the-printing-press-for-politic/item/1059.

2. Yet the Pontiac schools remained highly, if not completely, segregated because of housing segregation and the drawing of attendance boundaries. See Jerry M. Flint, "U.S. Judge Orders Integration of All Schools in Pontiac, Mich.," *New York Times,* February 18, 1970.

Paul Ross

1. See "Strike Ends at Plant of U.S. Rubber," *Detroit Free Press,* August 7, 1947.

2. See Clark, *Disruption in Detroit,* 161–63.

Margaret Beaudry

1. "Local Store Boycott: Community Aroused Over Non-Employment," *Pontiac Herald*, October 14, 1957.

Joe Woods

1. See Loren Schweninger, *Black Property Owners in the South, 1790–1915* (Urbana: University of Illinois Press, 1997), 165.

2. See Nan Woodruff, *American Congo: The African American Freedom Struggle in the Delta* (Cambridge: Harvard University Press, 2003).

3. See Clark, *Disruption in Detroit*, 20–22.

4. See Clark, *Disruption in Detroit*, Chapter 6, "'A Severe and Prolonged Hangover,' 1956–1957."

5. For a local reflection on the Pontiac bus bombings, see https://michiganadvance.com/2021/08/30/on-this-day-in-1971-kkk-bombs-empty-pontiac-buses-set-to-racially-integrate-schools/.

Les "Lucky" Coleman

1. Archival materials from this camp can be found at the Reuther Library: https://reuther.wayne.edu/node/5815.

2. For a discussion of the impact of automation on the auto industry during the 1950s, see Sugrue, *Origins of the Urban Crisis*, 130–38.

Gene Johnson

1. Calvin was buried in what was then called the Bounds Creek, Missouri Cemetery: https://www.findagrave.com/memorial/24754465/calvin-j.d.-johnson.

2. See James Loewen, *Sundown Towns: A Hidden Dimension of American Racism* (New York: The New Press, 2018).

3. See Chad Berry, *Southern Migrants, Northern Exiles* (Urbana: University of Illinois Press, 2000.

4. See https://www.wsha.org/members/madigan-army-medical-center/.

5. See https://www.mayoclinic.org/diseases-conditions/legg-calve-perthes-disease/symptoms-causes/syc-20374343. Far less was known about the disease in the early 1950s.

6. See Clark, *Disruption in Detroit*, Chapter 4, "A Post-Korean War Boom, 1953."

7. See Clark, *Disruption in Detroit*, 80–83.

Dorothy Sackle

1. See Clark, *Disruption in Detroit*, Chapter 1, "Shortages and Strikes."

L.J. Scott

1. See Lance Hill, *The Deacons for Defense: Armed Resistance and the Civil Rights Movement* (Chapel Hill: University of North Carolina Press, 2004).

2. See Danielle McGuire, *At the Dark End of the Street: Black Women, Rape, and Resistance—A New History of the Civil Rights Movement from Rosa Parks to Black Power* (New York: Knopf, 2010).

3. See Clark, *Disruption in Detroit*, Chapter 6, "'The Fifties' in One Year, 1955" and Chapter 7, "'A Severe and Prolonged Hangover,' 1956–1957."

4. See Sugrue, *Origins of the Urban* Crisis, 130–38.

Thomas Nowak

1. See https://www.nationalww2museum.org/war/articles/points-system-us-armys-demobilization.

2. The strike against Michigan Bell Telephone Co. began in April 1947. For a photo of women operators on the picket line in Ann Arbor, see https://aadl.org/N022_0048_003.

3. See Clark, *Disruption in Detroit*, Chapter 7, "'A Severe and Prolonged Hangover,' 1956–1957."

4. See Dan Georgakas and Marvin Surkin, *Detroit, I Do Mind Dying: A Study in Urban Revolution* (New York: St. Martin's Press, 1975); James Geschwender, *Class, Race, and Worker Insurgency: The League of Revolutionary Black Workers* (New York: Cambridge University Press, 1977); and the documentary film *Finally Got the News*, by Stewart Bird, Rene Lichtman, and Peter Gessner (Black Star Productions, 1970), available from Icarus Films: http://icarusfilms.com/if-fin.

5. See John Barnard, *American Vanguard: The United Auto Workers during the Reuther Years, 1935–1970* (Detroit: Wayne State University Press, 2004), 430–37.

6. See Thomas Sugrue, *The Origins of the Urban Crisis*, 114–18.

James McGuire

1. See Clark, *Disruption in Detroit*, 65–66.

2. See Clark, *Disruption in Detroit*, 80–83.

3. For photographs concerning this strike, see https://digital.library.wayne.edu/item/wayne:vmc29834.

4. See Clark, *Disruption in Detroit*, Chapter 7, "'A Severe and Prolonged Hangover,' 1956–1957."

5. See https://uawblacklake.com/.

Edith Arnold

1. For an article about the Hupp Motor Car Company, see https://www.motorcities.org/story-of-the-week/2020/the-hupp-motor-car-company-offered-great-advertising.

2. See Steve Meyer, *Manhood on the Line: Working-Class Masculinities in the American Heartland* (Urbana: University of Illinois Press, 2016).

3. See Clark, *Disruption in Detroit*, 72–78.

4. Clark, *Disruption in Detroit*, Chapter 7, "'A Severe and Prolonged Hangover,' 1956–1957."

James Franklin

1. See Beth Tompkins Bates, *The Making of Black Detroit in the Age of Henry Ford* (Chapel Hill: University of North Carolina Press, 2012).

2. See the U.S. Army Corps of Engineering website: https://www.usace.army.mil/About/History/Historical-Vignettes/Women-Minorities/112-African-American-Engineer/.

3. See Matthew F. Delmont, *Half American: The Epic Story of African Americans Fighting World War II at Home and Abroad* (New York: Viking, 2022), 223–25.

4. See Thomas Borstelmann, *The Cold War and the Color Line: American Race Relations in the Global Arena* (Cambridge: Harvard University Press, 2001), 33–35.

5. See Clark, *Disruption in Detroit*, Chapter 1, "Shortages and Strikes, 1945–1948."

6. See Clark, *Disruption in Detroit*, 80–83.

Ernie Liles

1. See David Welky, *The Thousand-Year Flood: The Ohio-Mississippi Disaster of 1937* (Chicago: University of Chicago Press, 2011); and the "Flood of 1937" entry in the *Encyclopedia of Arkansas*, http://www.encyclopediaofarkansas.net/encyclopedia/entry-detail.aspx?entryID=4878.

2. See Woodruff, *American Congo*.

3. See https://www.cityofbullshoals.org/BullShoalsDam.aspx.

4. See Clark, *Disruption in Detroit*, Chapter 6, "'The Fifties' in One Year, 1955."

Paul Ish

1. See Clark, *Disruption in Detroit*, 48–49.

2. Photographs of the 1951 Kansas flood can be found on the U.S. Geological Survey's website: https://www.usgs.gov/media/galleries/1951-kansas-flood.

3. See Clark, *Disruption in Detroit*, chapters 5–8.

Katie Neumann

1. For a description of Warsaw Park, see https://shelbyhistory.tripod.com/id33.html.

2. The Mount Clemens Pottery Company was party to a U.S. Supreme Court case in 1946 regarding unpaid work on both ends of the workday. See https://www.law.cornell.edu/supremecourt/text/328/680.

3. See Clark, *Disruption in Detroit*, Chapter 1, "Shortages and Strikes."

4. See Ryan Pettengill, "'Fair Play in Bowling,' Sport, Civil Rights, and the UAW Culture of Inclusion, 1936–1950," *Journal of Social History* 51, no. 4 (2018): 953–79.

Conclusion

1. See Jack Metzgar, *Bridging the Divide: Working-Class Culture in a Middle-Class Society* (Ithaca, NY: ILR Press, 2021).

2. See Clark, *Disruption in Detroit*, Chapters 2, 4, and 5.

3. See Peter Friedlander, *The Emergence of a UAW Local, 1936–1939: A Study in Class and Culture* (Pittsburgh: University of Pittsburgh Press, 1975); and Steven Rosswurm, "The Catholic Church and the Left-Led Unions: Labor Priests, Labor Schools, and the ACTU," in Steven Rosswurm, ed., *The CIO's Left-Led Unions* (New Brunswick, New Jersey: Rutgers University Press, 1992).

4. See Barnard, *American Vanguard*, 263–264.

5. See Clark, *Disruption in Detroit*, 107.

6. See Jeremy Milloy, *Blood, Sweat, and Fear: Violence at Work in the North American Auto Industry, 1960–1980* (Vancouver: University of British Columbia Press, 2017).

7. See Chad Berry, *Southern Migrants, Northern Exiles* (Urbana: University of Illinois Press, 2000), 107–109.

8. Barnard, *American Vanguard*, 264, 308.

9. See for example Boyle, *The UAW and the Heyday of American Liberalism*, 107–131; Sugrue, *Origins of the Urban Crisis*; and Lewis-Colman, *Race Against Liberalism.*

10. See Althea Prince, *The Politics of Black Women's Hair* (London, Ontario: Insomniac Press, 2009); Ayana Byrd and Lori Tharps, *Hair Story: Untangling the Roots of Black Hair in America*, 2nd ed. (New York: St. Martin's Griffin, 2014); and Emma Dabiri, *Twisted: The Tangled History of Black Hair Culture* (New York: Harper Perennial, 2020).

11. See Chapter 1, "The Rightness of Whiteness," in Nancy MacLean, *Freedom is Not Enough: The Opening of the American Workplace* (Cambridge: Harvard University Press, 2006).

12. For a discussion of Henry Ford's recruitment of Black workers from Black churches after World War I, see Beth Bates, *The Making of Black Detroit in the Age of Henry Ford* (Chapel Hill: University of North Carolina Press, 2012), 54–57.

13. For a discussion of discrimination in the Detroit building trades, see Sugrue, *Origins of the Urban Crisis*, 114–118.

14. See "Local Store Boycott: Community Aroused Over Non-Employment," *Pontiac Herald*, October 14, 1957.

15. On this issue, see Clark, *Disruption in Detroit*, 63; Sugrue, *Origins of the Urban Crisis*, Chapter 4.

16. See Stephen Meyer, *Manhood on the Line: Working-Class Masculinities in the American Heartland* (Urbana: University of Illinois Press, 2016).

17. See Dorothy Sue Cobble, *The Other Women's Movement: Workplace Justice and Social Rights in Modern America* (Princeton: Princeton University Press, 2004); Betty Friedan, *The Feminine Mystique* (New York: W. W. Norton, 1963); and Elaine Tyler May, *Homeward Bound: American Families in the Cold War Era* (New York: Basic Books, 1988).

18. William Chafe, *The Unfinished Journey: America since World War II*, 6th ed. (New York: Oxford University Press, 2007), 120–121.

Interview List

Edith Arnold	November 7, 2003. Local 653 Union Hall, Pontiac, Michigan
Margaret Beaudry	June 24, 2002. Ms. Beaudry's home, Waterford, Michigan
Elwin Brown	August 7, 2003. Local 653 Union Hall
Les "Lucky" Coleman	August 29, 2000. Local 849 Union Hall, Ypsilanti, Michigan
James Franklin	September 22, 2000. Mr. Franklin's home, Ypsilanti, Michigan
Paul Ish	June 18, 2002. Local 653 Union Hall
Arthur E. (Gene) Johnson	July 17, 2002. Local 653 Union Hall
Ernie Liles	May 27, 2003. Mr. Liles's Home, Sterling Heights, Michigan
James McGuire	August 24, 2000. Local 849 Union Hall
Emerald Neal	August 21, 2000. Local 849 Union Hall
Katie Neumann	March 18, 2002. Ms. Neumann's home, Shelby Township, MI
Thomas Nowak	September 20, 2000. Local 849 Union Hall

Paul Ross	May 20, 2003. Local 653 Union Hall
Dorothy Sackle	June 14, 2002. Ms. Sackle's home, Westland, Michigan
L.J. Scott	October 27, 2003. Mr. Scott's home, Detroit, Michigan
Joe Woods, Jr.	June 28, 2002. Local 653 Union Hall

Index

DANIEL J. CLARK is a professor of history at Oakland University. He is the author of *Disruption in Detroit: Autoworkers and the Elusive Postwar Boom*.

The University of Illinois Press
is a founding member of the
Association of University Presses.

University of Illinois Press
1325 South Oak Street
Champaign, IL 61820-6903
www.press.uillinois.edu